The Citi Commonsense
Money Guide
for Real People

The Citi Commonsense
Money Guide
for Real People

Pay down your debt
Make the most of what you've got
Put away a little something for the future

Edited by Dara Duguay
Director, Citigroup Office of Financial Education

RODALE

Mention of specific companies, organizations, or authorities in this book does not imply endorsement by the author or publisher, nor does mention of specific companies, organizations, or authorities imply that they endorse this book, its author, or the publisher.

Internet addresses and telephone numbers given in this book were accurate at the time it went to press.

Rodale books may be purchased for business or promotional use or for special sales. For information, please write to:

Special Markets Department, Rodale Inc., 733 Third Avenue, New York, NY 10017

Printed in the United States of America

Rodale Inc. makes every effort to use acid-free ♾, recycled paper ♻.

Book design by Joanna Williams

Library of Congress Cataloging-in-Publication Data

The Citi commonsense money guide for real people : pay down your debt, make the most of what you've got, put away a little something for later / edited by Dara Duguay.
      p.   cm.
   Includes index.
   ISBN 13 978–1–59486–348–6   hardcover
   ISBN 10 1–59486–348–2   hardcover
   1. Finance, Personal.   I. Duguay, Dara.   II. Citigroup (Firm)
   HG179.C5658   2007
   332.024—dc22   2007004126

Distributed to the trade by Holtzbrinck Publishers

2   4   6   8 10   9   7   5   3   1   hardcover

In keeping with its commitment to financial education,

other than funds used to satisfy administrative costs associated with the

publication of the book, Citigroup will donate all profits from this book

to not-for-profit organizations and programs that support and

teach financial education.

CONTENTS

ACKNOWLEDGMENTS

We'd like to thank the following employees for their commonsense contributions:

Grace Accardi

Shameem Ahmed

John Carroll Atwood, Jr.

Ronni Burns

Galen Burson

Jennifer Cohen

Richard G. Cohen

Douglas Davis

Deonna Decker

Dana Deubert

Jack Erickson

Maureen Forsman

Brian Franklin

Wendy Garcia

Lawrence A. Greenberg

Leeann M. Haight

Denene M. Hisgen

Jeff Hollander

Eliot S. Howell

Sara Jankowiak

Jackie Jelen

Eric Johnson

Donna Kiger

Jason Korosec

Barry Levine

David S. Lopez

Virginia Ann McBride

Mike Militello

Rachele Nicoletti

Tim Paul

Jack S. Pyle

Robert B. Seaberg, Ph.D.

Stacey Sechrest Carder

Ben Shapiro

Susan B. Silberman

Patricia Smith-Strawder

Brian Steel

Gary Wei

Amy Wilson

Walter L. Woodrick

Barbara Zakin

DISCLAIMER

This book is intended as a reference volume only. The information contained in it is provided only for informational purposes. It is not intended as a substitute for any advice you may receive from a professional financial advisor. Each individual's circumstances may be different. All forms of financial investment pose some inherent risks, and, as with all investments, past performance is no guarantee of future results. Individuals should seek legal and tax advice or other professional or expert advice or assistance based on their particular circumstances from an independent professional. THE PUBLISHERS, CITIGROUP AND ITS AFFILIATES, AND THEIR RESPECTIVE OFFICERS, DIRECTORS, AND EMPLOYEES SPECIFICALLY DISCLAIM ANY LIABILITY FOR ANY DAMAGES (WHETHER DIRECT OR INDIRECT, SPECIAL, GENERAL, OR CONSEQUENTIAL) OR LOSS (INCLUDING LOSS OF BUSINESS AND PROFITS, OR RISK, PERSONAL OR OTHERWISE), WHICH IS INCURRED AS A CONSEQUENCE, DIRECTLY OR INDIRECTLY, OF THE USE OR APPLICATION OF ANY OF THE CONTENTS OF THIS PUBLICATION, WHICH CONTENTS ARE PROVIDED "AS IS."

References to persons, names, incidents, or dialogues in illustrative stories are fictional. Any resemblance to actual persons, living or dead, is coincidental. Mention of specific companies, organizations, or authorities in this book does not imply endorsement by the author or publisher, nor does mention of specific companies, organizations, or authorities imply that they endorse this book, its author, or the publisher. Neither the information nor any opinion expressed constitutes a solicitation for the purchase or sale of a security or other investment or financial product. Internet addresses and telephone numbers given in this book were accurate at the time it went to press.

Important Additional Information Concerning Financial Products and Investments

In this publication you may read about various types of financial products and investments. There are a number of things to think about whenever you are considering financial products, investment styles, and services. A few of them are mentioned here, and others may be noted in the chapters and illustrations you may read. You should always consult a trusted and qualified advisor before making any decisions.

Citigroup, Inc., its affiliates, and its employees are not in the business of providing tax or legal advice, and this book is sold with the understanding that the publisher and author are not engaged in rendering such advice. These materials and any tax-related statements are not intended or written to be used, and cannot be used or relied upon, by any taxpayer for the purpose of avoiding tax penalties. Tax-related statements, if any, may have been written in connection with the "promotion or marketing" of the transaction(s) or matters(s) addressed by these materials, to the extent allowed by applicable law. Any taxpayer should seek advice based on the taxpayer's particular circumstances from an independent tax advisor.

Investment

Although this note is not all inclusive, investing carries unique risk. The stories and hypothetical examples in this material are for illustration only and should not be considered an individualized recommendation or personalized investment advice. The types of securities mentioned and investment strategies described may not be suitable for everyone. Each investor needs to review and decide, based on their own particular situation, the type of investments and investment strategies that will best meet investment objectives, risk tolerance, and investment strategy. Borrowing against securities may not be suitable for everyone.

If the value of securities used as collateral in a loan declines below a minimum level, you may be subject to a collateral call without specific advance notice, requiring you to provide additional cash or securities or resulting in the forced sale or liquidation of the securities or other assets, without the ability to choose which assets are sold or any extension of time to meet the collateral call. The sale of securities may have tax consequences. A concentrated portfolio holding a single or a few securities may be subject to greater risk of a collateral call than a diversified portfolio; a diversified portfolio will tend to be less subject to a sharp decline resulting from the negative performance of a single security. Diversification is a strategy that does not guarantee a profit or protect against loss. International investing may not be suitable for every investor. There may be additional risks associated with international investing involving foreign, economic, political, monetary, and/or legal factors. Dollar cost averaging, like any consecutive payment investment strategy (averaging payments over time to help reduce market volatility), is a strategy that does not guarantee a profit or protect against loss. There are unique issues associated with the use of online trading systems, including system interruptions, exposure to price volatility, and order execution delays. Prior to engaging in online trading, you should review the limits and risks of online trading and discuss them with your advisor.

Stocks, Bonds, and Other Financial Products

Although this list is not all-inclusive, investing in stocks, bonds, or other financial products may carry unique risk, including the possible loss of principal. As is the case with all investments, past performance is no guarantee of future results. Specific investments may not be suitable for all investors, and careful consideration should be given to individual investment objectives, risk tolerance, and investment strategy before engaging in any transaction. Preferred securities can be called prior to maturity, which may reduce yield if purchased at a premium. Preferred securities may be subject to other call features or corporate restrictions that may have an effect similar to a call. Prices may fluctuate, reflecting market interest rates and the issuer's credit status. Mortgage-backed securities have the possibility of premature return of principal due to mortgage prepayment, which can reduce expected yield and lead to price volatility. Investments in high yield or distressed securities involve a substantial risk of default and/or loss of principal and may be more difficult to sell prior to maturity than investment-grade securities. Bonds are subject to interest rate risk. When interest rates rise, bond prices fall; generally the longer a bond's maturity, the more sensitive it is to this risk. Bonds may also be subject to call risk, which allows the issuer to retain the right to redeem the debt, fully or partially, before the scheduled maturity date. Proceeds from sales prior to maturity may be more or less than originally invested due to changes in market conditions or changes in the credit quality of the issuer. Municipal Bonds may be subject to state and local taxes and/or the alternative minimum tax. Certain gains, if any, are fully taxable. **When considering any mutual fund, review the investment objectives, risks, charges, fees, and expenses of the fund carefully before investing. The prospectus contains important and more complete information about these factors and other information about the fund. Read the prospectus carefully before you invest.** Future investment return and principal value will fluctuate so that an investor's shares, when redeemed, may be worth more or less than their original cost. Money market mutual funds are not insured or guaranteed by the Federal Deposit Insurance Corporation or any other government agency. Although they generally seek to maintain a stable net asset value of $1.00 per share, there can be no assurance that a fund will be able to do this. Indexes are unmanaged, do not incur management fees, costs, and expenses, and cannot be invested in directly. CDs are FDIC insured only up to $100,000 per deposit, per institution, offer a fixed rate of return, and are subject to change and availability.

Annuities and Insurance

Annuities are long-term investments often intended for retirement planning. Taxes may be due upon withdrawals from the annuity contract. Withdrawals may be subject to a significant federal penalty tax if made before a certain age or event and are subject to qualified retirement plan provisions. An investor should consider the funding options' investment objectives, risks, charges, and expenses carefully before investing. The prospectus contains this and other information about the funding options. Read it carefully before investing. Life and long-term care insurance are medically underwritten. A policy change may incur fees and costs and may also require a medical examination. You should not cancel current coverage until new coverage is in force. Surrender charges may be due on an exchange of one life insurance contract for another. Surrenders may be taxable. You should consult your own tax advisors regarding tax liability. Life insurance products are not insured by the FDIC or any other federal agency. The investment return and principal value of variable life insurance will fluctuate, so that your account value, when redeemed, may be worth more or less than the premiums you paid. In addition, there are significant fees and charges associated with variable life policies. There may be partial and/or full surrender charges for early withdrawal from variable life policies. Consult your tax advisor about the income tax consequences when the life insurance death benefit is paid to an entity other than an individual. The death benefit may be affected by premiums paid and investment performance. Policy loans and withdrawals will affect the cash value and the death benefit of the policy. Policy loans and withdrawals are subject to certain limitations.

FOREWORD

I started my career on Wall Street as a runner, getting paid $35 a week. My wife and I lived with her parents and my mother before I became a broker and before we could afford a place of our own.

It's humbling to think about those days when my mother was my only client. In the beginning, you have your plans, your hopes, and your family and friends, but little else. Five decades later, Joan and I are fortunate to have come a long way indeed.

When people ask me what was the secret to my success in financial services, my answer is always twofold: "First, do your homework." Whether you're running your own business or balancing your checkbook, there are always ways to improve your bottom line, stay on top of developments and opportunities, and keep an eye on the future. The second part of my answer is "Do the right thing."

Doing the right thing can mean many things—getting a handle on your debt, saving more than you spend from your salary, or planning for the unexpected. Whatever it means for you, the most important step you can take is educating yourself.

As my friend and Citigroup colleague Bob Rubin likes to say: few things in life are certain. But one thing I'm sure of is this—when it comes to your personal finances, the more you know about how money works, the more you can make it work for you. That's what *The Citi Commonsense Money Guide for Real People* is all about.

And that's why we published it. We believe that as the leading financial services company in the world, we have a responsibility to share the lessons we've learned and the expertise we've gained so people everywhere can manage their finances wisely. We are among the world's leaders in the area of financial education so people can plan for their futures and someday live the dream of financial freedom.

I'm going to ask you to keep one thing in mind as you read this book—money can do a lot of things, but it will never love you back or solve all your problems. That said, when you get smarter about handling your money, you'll have more time to spend on the things that really matter.

—Sandy Weill
Citigroup Chairman Emeritus

INTRODUCTION

The Citi Commonsense Money Guide for Real People is not a book that aspires to make you a millionaire.

What it does aspire to do is show and teach you how you can live comfortably and responsibly on whatever money you have, with a reasonable level of credit and debt, saving regularly, dealing with the curveballs life throws you, and learning all the time how to do all this a little better.

You don't need an MBA, a fancy calculator, a computer, an aptitude for math (though it will help if you can add, subtract, multiply, and divide). You just need some common sense, a willingness to look honestly at yourself and your life—particularly its financial aspects—and an openness about education.

We think that education—specifically financial education—is the magic formula. And it isn't even so magic.

This book seeks to help you tackle the many aspects of personal financial management in a sensible, consistent, easy-to-implement way. Its underlying principle is that education is the key to better managing your debt, to making credit work to your benefit, to finding the right way to manage your finances, and to dealing with those unexpected situations that linger around every turn in the road.

We would be the first to point out that any one of the chapters in this book could be a whole book—or in some instances a whole shelf of books—on its own. It is by no means the definitive text on mortgages, college savings plans, debt management, or investing. Rather, it is a starting point that will show you how easy it is to learn more, try more, and do more to solve your financial dilemmas. And once you've done that, we hope you will then teach your children, brag to your friends, and tell your mother or your aunt or your sister how you did it and why it works.

Here's how we've set up this book.

The Citi Commonsense Money Guide for Real People is divided into three major parts. The first, "Get Back on Track," takes a look at several financial situations where people often find themselves backed up against a financial brick wall. Are you one of those people who live from paycheck to paycheck, always juggling, never able to save or get ahead? Maybe you've missed a couple of car or mortgage payments. Or maybe you find yourself facing a huge college tuition bill. It could be that your credit profile is holding you up or that you're drowning in debt. "Get Back on Track" suggests some practical ways to deal with these situations.

The common thread throughout the first section is our belief that in order to fix your financial problems, you've got to own up to them. A common first reaction to a financial dilemma is to do nothing—or even to run and hide. This reaction is entirely understandable. Avoiding the problem makes it disappear—for the moment. Unfortunately, this all too often contributes to further escalation of the situation. Ignoring financial problems is not the answer. Dealing with them is. Financial dilemmas, while grim, are not life threatening. You can turn them around.

The second part of the book we've called "Basic Training." We're talking about raising kids, owning homes, investing responsibly, and planning for the future. There's no right or wrong way to do any of these things. Our Commonsense Considerations will give you some further ideas.

The third and final part focuses on those unexpected "Curveballs" life throws at you. Right when you think you've got it down, something always comes along that disrupts your financial equilibrium, or your money routine. It could be someone stealing your credit card. Or the double-whammy of emotional and financial stress that comes from a divorce or losing a spouse. Sometimes it's an event that on the surface seems to be a joyful one, like a wedding or an inheritance, but that still threatens to topple your system. We haven't covered every possible situation in this section, of course, but we hope we've given you an idea of how to deal sensibly with anything that might arise at any time in your life.

We wrote this book to inspire you as much as to inform you. By that, we mean that while you're reading it, maybe it will give you an idea or two about how to tackle a financial problem that we haven't covered. We're providing this information for general educational purposes and not as personalized advice. But we think everyone can learn something from it.

We also wrote this book to emphasize that there are many solutions to any financial puzzle. We're not advocating one accounting or legal or financial option over any other. You may have to try many to find the one that works for you. But we encourage you to keep trying.

What we do hope you will appreciate when you finish reading this book is our faith and belief in the power of financial education. It's never too late to learn, and because of this, it's never too late to get your financial life in order. We don't want to discourage anyone from starting a savings account, whether they're 6 years old or 60. It's never too late to pick yourself up and clear up your debt, learn to save money, start an education or retirement fund, learn, and then learn more. We think financial education is a lifelong endeavor.

That's because we truly believe *knowledge is your greatest asset*^{SM}.

—Dara Duguay

PART

Get Back on Track

No surprise here, but *The Citi Commonsense Money Guide for Real People* is all about—common sense. It's great to be planning for your child's college education, investing in the stock market, or saving for that anniversary cruise. But if you're carrying a crushing amount of debt, if the collection agencies have your number on speed dial, if you've skipped a car payment or two or maybe three, then you need to rethink your priorities. It doesn't make much sense to be planning for the future, as smart an idea as that may seem, until you've cleaned up your past.

That's what Part 1 of this book is all about. It demonstrates how you can get your financial house in order. This includes how to deal with coming up short every month, what to do if you've missed a few mortgage payments, or how to pay for that college tuition bill even if you haven't saved a penny toward it. It stresses the importance of making a plan—and then following through on it.

CHAPTER 1

Making Your Financial Plan

The Citi Commonsense Money Guide recognizes that your time is short and your money is tight, and that there are lots of ways to solve a financial problem. You might have one, two, or even more financial challenges. Maybe you're overextended on your credit cards. Or perhaps you have missed a few payments on your car or mortgage loans and are overwhelmed by the prospect of catching up. Maybe you're not sure how you really spend your money. You think what you need is more money, which may be true, but even more, you need a new system for spending your money. You need a plan, and you need to figure out how to make that plan work.

When it comes to money matters, most people lack a plan, even though they may have carefully thought through other aspects of their lives, such as their careers or how they want to raise their children. A financial plan provides a map and a sense of direction. No matter what your money challenges are, even if you don't think you have any money challenges, a plan is the one tool you can use. You can write it out on the back of an envelope and stick it on your refrigerator with a magnet, or you can more formally type it up and distribute it to your family and financial advisors. Paste it inside your checkbook, or make it into a screensaver for your computer. A plan costs nothing to put together, and it can mark the start of a whole new financial life for you.

This first chapter offers guidance on setting your goals and making your plan.

Opening the Door to Discussion

Kay's childhood included private music lessons, summer camps, her own car when she turned 18, and a fully paid college education. After she graduated, she found a job as an office assistant at a nonprofit theater company. There, she met Marc, a set designer who had grown up in a working-class family. He liked to boast that he had put himself through college on steak sauce, because he had financed his education with restaurant jobs, including dishwasher, waiter, and, ultimately, maître d'. Kay and Marc were immediately attracted to each other and, after a few months, decided to move in together. They felt no pressure to get married, though they thought they might like to start a family—someday.

The couple's salaries were modest but sufficient to support their lifestyle. Kay was quite determined to make it on her own, without additional support from her parents. Sharing the rent, utilities, and food costs with Marc helped a lot. The first summer they were living together, they rented a small cottage for a week's vacation in a beach town about an hour's drive away. It was there that they had their first serious discussion about their future together.

Kay's older sister had sent Kay a magazine article about marriage between people from economically and socially diverse backgrounds. It predicted a bleak future for pairs in which one partner had grown up in a wealthy environment and the other hadn't. Kay took the article along on vacation, and after she finished reading it, she gave it to Marc to read. She was ready to dispute it point by point.

Marc didn't say much about the article for a day or so, so Kay decided to initiate a discussion, asking what he thought about it. Marc was quiet for a minute. Then he said that when he designs a set, he doesn't start by nailing wood together. He starts by reading the play and talking with the director and stage manager. Then he does some research and makes several sketches. Next he shows the designs to the team and asks for their reactions before building a model that incorporates their suggestions. He develops a budget, investigates sources for materials, and draws up a step-by-step plan for actually building the set. And even once the set is done, it might need some adjustment when rehearsals for the production begin. It's a process, he said. The best thing about the process, Marc said, is that every time he builds a set, he learns a little more about the play, about his craft, and about himself.

By the same token, Marc explained, he wouldn't want to start a life with someone without making a plan. This would involve creating a list of goals and discussing them with Kay to find out how important those goals were to her and whether she had any to add to the list. Then he'd want to figure out how to achieve those goals. So in the end, Marc said, where they'd come from wasn't as important to him as where they were headed.

Kay liked this answer. She felt lucky to have found Marc, and she looked forward to being the exception to the article her sister had sent.

Commonsense Considerations

Marc and Kay might have used the following goal questionnaire as a tool for starting their money conversation. If you are single, it can help you draft a list of your priorities. For couples, it can be an enlightening exercise for learning more about your partner's priorities. Without consulting each other, rate each of the statements below according to how true it is for you on a scale of 1 to 5, with 1 being not at all true of you and 5 being very true of you. Add three unique goals of your own, and compare your answers to those of your partner.

1. I would like to start a family.
   1   2   3   4   5
2. I would like to save for retirement.
   1   2   3   4   5
3. I would like to travel.
   1   2   3   4   5

4. I would like to save on taxes.
    1   2   3   4   5

5. I would like to pay the college tuition for our child(ren).
    1   2   3   4   5

6. I would like to pay down debt and/or remain debt-free.
    1   2   3   4   5

7. I would like to save a predetermined amount of money.
    1   2   3   4   5

8. I would like to purchase a new vehicle.
    1   2   3   4   5

9. I would like to purchase a new home.
    1   2   3   4   5

10. I would like to be able to support elderly parents.
    1   2   3   4   5

11. I would like to be able to pass on an inheritance.
    1   2   3   4   5

12. I would like to be able to buy designer clothes.
    1   2   3   4   5

13. I would like to be able to buy high-end electronics.
    1   2   3   4   5

14. I would like to pay off student loans.
    1   2   3   4   5

15. I would like to pay off medical bills.
    1   2   3   4   5

16. I would like to build an emergency fund.
    1   2   3   4   5

17. I would like to (fill in the blank).
    1   2   3   4   5

18. I would like to (fill in the blank).
    1   2   3   4   5

19. I would like to (fill in the blank).
    1   2   3   4   5

A Man, a Van, and a Plan

George worked in a luxury apartment building, where he was required to live—rent-free—because of his job. His wife, Zola, and their 5-year-old daughter, Myra, lived in the apartment as well. Zola was a stay-at-home mom because she didn't feel comfortable leaving Myra with baby-sitters and none of the family's close relatives lived nearby.

George was a real Mr. Fix-it, both on the job and at home. He owned a panel van of which he was very proud, and in his time off he often helped his friends with carpentry chores, hauling 2 x 4s and Sheetrock in the back of the van. For many years, the family lived comfortably enough within their means. Zola, who laughingly called herself "math-phobic," handled all the domestic chores except for the family finances and bill paying, which she left to George.

Then trouble came knocking. The owner of George's building hired a new management company, and the agent assigned to the building did not get along with George. It seemed to George that this agent was collecting evidence in order to fire him, and he was paralyzed with panic. He was so consumed by the thought that he was going to lose his job that he let more than a few bills slip by. The overdue notices quickly followed. George shoved them into a drawer. He developed painful migraines and had to lie down for several hours in a dark room every afternoon, unable to work.

Zola was unaware that George was not paying the bills. She saw there was more money in their bank account and assumed it was hers to spend. She bought Myra some new clothes and expensive toys that ordinarily she might have thought twice about purchasing, and she put some money down on a leather chair as a surprise for George's birthday.

George continued to try to do his job as best he could. Finally, he couldn't stand the pressure anymore and contacted his union representative. The representative told him there was not much he could do as long as he was still employed, but suggested that George might want to look for another position if he felt unhappy where he was working currently. He also gave George the name and number of a financial consultant who was contracted by the union to help members get their financial houses in order. George made an appointment.

The financial consultant, Roy, asked George whether he had any particular financial goals in mind. George told him that he was very worried because if he lost his job, he would also lose his home. Rather than reassure George that this would never happen, Roy asked him what options he thought he might have if this happened. George replied that he didn't think he had any. Without any savings and with the pile of unopened bills in the desk drawer and no idea where the household money was going, George felt like he was in the path of an oncoming train.

The consultant then explained to George that he was happy to help him, but that the first thing George was going to have to do was help himself. This meant facing up to the possibility that he might soon be out of a job and home. Rather than running and hiding, George had to consider not just the consequences, but also the potential solutions to this setback. Then George should pick the most attractive option and pursue it. Roy was sure that with George's experience and skills, he would be able to find a similar position. But George also had to consider whether this was something he wanted. Maybe it was time for a change. Roy urged George to discuss the situation with Zola and to make a list of possible outcomes. Then Roy would discuss with him how to implement the ones that seemed most favorable.

George returned home with a firmer sense of confidence and sat down that evening with Zola to confess to her what was happening. She reminded him that one of his best friends from high school had more than once asked George whether he was interested in starting a handyman business that they could run out of George's van. It might be tough in the beginning while they were building a client list, but the prospects were promising. Through his friendships with other superintendents of neighboring buildings, George thought he would be able to get many referrals. It was something he could start right away on weekends and evenings and, over time, grow into a full-time business. He already had the van, after all.

Zola also said that once Myra was in full-time kindergarten, she would be willing to look for work, perhaps in the school system so that she could still have time with her daughter over school vacations. And she didn't really mind moving—maybe they could get an apartment with a little more light. George then went to the drawer where he had been putting the bills and notices and pulled them all out. Zola's eyes grew wide when she saw them, but she told George she would help him open and sort them all so they could try to figure out how much they owed.

George went to bed that night feeling better about his future than he had in a long time. Looking ahead and making a plan seemed to be a better medicine for his migraines than anything his doctor could have prescribed.

Commonsense Considerations

As George found out, the best way out of a financial dilemma is to make a plan that lays out your options. It's easy to make a financial plan. Here is how you do it.

- **Start as soon as you can.** Tomorrow is good. Now is better.
- **Set realistic goals.** Identify what you want, when you want it, and how much it will cost.
- **Divide your goals into short-term and long-term.** Anything that you think can be accomplished in a year or less is short-term. Everything else is long-term. For example:

SHORT-TERM GOALS	LONG-TERM GOALS
Pay all bills on time	Set up a retirement fund
Take a nice vacation in six months	Buy a house
Reduce debt on credit cards Consolidate credit cards when feasible	Improve credit rating
Buy a new computer	Learn something about investing

The "Setting Financial Goals Worksheet" on page 281 can help guide you through this process.
- **Devise strategies.** This is where your financial education comes into play. You need a workable plan to reach every one of your goals. You may have to do some research to figure out your options. Or ask for some help.
- **Budget your plan.** This means you have to figure out how much each goal is going to cost and find a way to fund it. It may cost nothing, or the expense may be substantial. It may take a short time or a lifetime

to find the money. However, you will need to commit to putting away a certain amount of money on a regular basis to fulfill your plan. How much will that be, and how does it break down? Do you want to throw all your resources toward one goal at a time until it is achieved and then move on to the next, or split your resources and work simultaneously on all your goals? It's up to you to make these choices.

- **Review your plan regularly.** Do your goals need revision? Be disciplined but flexible. Think ahead and be creative. You may want a pie-in-the-sky goal that you can aspire to achieve, but don't have so many that you will feel discouraged if you can't attain all of them.
- **Put your plan in writing** and keep it in sight.

CHAPTER 2

Making Do between Paychecks

Many hardworking Americans spend every cent they earn—if not more. Living close to the edge is, for many, a way of life that they feel helpless to change. The solution for some is to take on second jobs to help pay the bills and support their lifestyles, though this may be a difficult if not impossible option for others. Educating yourself about managing the money you have and how to use it efficiently is another alternative.

Is living from paycheck to paycheck a cycle that can't be broken? The answer is no. Is it ever possible to get ahead financially? The answer is yes. It takes commitment and fortitude, but if you face up to your situation, then frame a plan to change it, you can, over time, fix it. Here's how one couple did just this.

Saving a Dream

Luis and Angie managed to squeak by every month. Luis worked for a landscaping company and Angie was a dental assistant at a busy clinic. They had met and married when they were in their mid-20s and were looking forward to starting a family soon—if only they could figure out how to afford it.

They simply didn't know where to start. It seemed like every penny they earned paid their bills and their living expenses, with no room to spare. They couldn't figure out how to afford a puppy, much less a baby. Yet all their friends around them seemed to be having children, buying starter homes, driving around in late model cars. "What are we doing wrong?" they wondered.

One weekend, Angie's older sister Rosie came for a visit. She had studied accounting in high school and worked as a bookkeeper for a shipping company. "Let me take a look at your finances," she suggested. Although Luis was at first reluctant to open up what he considered highly personal information, he agreed to sit down with her. When she asked to see the couple's bank statements, they laughed. "Are you kidding? We don't even have a bank account!" Rosie tried to contain her surprise as she learned that Luis and Angie used a check-cashing service to cash their paychecks and purchase money orders to pay their basic bills.

"Well, at least you're starting out with no debts," Rosie said. "But no savings or investments either," added Angie.

With Rosie's guidance, the couple drew up a list of their inflows and outflows and looked at their financial profile for the first time. Their combined household annual income was about $50,000. Housing costs were low, with rent just one-quarter of their monthly income. Rosie explained that debt and housing are typically the expense categories where people find themselves overcommitted. In Luis and Angie's case, these areas were under control. What they needed was to figure out how to squeeze more mileage out of their income by making smart lifestyle changes.

Rosie thought it might help if Luis and Angie kept better track of their money in order to try to identify ways that they could reduce expenses. Although the couple knew how much each earned every week and what they spent on rent, phones, food, and transportation, Rosie felt the rest was falling between the cracks. She strongly urged them to open a checking account, not just because the check cashing services they used were expensive, but also because a bank account offered opportunities to see where their money was going. As an added bonus, their paychecks could be deposited directly. If they satisfied the minimum balance requirement, they might even avoid monthly and per-check fees. She also thought they should look into obtaining a credit card in order to establish a credit history.

Luis told Rosie they would try her program. He and Angie chose to open an account at the local branch of a large bank that was advertising a promotion for free checking. Over the next few weeks, they figured out how to write checks and how to balance their checkbook. They obtained a debit card and started to use it to pay for groceries because they felt it was safer than cash and easier to track on the monthly statement, which they carefully matched up to their receipts. They also learned how to electronically transfer money from the checking account to a savings account that they had also opened. In fact, they pledged that as soon as their paychecks were deposited they were going to take a certain amount and move it right into savings.

Over the phone, Rosie explained how they should use their monthly statements to closely track their expenditures. She said they should think of each month's statement as more than a record to document what checks they had written—they should consider it as a tool to analyze and control spending. She suggested they sit down every month to review these statements and try to brainstorm new ways to put away savings.

Within six months of opening their bank account, Luis and Angie found that they were not only paying all their bills, they were much more conscious and conscientious about their spending. With the monthly bank paperwork, they could now account for their money, and they were able to better regulate their purchases. To their surprise and delight, the money accumulated in savings topped $1,000. When they called Rosie to report this momentous event, she offered to help them build a more formal budget and explain some principles of long-term financial planning. Luis immediately extended an invitation for Rosie to come and visit again. After all, thanks to her, their financial outlook was certainly "rosier."

Commonsense Considerations

When it comes to saving money, every little bit counts. Minor reductions in everyday expenditures can make a big difference. Like Luis and Angie, you too can uncover ways to be more efficient with your money

- Automatic payment is a simple process that can be set up online or over the phone with a bank representative. Using it for recurrent bills saves time and money and helps avoid costly late fees or interest charges.
- Home lunch is invariably less expensive than take out; take out is less expensive than sit-down restaurant service. "Brown bagging" is a great way to save money. So is cutting down on meals eaten out. Challenge yourself to find interesting, more economical restaurants. You could also make a resolution to skip dessert and coffee for a year and see the difference this makes in your wallet (and your waistline).
- Try putting yourself on a "latte diet." Decide how much you can afford to spend per month on designer coffee and buy a gift card for that exact amount. Or just brew your favorite brand of coffeehouse coffee—it's much cheaper per cup than purchasing it at the cafe.
- Carefully examine monthly phone, cable, and Internet bills. Would your Internet service be less expensive if it were bundled with your cable or telephone and wireless lines? Do you need high-speed, or could you be more patient and save money? Do you have a shared family plan where there's no charge between callers subscribing to the same service provider? Stay on top of new plans and offers.
- It's good economy—not to mention sound ecology—to turn off lights and minimize air-conditioning and heating. Call your utility company to see if they offer a free audit to help customers cut costs. Make house rules about using appliances—like making sure that the dishwasher is full before it is turned on and that lights are always off in unoccupied rooms.
- Target transportation for reducing spending. Is carpooling a possibility? Are there public transportation alternatives? Do you know exactly how much it costs you to drive your car? Add it up—then figure out where to cut.
- Examine bills (including a monthly line-by-line review of credit cards) and eliminate expenses like phone service features you don't use, gym memberships you don't utilize, or subscriptions to magazines that you don't have time to read.
- Brainstorm with family and friends; check money-saving tips in local newspapers and online; and set goals and stick to them.

Educating Yourself Out of Debt

Allan's stomach turned upside down every time the telephone rang. He never answered it, because it was usually somebody calling about a debt. Allan had a wonderful wife, two great kids, and a good job that afforded him a decent living. But there was always something competing for his money, whether it was the electric bill or the roof that needed to be replaced or hockey equipment for his boys. It was a constant juggling act.

Allan lay sleepless in bed at night, his mind always returning to the fact that he needed to make more money. It wasn't any one problem that had caused him to fall behind in his payments; it was all the everyday expenses that had dragged him to his current state of delinquency.

Then one day, a friend called to invite Allan to a financial education seminar. Normally this would have been the kind of invitation that Allan would turn down without a thought, but recalling the previous evening's sleeplessness, he accepted. Although he walked into the seminar doubting he would really learn anything, he walked out with nothing less than an intense desire to learn more.

The seminar was the first time Allan actually ever had formal instruction in money management. The speakers talked about using time and consistency in investing, how to eliminate debt, and how to defer taxes. They suggested strategies and took questions from the audience that clarified aspects of managing money. They pointed out how important it is to pay yourself first—put money away from every paycheck before tackling the bills. They talked about keeping a mortgage affordable and staying on top of rates. They summarized ways to defer taxes with retirement accounts and discussed how to establish an emergency fund—something Allan had never thought he could afford.

With the financial seminar as his inspiration, Allan sought out additional ways to educate himself. He went to his local library, where he took out a number of books written by well-respected financial experts and read back issues of a monthly magazine that focused on how to manage money. He subsequently established a relationship with a professional financial advisor who helped him develop a plan to reach his financial goals. He now has a growing savings and investment account, and he has refinanced his mortgage. He knows that being educated and having a plan is half the battle. And he sleeps soundly—every night.

Commonsense Considerations

Here are some time-tested principles of money management Allan learned that might help stretch that paycheck beyond your basic expenses.

- **Start by embracing the principle of paying yourself first.** No matter how little or how much you earn, you should automatically put a set amount in your savings account. This way, you can work to build up your savings.
- **Find a way to save $100 to $150 monthly.** Track your expenses carefully for a month and then sit down to evaluate them. An obvious first place to look to cut would be services or products that you don't use or can stretch between uses, like visits to the barber or beauty salon, custom car washes, dry cleaning, or recreational shopping. If you still can't come up with the money, you may have to resolve to make a lifestyle sacrifice for a limited period until you meet your goal.
- **Make sure your mortgage has the best rate and terms possible.** Keep an eye on rates and offers and refinance when it makes economic sense. Be sure to ask your lender for the true cost of refinancing, including points and fees, and for payoff terms.
- **Arrange to pay half your mortgage every two weeks rather than paying once a month.** This allows more money to go to principal than interest, paying off the mortgage sooner (and saving you interest on that principal) than the scheduled term. Or arrange to make one additional mortgage payment per year, in conjunction with an annual bonus, tax refund, or end-of-year savings.
- **Invest intelligently.** Consider the advantages of tax-deferred investments, such as retirement accounts, where you have no income taxes to pay now and interest is reinvested to increase the base so that additional earnings can accumulate. Taxes are due when money is withdrawn, and early-withdrawal penalties may apply.
- **Establish an emergency fund, and give it special status.** You should aim to accumulate three to six months' of living expenses. Keep these

funds liquid but not too readily available and use them only to pay for serious, unexpected situations.

For further guidance, check out Chapter 8, "Dispatching Debt," Chapter 9, "Building a Budget," and Chapter 17, "Saving Your (Financial) Life."

CHAPTER 3

Driving Away Car Loan Problems

Americans love their cars. But few love the cost, which can average more than $28,000 for a new car and nearly $13,000 for a used vehicle, according to the National Automobile Dealers Association. For many, at these prices, financing becomes a necessity. After mortgages, auto financing is the most expensive loan most Americans carry. When you add in related costs such as insurance, gas, registration fees, and maintenance, the total cost of auto ownership is considerable.

A car loan is a serious obligation. It's a contract, and inability to make timely payments can wreck your credit rating or trigger even more dire consequences, such as repossession. You may then have to pay off the entire loan balance in order to get the repossessed vehicle back. Or you might find that the vehicle has been sold at dealer auction for wholesale or below wholesale price.

If a dealer or lender sells a repossessed vehicle for less than what is owed, the difference is known as a deficiency balance. Assuming the dealer or lender has followed correct procedures for repossessing the vehicle (which may include posting required notices and conducting a commercially reasonable sale), they can sue you in court for the deficiency and receive a judgment to enforce payment. Even if they fail to follow procedures, or wrongfully deny your right to reinstate the contract, and are not entitled to a deficiency judgment, you must be prepared to go to court to show what they did wrong.

The easiest way to avoid this bleak scenario is, of course, to make sure the loan you obtain is well within your means to pay and then make timely payments on it. But sometimes circumstances can spiral out of control. What should you do then?

The Odyssey

Diane and Roger decided they would like to request unpaid leaves of absence from their jobs to take a cross-country trip. To save costs, they would stay with friends and at public campsites. They didn't feel that either of their current automobiles, both which had been purchased used, would be reliable or comfortable enough to make this journey. Neither car had functioning air conditioning, and both had various idiosyncrasies—on one, the trunk was held shut with a bungee cord; on the other, the passenger side door wouldn't lock. Both had required extensive mechanical repairs in recent years and were prone to breaking down, often at the most inconvenient times.

Roger browsed automotive magazines to check out the latest designs while Diane perused consumer publications that rated safety, fuel economy, and reliability. They narrowed down their choices to two or three models and headed over to the local dealership to take a look. They were hoping to make their purchase within the next month or so, preferably before they sank any more money into repairs on their older cars and in plenty of time to get acclimated to the new car before their trip. They had made some preliminary calculations on the back of an envelope to figure out how much they could afford and were confident they would be able to avoid being "taken for a ride." One item they agreed they would purchase was a service contract, which they felt would be added protection against breakdowns.

As soon as they walked into the showroom, a friendly salesman offered to pre-qualify them for a loan. They reckoned it wouldn't hurt and gave him the necessary information. It turned out their combined incomes and solid credit score made them eligible for a larger loan than they had planned on. When the salesman heard that Diane and Roger intended to drive the car across the United States, he convinced them they would need a roomy vehicle.

After considering several options, Diane and Roger zeroed in on a full-size car with all the bells and whistles. Not only would it hold all their luggage and camping equipment, they could also fit their bicycles in the back if they put the seats down. The color they wanted was in stock, though there was only one left, which added to the pressure to purchase the car immediately.

They chose to offer one of their cars as a trade-in, even though they were able to get only $400 for it. After the salesman deducted their down payment, the remaining balance on the loan translated into a monthly payment of about $800. Although they had vowed they'd shop around for the best deal and the best financing, they didn't want to lose the opportunity to buy this model. Within a matter of days, Diane and Roger found themselves the new owners of a new car, with a whole new monthly expense to figure into their household budget.

Diane and Roger enjoyed the novelty of their new car. The first time they took it to their favorite service station they were still so enthralled they barely noticed that it cost nearly $50 to fill the tank. When their son suggested they might be able to buy gas cheaper at another service station, they just laughed. "We just spent a lot of money on this car," Roger said. "A couple more cents a gallon isn't going to make that big a difference."

The couple plunged ahead, planning their trip, contacting friends and relatives across the country they hoped to visit, and plotting a route. Then, the unexpected happened. On one of their regular bicycle rides Diane fell off her bike and broke her leg in two places. She was told to stay in bed for 6 weeks, only venturing out to the doctor's office for physical therapy, and was not permitted to go to work for at least another 2 months. Immediately, the couple's income was reduced by almost half, and they had to put their cross-country plans on hold.

Diane's injury did not cause an immediate impact on their bank account because they had been building up funds in anticipation of their trip. Roger was able to manage their bills on these savings and his income alone. Additionally, they had made the first quarterly payment for their car insurance, so that expense was covered. But without Diane's full income, their resources started to become strained.

When the bill for the car payment arrived, Roger started to worry about how they would manage until Diane got back to work. He set it aside.

Four weeks later, another bill arrived—and Roger suddenly remembered the previous month's bill. Sure enough, a large penalty had been added to the overdue amount. Although she was still not able to get around easily, Diane felt pressured to get back to work to help cover the bills that were piling up. Staying home until she fully recuperated was no longer an option.

Roger was now experiencing buyer's remorse about the new car. He felt it was ridiculous that his wife should have to return to work so that they could pay for the vehicle. The price of gas seemed to be rising every day, too. Why hadn't he paid more attention to the average-miles-per-gallon signs posted on the showroom models? Why hadn't they just done what they always did and bought a sound used car? Not only that, he was paying almost $100 a month for the service contract to cover a car that was now going nowhere.

Diane recognized these issues were too overwhelming to deal with on their own. She sought credit counseling.

The counselor, Kim, took the initiative to call the company that had financed Roger and Diane's car loan. Since only a few payments had been made, options were limited. New cars depreciate by several thousand dollars as soon as they are driven off the lot, so even though the car still looked and even smelled new, Diane and Roger would lose at least their down payment if they put it up for sale to cover the loan. Despite this, Kim suggested they try to sell the car and buy something cheaper. Although they would be left with a balance on the current loan, they had the cash flow to cover the deficiency plus a more modest loan on a used car.

Kim then suggested another alternative: If they could come up with two more payments, their bank could request a double deferment on the loan. This would push two payments to the end of the loan and give them more time to stabilize their financial situation.

Later that week, Roger called Kim to say they were able to shift some money from their emergency savings to make the two payments. Diane would return to her job so their cash flow would stabilize. Their trip, however, was put on indefinite hold, since they could no longer afford to take the unpaid leaves they had planned. For now, Diane and Roger would have to be content with biking and camping closer to home, instead of across the country, in their new car.

Commonsense Considerations

Roger and Diane might have been in less of a predicament if they had kept these steps in mind before heading to the showroom.

- **Start with an honest assessment of your credit history.** You may wish to work on clearing it up before you even think about what kind of car you'd like to buy. A better credit rating can mean a lower rate—and the option of spending a little more. Use the time while you do this to bargain hunt for your dream car at a fair price.
- **Figure out your current finances—and project into the future.** How much do you want to pay? Does that number match what you can actually afford to pay? What if you suffer a reversal? Make sure that you'll have enough income left over to cover your current monthly living expenses and that you have enough in the bank to cover at least two payments if for some reason you do not receive your paycheck.
- **Calculate your related expenses.** Though that SUV may have caught your eye, additional costs for gasoline may steer you toward a more fuel-efficient vehicle. A larger vehicle may be more expensive to insure and can even mean surcharges at parking facilities and car washes. These costs add up!
- **Calculate total costs.** Remember, although you may pay less every month for a loan that is longer, you will pay more in interest over the life of the loan than for a shorter loan with higher monthly payments. The difference between a 3- and 5-year loan commitment may be more than you want to spend. Consider the total cost, with interest, as well as the monthly cost.
- **Shop around for loans.** Inquire at local banks and financing companies, as well as the dealer rates. Then, do yourself a favor and keep track of what loans are available to you. Record the providers, interest rates, lengths, and terms. See how they stack up.

SAMPLE FINANCING COMPARISON

This example will help you compare the difference in the monthly payment amounts and the total payment amounts for a 3-year and a 5-year credit transaction. Generally, longer terms mean lower monthly payments and higher finance charges. Review your monthly spending plan to make sure you have enough income available to make the monthly payment. You'll also need to factor in the cost of automobile insurance, an expense that may vary depending upon the type of vehicle.

	3 YEARS (36 MONTHS)	5 YEARS (60 MONTHS)
Amount Financed	$20,000	$20,000
Contract Rate (APR)	8.00%	8.00%
Finance Charges	$2,562	$4,332
Monthly Payment Amount	$627	$406
Total of Payments	$22,562	$24,332
Down Payment	10.00%	10.00%

Note: All dollars have been rounded for the illustration. The numbers in this sample are for example purposes only. Actual finance terms may be different and will depend on many factors, including your credit worthiness.

Source: Understanding Vehicle Financing, reprinted with permission of the American Financial Services Association Education Foundation, all rights reserved.

Deals on Wheels

Skip had pined for a light truck for several years and finally felt he could afford a late-model used vehicle. He shopped around carefully, answering ads in the local papers, posted on bulletin boards, and on the Internet, but finally found what he thought he wanted at a small used dealership that was located on the access road to the local highway he took every day to his job. It was a cherry red, 2-year-old pickup priced at $15,100.

Skip had already agreed to sell his sedan to a colleague at work and planned to use this money as a down payment. He realized that the terms for used cars were not as good as for new cars, but was convinced he would still save money over buying a new car. He asked to examine the buyer's guide for the truck, which wasn't posted. He was told that by law, the dealer didn't have to post it but the salesman would be happy to answer any questions he might have. Skip found out the truck was being sold without a warranty, but that there were no major mechanical or electrical problems with the vehicle. According to the salesman, even though the truck was being sold "As Is," if anything went wrong over the next three days, or even if Skip changed his mind, he could return the pickup, no questions asked.

Skip inspected the truck with the help of a checklist he'd torn out of a magazine. He took the pickup for a test drive with the salesman riding next to him. He immediately fell in love with the truck and decided not to bother asking for the maintenance log or if he could take it to an independent mechanic. Deciding that payments stretched out over 3 years would be the most manageable, he signed the papers and drove away.

He didn't get far. About 20 miles down the road a burning smell filled the air, and the truck's temperature gauge shot up to the red zone. When Skip pulled the truck over and popped the hood, and a huge cloud of smoke wafted out. Skip left the hood open and set out on foot to find a service station that might give him a tow.

When Skip drove up to the used car lot—this time in the passenger seat of the tow truck—the salesman he had dealt with just an hour or so earlier seemed a lot less friendly. The salesman was sure the problem was a "minor" thing that Skip should just take care of. Skip explained he had just taken "care of" a $50 tow bill and that was about the extent of what he wanted to take care of. The salesman reminded him that he had purchased the truck "As Is" and therefore the dealership was under no obligation to fix it.

Skip, who was normally mild-mannered, was rapidly reaching a boiling point. He asked to speak to the manager. While he was waiting, another customer approached and suggested he check out the buyer's guide to see what rights he had. Skip explained there was no buyer's guide. The customer told him that was something to bring up with the manager when he showed up. But he also told Skip that unless the salesman had put the promise to take the truck back in writing, the verbal agreement probably wouldn't hold up.

When the manager came in, Skip tried to stay calm as he explained what had happened. When the manager heard that there was no buyer's guide, he shook his head. "We always post a buyer's guide," he said. He went to the computer, tapped a few buttons and printed a new one. He looked at it for a few seconds before handing it over to Skip. "Looks like it's your lucky day," he said. The box next to "As Is—No Warranty" was clearly not checked.

Skip was greatly relieved and appreciated the manager's honesty. It turned out that all that smoke and burning smell had resulted from the snapping of a belt that was easily fixed by the mechanic right next door. As Skip drove away from the lot he could see the manager having a heart-to-heart talk with the salesman who had sold him the truck. Skip was sure this experience taught both he and the salesman a lesson they wouldn't forget.

Commonsense Considerations

If you run into difficulty with or have questions about any of the terms or conditions of your contractual obligations, don't run and hide. Know that you do have options—but so does your lender. The sooner you face up to your situation, the better your chance of a favorable outcome.

- Involuntary repossession can occur if you fail to make timely payments. Repossession does not relieve you of your obligation to pay for the vehicle. In some states the law allows a creditor or assignee to repossess your vehicle without going to court. A creditor or assignee may take the vehicle in full satisfaction of the credit agreement, or may sell the vehicle and apply the proceeds from the sale to the outstanding balance on the credit agreement. This second option is more common. If the vehicle is sold for less than what is owed, you may be responsible for the difference.
- Talk to your creditors. In their publication *Understanding Vehicle Financing*, the American Financial Services Association Education Foundation (AFSAEF) recommends that you contact your creditors to explain your situation and the reason your payment will be late and to suggest that you are open to working out a repayment schedule.
- The AFSAEF also suggests that, if necessary, you should seek the services of a nonprofit credit-counseling agency that may be able to mediate between you and your lender.

CHAPTER 4

Mortgage Matters

It's a cliché, but, yes, owning a home is the American Dream. According to the Department of Commerce's Census Bureau, the U.S. homeownership rate has been close to 70 percent for several years. For many, their home is their greatest asset. It is at once an emotional and financial investment. Because of this, its value should be carefully guarded.

A mortgage, however, is not an asset. It is a liability and must be taken seriously. Every day, homeowners unnecessarily risk losing their homes by not making their mortgage payments. Foreclosure has an immediate personal impact and can affect a borrower's ability to buy a home in the future.

Happily, there are strategies to avoid defaulting on a mortgage and facing foreclosure. It's critical to understand these options in order to save your home. It's even more important to learn how to avoid foreclosure in the first place.

Flying Low, Flying High

Kyle was in big trouble, and he knew it. A pilot for a private airline that catered to corporate business travelers, he had been able to buy a large home in an upscale neighborhood a decade ago, and he mortgaged it to the maximum amount possible. Over the years, he had maintained his property in a meticulous fashion and paid his mortgage like clockwork. But 9 months ago, the owner of the airline had some financial difficulties, putting Kyle out of work. Kyle could have found another job while the company was reorganizing, but he felt an allegiance to the company and especially its executive clientele, so he preferred to wait it out.

During this period, Kyle had only two sources of income: unemployment benefits and rental income from tenants who lived in the basement apartment of his house. This was just enough to pay for his utilities, food, and incidental expenses, but not much more. He was not able to afford his largest obligation, his mortgage, on this reduced income. Kyle reasoned that he could get away with skipping a few payments and as soon as he got back to work he would catch up.

Unfortunately, reorganizing the company took longer than he anticipated, and Kyle's creditors, including several credit card companies, started closing in on him. He consulted a friend, an attorney, who recommended filing for bankruptcy to discharge his credit card debt. In the meantime, Kyle's mortgage payments continued to fall further and further behind. He received notice that the bank had started default management procedures, a precursor to initiating foreclosure proceedings. Because bankruptcy does not prevent a lender from foreclosing a property on which there is a first or second mortgage (such as a home equity mortgage), the borrower risks foreclosure even after final resolution of the bankruptcy case. In fact, if Kyle did not make his mortgage payments while the bankruptcy case was active, the lender could even seek approval from the bankruptcy court to foreclose against the property while the bankruptcy was still in effect.

Although the bankruptcy severely downgraded his credit score, it allowed Kyle to put more of his income toward his mortgage loan. And it turned out that his previously regular payment history worked in his favor. His bank's default management department agreed to work with him to see what could be done to help him avoid losing his home.

It was clear that it was going to take a great deal of work to assist Kyle. The loan was now more than 9 months in arrears. Although the typical time frame for referring a loan to foreclosure is 4 months after the initiation of default management procedures, the bankruptcy had stalled the collection and foreclosure process, allowing the mortgage to run 9 months past due. Kyle asked his family to advance him a personal loan, which they agreed to do with the stipulation that it would be repaid once he was working steadily again. Because of this loan he was able to offer the bank a substantial payment of $15,000 toward the default on the property.

Kyle's bank officer then suggested he consider a loan modification, a revision of the defaulted loan that could help pay down past-due amounts by adding a portion of the delinquency to the current unpaid principal balance. But there were complications. Kyle's loan had been sold to another lender. His original bank no longer "owned" the loan. It was just acting as the servicing agency, or the entity that collects the payments owed on a mortgage on behalf of the lender or investor holding and owning the loan.

The modification plan that Kyle's bank suggested was well beyond the new lender's guidelines. The new lender indicated that because of the magnitude of the default, Kyle's best course would be to sell the property. His bank officer then went to bat for him, pointing out that Kyle had $15,000 to put toward the default and that the property was well maintained. Fortunately, the investor agreed to give Kyle a second chance to save his home.

Kyle's bank then argued that it would be best for all parties if Kyle was put on a repayment plan through modification of his loan. Kyle would pay the $15,000 as a down payment and would be responsible for 12 payments of his previous monthly amount plus an additional $1,000. This would result in the delinquent amount being paid off after one year.

Kyle knew this additional amount would be hard to swing. The house was so important to him that he decided he could make some temporary lifestyle adjustments to afford it. He gave up his car, which was leased, and started taking public transportation. This immediately freed up $450 a month. When his tenants in the downstairs apartment moved out, he took the opportunity to charge a higher rent to the subsequent renters. And he tightened his belt on other living expenses.

Kyle was relieved when he got the call to return to work. He called his bank officer to report that things were "looking up" and thank him for stepping in when he needed the help.

Commonsense Considerations

Throughout negotiations, Kyle's bank representative was able to point out to the new holder of the mortgage that prior to his financial crisis, Kyle had been making consistent payments for several years, and that it was likely this pattern would continue.

If you are experiencing difficulties and find it hard to make your monthly mortgage payments, you should communicate the facts to your lender or the firm servicing your mortgage—the sooner the better. Extenuating circumstances might include unemployment or a job change that caused a decrease in your income, illness, divorce, or a recent death in your immediate family. Many lenders will appreciate that you contacted them and assist you based on their investor or insurer guidelines on your loan.

Here are some of the options that may allow you to keep your home:

- **Forbearance,** which is a temporary suspension of payments to allow you to bring your account current, can be offered if your financial situation is temporary and you will be able to afford your mortgage payments in the near future.
- **Repayment plans** suggested by the lender where you make more than one payment per month until the loan is brought current. For example, a payment plus one-quarter more.
- **Modification,** or the elimination of past-due amounts by adding all or a portion of the delinquency to the current unpaid principal balance. Term extensions and interest rate adjustments may also be considered, when necessary, in order to create an affordable payment.
- **Claim advance,** if your loan includes mortgage insurance. The lender can determine if you qualify for a loan from your mortgage insurance company to bring the account current.

Letting Go to Stay Ahead

Annie and Carl had inherited Annie's grandmother's large, colonial-style house in the 1960s and raised six children in it. Along the way they had taken out a mortgage to provide the cash flow to finance upgrades, pay college tuitions, and provide tax relief. Carl retired from his job as a free-lance sound recording engineer when he turned 65, and Annie took an early-retirement package 2 years later when the nonprofit company she was working for underwent an internal reorganization. Both were quite involved in community and charitable endeavors and weren't really paying attention when interest rates started to creep up after several years of being relatively flat. Because interest rates were falling when they financed the house, they had signed up for an adjustable rate mortgage, which had been a smart financial move at the time.

One day when they were in the dining room paying bills, they noticed that their payments had jumped up by more than $300 over the same month the year before. At the same time, the price of heating the house was going through the roof. Although they were quite diligent about keeping the thermostat low, the house was old and drafty and the heating system inefficient. They were genuinely shocked to open a bill for $1,400 for a single month of natural gas.

Annie and Carl might have considered selling the house, even though it had been in the family for more than a century, but there was an added wrinkle. Their youngest son, Rickie, was a "boomerang baby" who had returned home after college and never left. He lived in a room they'd fixed up for him in the basement, working at a series of low-paying jobs that never seemed to last for more than a few months. If they sold the house and downsized, what would become of Rickie?

Everyone in the family, of course, had an opinion. Their eldest daughter was married to a commercial real estate developer who was convinced that the house could readily be broken up into condominiums and sold for a huge profit. Their next daughter, Amy, was deeply emotionally attached to the house and burst into tears any time the suggestion of selling arose. One son urged them to look into taking a second mortgage or line of credit, and another thought it might make sense to rent the property and move to Florida until interest rates settled down again. Rickie's twin brother, who was a paralegal, brought up the possibility of a reverse mortgage that sounded intriguing. He didn't know much about reverse mortgages other than you have to be at least age 62 to apply for one, but he thought the topic might be worth investigating.

Annie and Carl decided to educate themselves about reverse mortgages. They went to the library, where a research librarian helped them do an Internet search and showed them the section where personal finance books were shelved. Reverse mortgages, they found, come in assorted shapes and sizes. But basically, a reverse mortgage is just what it sounds like—an inside-out mortgage.

With a regular mortgage, the bank advances you the money to purchase the house and you pay back the loan gradually, over time. With a reverse mortgage, the bank pays you the value of the house, either in a lump sum or over time. Then you (or your estate) pays this back with interest at the end of the loan period. Since you are still the owner of the house, a reverse mortgage doesn't get you off the hook for paying utility costs such as heating and electricity, or property taxes. As for the amount that can be advanced through a reverse mortgage, this depends on the value of the house and your age. Believe it or not, the amount you can get is greater the older you are. If you have a current mortgage, you can use the reverse mortgage money to pay it off or do this with other resources you may have, but you can't have both a conventional and a reverse mortgage.

Initially, this seemed like an attractive proposition to Annie and Carl. They liked the idea of the debt limit—that the amount of the loan could never exceed the value of the house. If real estate values crashed, it wouldn't be their problem—it was the bank's loss. And Rickie could stay put.

Then, a few clouds appeared that shed some rain on their plans. First, their son-in-law pointed out that it was his understanding that Annie and Carl could never add the name of one or any of their children (or anyone, for that matter) to the title of the house. That meant if they decided to take an extended trip or move to warmer environs for the winter and wanted to rent out the house in their absence, they might be considered in default. Under the terms of some reverse mortgages, they would have to stay put.

Annie and Carl needed a third-party opinion to help balance their options, so they called their accountant, Georgina. She asked them to try to set aside the emotional issues while evaluating the facts. How much would it cost them just to stay put? Annie and Carl were pretty sure that just keeping up with the mortgage would be an increasing struggle. What could they get for their house now? They said they believed that the house was worth more than it ever had been, but they were unsure that this value would hold. Right now it was in a good school district, and this made the neighborhood particularly attractive to couples with young children. It was rapidly becoming clear that perhaps the best option was to sell the house and purchase a comfortable but more modest home, or even rent and use some of the proceeds to resettle Rickie in his own apartment.

When they explained this analysis to their children, they allowed each one to voice an opinion but stayed firm on their decision. Just as they were about to put the house on the market, Amy, their younger daughter, came forward. She had convinced her husband to relocate his business to her hometown, and the two of them were interested in buying the house "to keep it in the family." While this pleased Annie and Carl, they told Amy that they were going to move ahead with their real estate agent to see what kind of price they could get for the house. They did not want Amy's brothers and sister to think they had cut her a deal, so once there were some offers on the house, Annie and Carl would negotiate a price. If Amy and her husband didn't want to meet that price, the house would be sold to the highest bidder.

Annie and Carl felt like they had made some monumental decisions, but firmly believed they had chosen the best options for themselves and their entire family. The last thing in the world they wanted was to lose their house to the bank through defaulting on their mortgage, and now they realized that sometimes to hang on, you've got to let go.

Commonsense Considerations

Annie and Carl considered their mortgage payment an important obligation, well worth their attention. Recognizing that your home is at once an asset, a liability, and an investment will pay in the end. Even if you do go into default, there are still options that your lender may allow you to explore. For instance:

- **Short sales** occur if you can no longer afford your home and the property sales value is not sufficient to pay your loan in full. In a short sale, the lender may be able to accept less than the full payoff as settlement in full for the account.

- **Loan assumptions** are another option. If you can find a qualified buyer who would like to assume your mortgage loan, the lender may allow this transfer of ownership.
- **Deed in Lieu** is when you have had the property listed for sale at fair market value for 90 days with no activity. The lender can review the account to accept a "deed in lieu" of fulfillment of your mortgage obligation. If you qualify, the lender would agree to accept the property as settlement.

See also Chapter 12, "Home Sweet Home Loans."

CHAPTER 5

Covering College Costs

Paying for a college education is a major concern for students. Many fear that the debt they incur—and risk of joblessness after incurring it—might more than offset the benefits of a higher education. According to one survey of college students undertaken by the Partnership for Public Service, graduating seniors rank college debt and joblessness among their greatest fears. Yet without that college degree, career options and income are severely limited over the long term. College graduates earn 73 percent more than high school graduates, on average, says a report from The College Board. It's a Catch-22 that confounds many.

Parents, too, are concerned. Costs to attend a 4-year public institution more than tripled between 1985 and 2005, topping $5,000 (including tuition and fees) a year. Four-year private institutions are considerably more expensive, coming close to $20,000 a year. Even families who started planning when their children were still in diapers can be caught short.

2005–2006 AVERAGE ANNUAL SCHOOL EXPENSES

SCHOOL TYPE	TUITION AND FEES
Four-Year Private	$21,235
Four-Year Public	$5,491
Two-Year Public	$2,191
Room and Board (approx.)	$7,791

Source: Making the Grade, Smith Barney, 2005

While many parents place a high value on higher education, some are not able to make room in their budgets to save the necessary funds, or prefer to wait and see if college is the right choice for their offspring before committing to pay for it. Staying on top of tuition costs requires a collaborative approach among parent, child, and the institution the child wishes to attend. When those college catalogs start arriving in the mail, it's definitely time to figure out a plan that will send your child to the top of the class—without bottoming out your bank account.

Third One Lucky

Kevin and Margie's youngest child, Emma, was a senior in high school. The couple had managed the cost of putting their eldest son through state university, and their middle boy was enrolled at the local community college. They had long made clear to their children that they were happy to cover tuition costs for undergraduate education, but the children were responsible for paying their own room and board and pocket money. Both boys had held jobs during the school year and had worked all summer.

Now, Kevin and Margie felt tapped out. The irony was the good news that Emma had maintained a high GPA throughout high school and was an attractive candidate for a top-tier private university. It was beginning to look as if Kevin and Margie might have no choice but to raid their retirement funds to cover Emma's college costs.

Because they were unsure how to do this and what the consequences might be, Kevin and Margie tried to do research. They came up with conflicting information. To clear up the confusion, they made an appointment with their local bank's financial center branch representative.

In reviewing Kevin and Margie's financial situation, Andy, the representative, saw that the couple's commitments to their older children's education had left them barely able to keep up with their own retirement plan contributions and daily living expenses. Andy suggested that since Emma excelled academically, she might qualify for a scholarship. Exploring this option should be their first step, before moving on to consider loans or plundering their tax-shielded savings. A good place to start was with their respective employers.

Margie worked as a bookkeeper for a doctor's office; Kevin's company was part of a large multi-national corporation. Kevin contacted his human resources department and found out the company, in fact, offered a college scholarship program for children of employees. Kevin obtained the necessary forms, and they were in the mail the day Emma sent off her last college application. The scholarship amount, which was awarded in the spring, was sufficient to subsidize the contribution Kevin and Margie were able to make. Emma was further inspired to do well at college in order to qualify for annual renewal of this award.

Commonsense Considerations

There are a large variety of scholarships available to support educational goals. Close to $3 billion is given to qualified students every year in the United States.

Here are some avenues parents and students should investigate to identify and locate scholarship programs.

- There are numerous catalogs and listings available both on the Internet and in book form. Take a rainy afternoon to surf the Web or browse your local bookstore.
- Your child's college or guidance counselor should have comprehensive information on available scholarships as well. Give a call or make an appointment.
- Keep your eye out for scholarship solicitations in your local newspaper. Investigate potential local resources in your community by calling your local librarian or city or town hall.
- Do you belong to a union, a professional or trade association, a club? If you don't ask, you'll never know what they might have to offer. Don't forget to contact your church, synagogue, or mosque as well.
- Don't overlook (or underplay) your child's special talent in ping-pong, tuba, or organic chemistry. If your child has a particular artistic, athletic, or academic gift, there may be a scholarship targeted specifically for supporting further education in this area.
- Ask at the local branch of the national chain stores where you shop if they have scholarship programs for customers' children.

Beware of scholarship scams. Services that offer to locate "secret" funds or that require a fee to identify scholarships may not be legitimate and should be regarded with appropriate suspicion.

Flagging Down Dollars

Nate, an industrious high school student with a passion for history, was accepted at a small liberal arts college with a prestigious history department. Although he was awarded a small scholarship by the school, it barely made a dent in his tuition and housing costs, and his father, who raised him alone, had no further resources to offer. Anticipating this lack of support, Nate had put away every penny he earned from the summer job he took after his junior year of high school: working as the flagman on a road crew repairing potholes—a hot and grueling but lucrative endeavor. The summer after his senior year, much as he would have liked to sit in the air-conditioned town library reading historical biographies, Nate again joined the road crew.

Although he was able to put away a sizeable sum, when he began his first semester at college Nate was still short of the amount he needed, so he researched additional income opportunities on campus. The option that most appealed to him was a Federal Work-Study program that would provide him a government-subsidized job. Through this program, Nate would be able to earn money for his education as well as for discretionary expenses. Nate applied for and was assigned a work-study job as an assistant to a well-regarded professor of Russian history. The job was a good fit. The professor took Nate under his wing and appreciated the quality of his research. Nate was able to balance work and school demands for the fall semester.

Right before winter break, however, Nate's father had a minor heart attack, and when Nate came home for the holiday, he was distressed to find his father struggling with the daily demands of life. He decided to stay home to nurse his dad back to health. He missed the first two weeks of classes and was not able to fulfill his work-study job obligation. After his father recovered, Nate tried to catch up on the missed class work. But doubling up time and effort on academic demands reduced the time

Nate had left for his campus job. Because he had been counting on this job to pay his remaining expenses for the semester, he sought advice from the financial aid office.

At the financial aid office, Nate learned that the normal process would be to apply for a federal loan before seeking private, possibly higher-interest, money. But since it was already halfway through the academic year, the best the financial aid officer at Nate's school could suggest was to see about obtaining a student loan from a bank. Nate's only other alternative, it seemed, was to take a leave of absence and try to build up his savings to re-enroll the next year. Nate decided he would rather stay in school.

The advantage of the private loan was that Nate could obtain the funds quickly. He was able to complete an online application and get an immediate affirmative response. The loan filled in the gap between college costs and the money he was losing due to his inability to work as many hours. By replacing his missing income, his loan allowed him to focus his time on his academics. Toward the end of the school year, Nate found out that he had been awarded additional scholarship funds toward the next year's tuition. And, best of all, he was offered an opportunity to work again with his mentor over the summer—this year, in the air-conditioned university library.

Commonsense Considerations

It's important to consider the benefits and the drawbacks of the various sources of financial aid available for paying educational expenses. If the money is not granted as a scholarship, gift, or grant outright, it must be repaid. Interest rates, fees, and repayment terms can vary widely. There also may be limits on the amount that can be borrowed.

Loan programs come in two forms: public, offered by the government; and private, available through private loan companies. Congress determines interest on federal loans. Private loans, which are less restrictive, charge higher rates that may reflect an applicant's creditworthiness.

Here are some details about the major sources of financial aid available for paying educational expenses.

Scholarships

- Scholarships do not need to be repaid. They are given to students who have demonstrated or shown potential for excellence in a certain area or discipline, such as academics, sports, or music. There are thousands of private scholarships available through various companies, organizations, and clubs. Financial need is not necessarily part of the criteria for receiving scholarships.

- Scholarships can be one-time payments or renewable. If you anticipate you will need support throughout your college years, it pays to look into scholarships that can be renewed provided you continue to meet the criteria.

Grants
- Grants are awarded to students who demonstrate a financial need based on formulas established by federal and state governments and/or the school. Grants, like scholarships, do not have to be repaid.
- Grants are available from the federal government, state government, schools, and private organizations.
- Pell Grants are the largest source of need-based gift aid and are funded by the U.S. government.
- Pell Grants are awarded only to undergraduate students who have not previously earned bachelor's degrees or professional degrees, though in some cases, a Pell Grant may be awarded to a student attending a post-baccalaureate teacher certification program.
- The U.S. Department of Education guarantees that each participating school will receive enough money to pay the Federal Pell Grants of its eligible students.
- To apply for a Pell Grant, you use a FAFSA, or a Free Application for Federal Student Aid, available from your financial aid office or on the Internet at www.fafsa.ed.gov/.

Federal Work Study
- The Federal Work-Study Program requires a student to have an established financial need. The amount of the award is determined when you apply for aid, based on the level of financial need and the funding level at the school.
- Federal Work-Study Program participants are guaranteed to earn at least the current federal minimum wage and may be eligible to earn even more, depending upon the job and the skills required.

- The total amount earned through the Federal Work-Study Program cannot exceed the award amount given by the financial aid office for the school year. Therefore, the number of hours you can work is limited.
- Federal Work-Study Program jobs can be on- or off-campus positions. Your school's financial aid office will have a listing of available positions. Where possible, students are offered on-campus jobs related to their fields of study. Off-campus jobs are sometimes available with private, nonprofit organizations or public agencies whose work is in the public interest.
- A major advantage of the Federal Work-Study Program is the real-life experience. You can draw on this work experience when seeking employment after graduation. You have a unique opportunity to show future employers that you are reliable and hard working and that you can balance work with the other demands of your life.
- Many colleges sponsor student employment programs independent of the Federal Work-Study Program. Sometimes you can still obtain on-campus employment through a school-sponsored program even if you do not qualify for Federal Work-Study. Your school's financial aid office can provide information and guidance about school-sponsored employment programs.

Federal Perkins Loans
- Federal Perkins Loans are among the lowest-cost loans available to both undergraduate and graduate students with exceptional financial need. A Perkins Loan is obtained through your school and is secured with government funds that you must repay directly to the school.
- The total amount you can borrow is limited to specific levels for undergraduates and at the graduate level (and may include any monies previously borrowed under this program as an undergraduate).
- There are no fees for a Perkins Loan. The school pays directly by check or credits your account during the academic year.
- Once you've graduated, you have a specified grace period (assuming you've been attending school at least half-time) and then a certain number of years to repay these loans.

Federal Stafford Loans
- Federal Stafford Loans can be either subsidized or unsubsidized. Subsidized Stafford Loans are awarded on the basis of financial need. Interest is paid by the government while you are in school and during periods of grace and deferment. Unsubsidized Stafford Loans are available to everyone and require payment on the interest on the portion of the loan while in school and during periods of grace and deferment, as well as during repayment.
- To be eligible for a Federal Stafford Loan, you must be enrolled as a full- or half-time undergraduate, graduate, or professional student and submit a FAFSA.
- Principal payments are not due while you are in school or during a grace period after graduation. A grace period (typically 6 months) also goes into effect when a student drops below half-time status or leaves school without graduating.

Federal Parent Loans for Undergraduate Students
- Federal Parent Loans for Undergraduate Students, known as PLUS loans, are available to parents of dependent undergraduate students and to graduate and professional students without a parental guarantee. They offer a solution for financing up to the full cost of education, less other financial aid awarded.
- Repayment of a PLUS loan begins after the loan is fully disbursed. However, certain PLUS loan providers allow parents to defer payments as long as the student is in school.
- Standard repayment terms allow up to a certain number of years to repay a Federal PLUS loan, in addition to any periods of deferment or forbearance.

Private Student Loans
- There are numerous private student loan programs offered through private companies and banks. Private loans (also known as alternative loans) help bridge the gap between the actual cost of an education and the amounts the government allows you to borrow in its programs.
- Because private lenders offer these loans, there are no federal forms to

complete. You can shop around to compare favorable terms to get the best deal for your particular circumstance.

- Private loans are typically sought when federal loans don't provide enough money or when more flexible repayment options are desired. For example, a parent might want to repay a loan over a longer period than available under a PLUS loan.
- The right loan for a student's situation should be determined with the lender.
- Parents considering an alternative loan may also want to consider a home equity loan.

Funding a college education has increasingly become a subject as critical to study as any college core course offering. Students paying for their education through scholarships, grants, and loans are in the majority on campuses across the country these days, and most students should be able to access the necessary funding. Research, analysis, paperwork, and perseverance are key to finding the best fit for an individual student and his or her family's needs.

For additional relevant information, see Chapter 14, "Being Smart About Saving for College," and Chapter 15, "Investing in Learning About Investments."

CHAPTER 6

Spend Less to Send Money

Since colonial times, economic opportunity and legal rights have made life in the United States attractive to people from other countries. Today, immigrants living and working in the United States are often the primary source of financial support for their relatives back home. The largest volume of money flows from the United States to Latin America, with some $30 billion transferred annually, according to a study sponsored by the Inter-American Development Bank. The study also found that more than 60 percent of the Latin American–born adults currently living in the United States send money home at least four times a year. Average amounts ranging from $150 to $250 are typically sent monthly. This is sometimes nearly all of the disposable income available to the family member living and working in the United States.

The money sent to family and friends is often quite significant—for many immigrants, constituting 50 to 80 percent of household income. The majority of these transactions take place outside the formal financial system. Many immigrants still rely on informal money transfer systems that require high service fees. In some instances, the money can disappear altogether when taken to less-than-reputable establishments. This chapter offers advice on the safest, most reliable ways to make such transactions.

Building a Promise

Ramon grew up in a rural area of Mexico, in a small house with concrete walls and a mud floor. His father would always tell Ramon and his two brothers and sister that some day he would build a nice big house for them. Even as a small boy Ramon realized this was more of a dream than a reality. Ramon promised himself that if he ever made any money, the first thing he would do would be to build a house for his family.

Ramon worked hard at his studies and, thanks to the attention of one of his teachers, when he was 14 he was given the opportunity to come to the United States on a scholarship program at a prestigious boarding school. After graduating, he returned to Mexico for a year and then applied to college in the United States. Once he'd obtained his degree, his student visa expired, so he applied for lawful permanent resident status and was granted the right to stay and work. He had an excellent job at a large bank in Los Angeles, and he opened a savings account where he started making regular deposits every time he received his paycheck.

After a few months, Ramon decided that his own financial position was stable enough that he could afford to send some money home. After all, he felt he owed his family something for raising him and for being understanding when he wanted to leave home. He wasn't sure exactly how he wanted to make this contribution. His father was getting on in years and would not be able to work much longer. Should he send a regular amount for his father to use any way he saw fit? Or would it make more sense to set up his brothers and sister in a small business that would not only provide them a living but might someday allow his investment to be repaid?

Then, he remembered the promise he had made as a young boy.

Ramon contacted his brothers and outlined his plan. He wanted the two of them to share responsibility for being the general contractors on his "secret project." He then spoke with his sister and took her into his confidence. She would be in charge of the finances and be his eyes and ears as the project unfolded.

Over the next several weeks, Ramon and his siblings laid down the groundwork for the project. His sister scouted a plot of land to buy, and his brothers put together a team to work with them. Ramon and his sister together developed a budget, and he continued to put away money from his earnings. Through the bank he worked for, he arranged to make orderly transfers of money into an account he set up in his home town that only his sister could access. All this time, Ramon continued to work and excel in his career.

When the building actually began, Ramon's brothers told their father they had been hired to work on a construction project. Their dad didn't suspect a thing. Ramon sent his sister a digital camera so she could record the progress of the project. Once construction got started, it seemed to go very fast. Ramon reviewed his sister's ledgers of expenditures and made sure the money was in the account when it was needed for materials and supplies or to pay the workers.

Ramon told his father that he would come home for Christmas that year and that he had a big surprise for his present. When he arrived at his home, his father asked gruffly where this "important present" was, obviously disappointed that Ramon didn't have it in his luggage. With a smile, Ramon helped his father into the taxicab that had brought him from the airport. They drove to the site of the house—his father's new house—that Ramon, with the help of his brothers and sister, had built. For Ramon, the look on his father's face was worth more than anything else his money could have bought.

Commonsense Considerations

Just as Ramon learned, it is important to carefully think through your own expectations for money you send out of the country. Why are you sending money home? Here are some typical scenarios:

- The money is a repayment or reimbursement to family or friends who financed your migration. In this situation, be sure that the amount being repaid (and the rate, if there is interest) is clearly understood and documented before sending any money back. Otherwise, it may be unclear when your obligation is fully satisfied. Consulting an attorney may help you to properly document the debt.
- The money is sent to voluntarily support family back home. Here, your remittance is really a gift. Once the money is sent, you should

not expect to receive anything in return. Your family or friends will not be paying you back.

- You are legally obligated to send money home, perhaps in response to a court order to support family. You should not expect to receive anything in return for these required payments and should carefully document them.

- Sometimes, money is sent as an investment in a family business. These situations are more complex than a remittance intended as a gift. Ideally, you should consult with an attorney in your own country or in the United States to advise you on how to clearly document the terms of your deal. There may be state and national laws that limit the amount of interest you can charge, another reason why you should work with a lawyer.

- Is your money being used to build or buy a home that you expect to live in after you return to your country of origin? Consider, then, such issues as who will own the house and who will live in your home while you are working in a foreign country? Who is responsible for paying the costs of upkeep and any real estate taxes? All of these questions need to be carefully considered, and, ideally, written down and agreed upon before you send money home.

Sending Safely

Until she was 30 years old, Joanelle had never left the small Caribbean island where she was born and raised. By then, she had been married and divorced and had two young daughters, who were 7 and 9 years old. She hated to leave them behind, but she knew her mother and sisters would take good care of them, and she promised she would come home to visit them as soon as she could. Then she boarded an airplane for the first time and flew to a large city in the United States, where her new employer was waiting at the airport for her with a cardboard sign that said "Welcome Joanelle," drawn in crayon by a child's hand. The children she was going to care for had made it for her.

Joanelle had been hired through an agency to be a nanny for the Weathers family. Mrs. Weathers was a business executive who worked long hours and traveled across the country, and Mr. Weathers was an important judge. They had two boys about the same age as Joanelle's girls.

Joanelle was given her own room in the Weathers' home. Her job was to help the boys get ready for school in the mornings and walk them there, then pick them up from school and take them to play dates or sports lessons, assist with homework and dinner, and sometimes baby-sit if their parents were going out. Mrs. Weathers said that while the boys were in school Joanelle could enroll in a course at the local community college or, if she preferred, work at a part-time job to earn extra money, as long as she could still pick up the boys on time. The Weathers were paying her a weekly salary and were paying her taxes, which they explained was very important. Because Joanelle didn't have to pay for room or board and had few expenses, it was her intention to send as much money as she could back to her mother to help the household.

Mrs. Weathers helped Joanelle open a checking account at the local back so that Joanelle could be paid by check. Joanelle could withdraw cash through an ATM machine or by writing herself a check and standing in line at the bank. She could also pay bills through the account, either electronically or with checks. It would be safer to keep her money in the bank than to walk around with it in her purse or keep it in her room.

Joanelle found her job easy and pleasant, even though she missed her girls terribly. They spoke on the telephone every Sunday. After just two weeks of working, Joanelle had already saved up $200. She put the cash in an envelope and mailed it off to her mother. During their weekly phone call, she told her mother to watch for the envelope.

When Joanelle called the following Sunday, her mother told her that the money still hadn't arrived. Joanelle told her not to worry; it could be that the mail service was slow. Another two weeks had passed, so she mailed off her savings, $200, again.

Now that Joanelle had been living in the United States for almost a month, she decided to look for a job she could do while the boys were in school. She found one at a local florist. So she was making even more money now. She decided that instead of sending it all to her daughters, she would try to save half of her salary from the flower shop to buy a ticket to visit her family when she had some time off. The rest she added to the amount she had been sending to her mother.

That Sunday, her mother told her again that neither of the two envelopes had arrived. Now Joanelle began to get worried. She decided to ask if Mrs. Weathers might help her find the letters.

Mrs. Weathers didn't exactly scold her for sending the money, but she was clearly upset that Joanelle hadn't come to ask for help earlier. She said that sending cash through the mail was always risky because there was no way to trace it and it could be easily stolen. She explained that, instead, Joanelle should have gone to the bank where she had her account and asked if they had a way to make a low-cost transfer to send money out of the country. She also warned Joanelle not to use one of the storefront money services, because they would charge too much money to send the $200 and might charge her mother to pick it up too.

The next day, Joanelle went to her bank and found out she could have the money sent to a bank near her mother's home. When she called that Sunday, she explained the procedure to her mother. First, she got the good news that both envelopes had been delivered in the mail just the day before. Joanelle hadn't put on enough postage for them to travel airmail, so they had taken the slow route. Both Joanelle and her mother were much relieved. Joanelle asked her mother to use some of the money to buy her daughters special treats. And she said to tell the girls she would be home to visit them very soon.

Commonsense Considerations

There are a variety of options for sending money home. Each has different features, fees, security, advantages, and disadvantages. You should make sure to always ask specifically about fees, if any, associated with the method you choose to use and how they are charged. Fees may be deducted from the amount sent or may be charged in addition to it. Additional fees or commissions may be charged for converting your money from U.S. dollars into the home currency. And the conversion rates may differ from company to company. Foreign exchange rates are often posted so you can compare them; if you don't see them, you should ask.

When money is being converted from one currency into another, the buy rate is the rate that the transfer company or bank uses to "buy" currency from you, and the sell rate is what is used when it "sells" the currency. The difference between the two rates is called the spread. Generally, if you convert U.S. dollars into your home currency, you will lose some value of it in the conversion. That's how the bank or transfer company makes money.

There is a chart on the next page to help you decide the best way to send your money.

SENDING MONEY OUT OF THE UNITED STATES

METHOD	HOW IT WORKS	FEES*	ADVANTAGES	DISADVANTAGES
Cash via mail or personal delivery	Send money with a relative, friend, or acquaintance, or put the money into an envelope and mail it.	Postage Fx	Low fees No rules	Vulnerable to loss or theft
Bank or post office money orders	Purchase a check that is then mailed or carried home.	Processing Fx	Low fees Can keep a copy for records	Limits on amount per money order Recipient bears cost of fx
Prepaid money or gift cards	Purchase the card here, to be mailed or carried home by a friend.	Postage Fx ATM charge	Security Low or no fees Value limited to amount stored on card	Can access money only through specified ATM or merchant
Money transfer companies (e.g. Western Union, MoneyGram, Vigo)	Most common way to transfer funds through Web site, telephone, or walk-in.	Sending fees Fx Pickup fees	Widely available in many countries Easy to use Available almost immediately	Higher fees
Wire transfer via SWIFT, ACH, or other bank networks	Arranged through your local bank by fax or the Internet or within bank systems.	Sending Fx Receiving	Secure process Available to any financial institution You don't have to be a customer of the bank	May take up to a week Tracking may be difficult If you don't have an account at the bank you may need to pay cash and will be charged higher fees
Bank internal transfers	You transfer the funds from the bank's Web site, ATM, telephone system, or teller.	Sending Fx Receiving	Automated sending at low cost to sender Real-time transfer	Bank rules vary Must have a bank account, which may have minimum requirements

METHOD	HOW IT WORKS	FEES*	ADVANTAGES	DISADVANTAGES
Dual/bi-national charge or debit bank accounts	A single account that can be accessed in two different countries. Works like a debit or credit card with two users, where primary account holder can share the account with someone in another country. Two statements are issued.	None	Free access to money in ATMs	Obligation to cover charges if other holder overdraws

*Fx = foreign exchange conversion and fees to sender or recipient

CHAPTER 7

Keeping Credit in Check

Just about every adult (and more than a few teenagers) in the United States has a credit card. Credit cards are without question a fast, efficient, and convenient means of payment. They are also instrumental in establishing a credit history, which plays an essential role in your ability to make large purchases such as a home or automobile, to get a job, or even to open a bank account.

The credit card industry facilitates almost 20 percent of all consumer spending in the U.S., or the equivalent of some $1.7 trillion, according to the U.S. Bureau of Economic Analysis. Consumer spending is a key component of the U.S. economy, accounting for a significant portion of the nation's Gross Domestic Product, a measure of the economic health of our country. This may be good for the U.S. economy—but can be a challenge for overextended individuals and their families.

Unfortunately, the line between credit card use and abuse is sometimes thin. When people spend more than they have the capacity to repay, big problems may result. If you are not fully educated about credit, you can mar your credit history for years to come.

Some signs of being overextended are obvious. Others are more subtle. Common warning signs include avoiding totaling your debt (and being unable to make an estimate that is within a few hundred dollars of being accurate), having maxed-out credit limits, having a delinquent account, needing cash advances or payday loans to pay bills, persistently paying only the minimum monthly, or experiencing a denial of a credit application. Is this you?

The Revolving Door of Revolving Credit

Len and Elaine came from farming families that stretched back generations, and their organic soybean farm had survived good times and bad. Now, during a long dry season that brought weeks of relentless sun and no rain, they were struggling daily to make ends meet.

Farming, while greatly romanticized in this country, is a notoriously fickle business. Farmers are dependent on prices often set in global markets by factors far beyond their control. Len and Elaine's financial problems had started when prices dropped at precisely the same time their property taxes had increased. This forced them to sell off some of their land just to pay their monthly expenses. Since money was so tight and their earnings were down, they had started using their credit cards to pay for necessities such as groceries, computer support for their business, fertilizers, and parts for farm equipment. In almost no time they racked up thousands of dollars in credit card debt, and for a year they had been consistently late with their payments.

Len and Elaine just couldn't catch up, no matter how hard they tried. Every day they felt themselves sinking deeper and deeper in debt. Selling their beloved farm started to loom large as their only option. This was an extremely painful thought.

One day they received a phone call from Adam, a manager in one of their credit cards' high-risk accounts department. Their account had been flagged for being consistently delinquent. Adam was calling to find out why their payments were late. As he listened to Elaine apologize and explain their problems, he realized this was a true hardship situation. Because of this, he was able to have a new payment plan authorized. He then recommended that they seek the advice of a professional credit counselor to advise them about their other debts.

Because of the cyclical nature of their business, it seemed likely that Len and Elaine would be able to work their way out of the debt hole they had dug for themselves. And their optimistic outlook was now supported by a change in the weather—and with the rain clouds, a silver lining.

Commonsense Considerations

Ideally, Len and Elaine should have contacted their credit card company when they first realized the extent of their financial difficulties. Take the initiative to work with your creditors to find the repayment arrangement that works best for you. The longer you wait to seek a resolution to your financial dilemma, the fewer options you may have and the harder it will be.

Most creditors offer a variety of payment options, including settlements. If you are having a difficult time paying your debts, qualified nonprofit credit counseling agencies can offer valuable assistance and may be able to help work out payment plans with all your creditors.

Educating yourself about your credit cards can help head off situations like Len and Elaine's before they happen. Here is a list of what you should know about every credit card you use. Most of this information can be found in your original credit card agreement detailing the terms and conditions for your credit card, on your monthly billing statement, and in card member fulfillment materials that accompany the card. If you can't find it, try calling the toll-free number on the back of your card. Customer service should be able to help you.

- **What kind of card is it?** Secured cards require a security deposit. Premium cards have higher credit limits than regular cards and may offer a package of extra features, like warranties, travel insurance, or emergency services.
- **What is its annual percentage rate, or APR?** The only way to truly compare credit card rates is using the APR. The APR is the finance charge (which includes interest and certain types of fees) over a year's time. Sometimes, credit cards can have different rates—a rate for purchases, a different rate for cash advances, and a third, even, if you transfer balances. Look to see if the rate changes after an "introductory APR" or if there are penalty or delayed APRs. A penalty APR is what's charged if you miss a payment date. Introductory rates are typically low rates that induce you to apply for the card

and then go up after a specified period of time. Similarly, a delayed rate may have no interest until after a specified time period.

- **Know your grace period.** This is the amount of time you have before interest rates start being charged or assessed on purchases, cash advances, and balance transfers. For example, for cash advances, interest often starts being assessed from the day the cash advance is posted to your account.

- **Figure out how your finance charge is calculated.** Different companies use different methods depending on your balance and the timing of your purchases and payments. Some have a minimum finance charge, no matter how little you have purchased.

- **What are the fees on your card?** These can be recurring, like an annual fee for having the card, or situational, like a fee for taking a cash advance, transferring balances, or making a late payment. Card companies also assess fees for exceeding your credit limit or paying your bill with a bad check or by telephone.

- **How do cash advances work?** Can you use an ATM to get an advance? What are the limits? How are payments credited? Keep in mind that payments you make may be applied to purchases before cash advances.

- **What additional features does the card offer?** Rebates on purchases, frequent flyer miles, extended or additional warranty coverage, car rental insurance, and charitable donations are examples.

> When you borrow money, the **interest rate** (typically expressed as a percentage amount) is what you pay to your lender as a cost of borrowing. The **finance charge** is a dollar amount that includes the interest plus any additional fees. An **annual percentage rate, or APR**, is an annualized representation of your interest rate. An **APY, or annual percentage yield**, takes into account the compounding of interest over a year's time and its effect on your debt.

Free Credit for Sale

When she was in graduate school, Paige learned much more than just what was taught in her academic courses. She would pay her bills by writing checks from her checking account, but then discovered that many companies accept credit cards as a form of payment. Authorizing automatic credit card payments eliminated the mad last-minute rush to bill paying centers, and, of course, it didn't matter how much money was in her bank account. This way, she was sure her utility and cell phone bills would be paid on time. She also found payment of other bills was made even easier because her credit card companies mailed her blank convenience checks.

When Paige graduated and entered the working world, she continued to juggle bills and credit card debt. She started paying one credit card with the convenience checks issued by another. She didn't expect to have to do this forever. But being a recent graduate, she was just starting out and her salary was low. She was confident that with time, as she got raises and work experience, things would be different.

Paige never analyzed her credit card statements closely enough to realize how the habits she had developed were creating significant debt. In fact, she barely looked at anything other than the minimum payment that was due, because that was the amount she would pay. She had no idea of the cost of credit or how long it would take to pay off a balance if she paid only the minimum. Because she had fallen into the minimum-payment habit, she ended up paying more in total interest over time.

As Paige's balances grew—along with her stack of bills—she found that opening her statements was becoming painful. Eventually the day arrived when Paige had maxed out her credit cards and couldn't obtain any more credit, even though she had filled out numerous applications. When she requested a copy of her credit report to find out why she had been turned down, she was dismayed to discover the true extent of her debt. There she was confronted with how many accounts she had and how much total debt she owed.

Without the option of obtaining additional credit cards, Paige panicked. For the first time, her income was all the money she had available to pay her bills. No longer able to use credit as an additional source of money, she decided to get a part-time job in the evening and devote the entire amount she earned to paying off her credit card bills.

Commonsense Considerations

If you don't know how much debt you can handle, it's easy to get in over your head. You can use the "debt thermometer" below to find out where your finances fall on the debt scale.

To figure out your debt-to-income ratio, divide your total monthly debt payments (including your mortgage and car payments, if you have these) by your monthly gross income.

The "Monthly Debt Percentage Worksheet" on page 284 will help you to calculate your percentage.

THE DEBT THERMOMETER

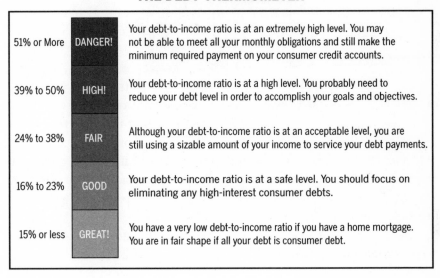

51% or More	DANGER!	Your debt-to-income ratio is at an extremely high level. You may not be able to meet all your monthly obligations and still make the minimum required payment on your consumer credit accounts.
39% to 50%	HIGH!	Your debt-to-income ratio is at a high level. You probably need to reduce your debt level in order to accomplish your goals and objectives.
24% to 38%	FAIR	Although your debt-to-income ratio is at an acceptable level, you are still using a sizable amount of your income to service your debt payments.
16% to 23%	GOOD	Your debt-to-income ratio is at a safe level. You should focus on eliminating any high-interest consumer debts.
15% or less	GREAT!	You have a very low debt-to-income ratio if you have a home mortgage. You are in fair shape if all your debt is consumer debt.

Source: CitiPro® Financial Needs Analysis

If you find yourself overextended, the following steps can help you work your way out of debt.

- Make a list of your creditors and your corresponding debt amounts. Then add them up to find out your total debt level.
- On your list, record the minimum payment. Starting now, try to pay more than this number. Paying even a small amount over the minimum reduces both the amount of interest paid on your debt and the time it will take to pay it off.

If you owe $12,000 on a credit card with a 15 percent APR and only pay the minimum every month until the entire bill is paid off, it will take 323 months, or almost 27 years. You will have paid $14,305 in interest alone—more than your original balance! However, if you add the following amounts every month to the minimum payments, look at the results:

ADD TO MINIMUM	PAYOFF TIME (MO/YRS)	TOTAL INTEREST PAID	INTEREST SAVINGS*
$0	323/26.9	$14,305	$0
$100	76/6.3	$5,190	$9,105
$200	45/3.75	$3,307	$10,998
$300	32/2.7	$2,444	$11,861

*Savings over paying just the minimum

- Put your credit cards away in a safe place where you won't be tempted to use them. Cease further usage until you get your debt under control.
- From time to time, you may get an offer of a "free" month, where you don't need to send in a payment. If this occurs, ignore the offer and continue sending in your payment.
- Make a priority list for paying off your cards, perhaps starting with the one with the lowest total balance. Starting small will give you a sense of accomplishment, whereas trying to tackle a larger balance may take longer and lead to discouragement.
- Apply the monthly payment from the card that has just been paid off to the next card in the list.
- Send your payment as soon as you get the bill. Some credit cards accumulate interest charges every extra day if you carry a balance from one month to another. Even if yours don't, it's good to pay immediately, before that money gets detoured into other expenses.
- Consolidate and refinance high-rate credit cards by shopping around for the best interest rate.
- Resolve to be a credit-wise user once you've cleared up your balances.

Clearing up your credit has many benefits. A major one is its effect on your credit report. Just as school report cards contain a cumulative total of academic performance, credit reports gather information about your financial performance.

A credit report is a very powerful instrument. Lenders and creditors, insurance companies, some government agencies, landlords, and employers are allowed to order your report. Landlords use your credit history to assess your ability to pay rent, and employers may use it to judge your potential risk to the company. A credit report should exist for anyone who has ever had any form of credit issued. They are compiled by credit bureaus that collect information about debt and repayments. Credit bureaus don't decide whether you will get credit. They just report data used by lenders to determine your creditworthiness.

> A **credit report** typically lists your name, address, and current employer, your credit history, your payment history, any accounts that have been turned over for collection, public records (such as liens filed or bankruptcies), former address and employment information, and the names of businesses that have requested your credit history in the last 24 months. A **credit score** is a number assigned by a credit rating company that reflects your credit history as detailed in your credit report. A **credit rating** is the ranking assigned to each score.

It pays to make sure the information in your credit report is accurate. Some 70 percent of credit reports contain errors that might cause consumers to be denied credit cards, car loans, and even mortgages, according to Bankrate. com. Credit reports should be checked at least once a year to make sure they are accurate. The sooner you spot an error, the faster you should be able to correct it.

If there appears to be an inaccuracy on your report, contact the credit bureau that issued it right away. You have the right to dispute any errors. By law, the bureau must investigate your complaint and should correct or remove any inaccurate information, usually within a period of 30 days. The bureau must then send a revised credit report to anyone who asked for a copy in the previous 6 months. At your request, the credit bureau will also send you a revised report.

You must explain the errors in writing to dispute inaccurate information. Include copies of documents that support your position, as well as a copy of your credit report with the inaccurate information clearly marked or highlighted. Keep copies of your letter and all enclosures. Submit this information online, or send it by certified mail and hold on to receipts. If you disagree with the bureau's conclusion, you can ask that future credit reports include your statement explaining your side of the story. However, if the negative information is accurate, there is nothing you can do to remove it.

It's also important to keep in mind that your credit rating can be marred by others—including a spouse, or a child who has authorization to use your credit card.

Till Debt Do Us Part

Jamie married her charismatic boyfriend, Robert, with no thought to how her choice of spouse would affect her credit. When they met, Robert worked full-time and moonlighted on weekends. Only after they married did Jamie realize she had joined in union not only with Robert, but also with his many debts. Jamie herself had worked consistently and paid her own way through college. She had very little debt and a clean payment record. Robert was just the opposite. He had several high-interest loans with finance companies, a sporadic work history, and a spotty bill-paying record.

However, Jamie was swept up by Robert's carefree attitude, and the couple recklessly spent, charged, and borrowed. They amassed a collection of credit cards, a total of 25 between them. Whenever they couldn't pay cash for an item, they charged it. They traveled often and bought new furnishings and expensive electronic equipment. In time, the minimum due became harder and harder to cover on their many credit card and loan balances.

Shortly after their marriage, Jamie was offered a better job in another state. While at first it seemed like an opportunity to generate more income, it actually generated even more debt for the couple. There were moving expenses and repair costs on Robert's car. And Robert was unable to find work. It wasn't long before the bills coming in each month exceeded Jamie's new salary.

The couple's financial problems escalated. They had their loans refinanced and lengthened the repayment periods to lower their monthly payments. The couple was jointly and individually obligated on the loans. Collections calls and letters became a daily reminder of the sad state of their finances. Credit card balances continued to climb, since each month the couple could pay only the monthly minimum—or less. The frequent collection threats, along with the stress of being the only one in the family working, made Jamie angry and resentful. The marriage began to crumble as Jamie and Robert argued over the lack of money and the nagging debts.

Jamie finally had enough of Robert's careless and haphazard financial life. She filed for divorce. During the separation, Robert skipped town— actually, the state—and all the creditors came after Jamie. Stuck with thousands of dollars of debt and unable to meet the couple's obligations, Jamie sought the assistance of a lawyer. She ended up filing for bankruptcy to clear all of the unsecured debts.

Following the bankruptcy, Jamie felt defeated and helpless regarding her credit situation. In trying to reclaim her financial life, Jamie realized that Robert wasn't the only one responsible for their financial affairs. She took a hard look at her own spending habits and pledged to regain her previous low-debt, good-credit standing. Jamie vowed to work consistently and keep her checking account on track. She pledged to pay her living expenses on time and keep her debt at a manageable level. In time, perhaps, she would be able to rebuild her credit reputation, and she felt it would be worthwhile to work hard to do so.

Commonsense Considerations

Credit scores are developed by independent companies, credit reporting agencies, and even some lenders. Used to evaluate your credit-worthiness, they reflect your current level of debt, your repayment history, and your outstanding credit applications. Your scores from various agencies may be different, depending on the scoring models used to calculate them.

In 2006, the three major consumer credit bureaus (Equifax, Experian, and TransUnion) announced that they had jointly developed a new consumer credit scoring model called VantageScore℠. VantageScore℠ ratings range from 501 to 990. Your rating is similar to the grades you would receive in a school:

GRADE	SCORE
A	901–990
B	801–900
C	701–800
D	601–700
F	501–600

Source: VantageScore Solutions, LLC

Although there are letter grades associated with VantageScore℠, lenders will continue to make their credit decisions based on the actual, more precise numbers generated. The accompanying grade scale is intended for consumer edification purposes. It is expected that many creditors will have made the transition to VantageScore℠ by the end of 2007.

Currently, one of the most well-known names associated with credit scores is the Fair Isaac Corporation, which generates FICO scores that range from 300 to 850. Almost half the population scores in the 700 to 800 range.

Actions like paying bills on time, paying off accounts, and keeping existing balances low improve your credit score. Missing payments and maxing out credit cards will, obviously, make it worse.

Various factors have different weights in calculating your total score. For example, the length of your credit history can either help or hurt you. The average consumer's oldest obligation is 14 years old, indicating that he or she has been managing credit for some time. In fact, Fair Isaac found that one out of four consumers who recently applied for credit had a credit history of 20 years or longer. For those consumers, this longevity will help to increase their scores. For the one in 20 consumers with a credit history shorter than two years, brevity will pull down their credit scores.

Payment history, amount owed, and type of credit (mortgage or student loans are considered good; new credit can be a negative factor) all impact the credit score. Credit bureaus can report information that is up to 7 years old, except for Chapter 7 bankruptcy information, which can affect your account for up to 10 years. Most inquiries will be removed within two years. In addition, bureaus can report your lifetime credit history if it's used to evaluate you for credit or life insurance valued at $150,000 or more, or for a job paying at least $75,000.

Credit scores are vital to your financial health. Your actions can affect your score, sometimes dramatically. Jamie's credit score, based on her bill payment history, outstanding debt, credit account history, recent credit application inquiries, and the credit cards she had, was marred during her marriage. Here are some ways to keep your credit score in good shape and maintain a sound credit history:

- Every month, pay at least the minimum payment due, on time. Pay more than the minimum every time you can.
- Don't overextend yourself. The fewer accounts you have open—whether they are loans or credit cards—the better.
- Don't spend income now you hope to make later.
- Avoid transferring balances unless you are truly getting a better interest rate.
- Notify creditors when you move, so bills arrive on time and you can pay on time. Even if for some reason you don't get your bill, you still owe the payment. If your due date is coming up and you haven't received a statement, call the customer service number on your credit card. The customer service representative can tell you your minimum payment and where to send the check.
- If you co-sign a loan for a family member or a friend, make sure you can afford to pay the loan. If you are asked to pay and can't, you could be sued, or your credit score could be damaged. You liability for the loan could keep you from getting other credit. Your could also forfeit any property you may have pledged to secure the loan.
- If you co-sign a loan, make sure you ask for and retain copies of all important papers, including the loan contract and any disclosure

statements or warranties. You may have to ask the co-borrower for these if the lender does not furnish them. You can ask the lender to agree to notify you in writing if the co-borrower misses a payment so that you aren't caught unaware by a large liability.

- If your co-borrower does fail to make payments, you should try to bring the account current as quickly as possible. You should back this up with a written statement to all three credit bureaus explaining the situation and then work to determine if the co-borrower intends to make up the missed payments.

See also Chapter 8, "Dispatching Debt."

Dispatching Debt

Credit is a necessity in today's society. Without access to credit, routine transactions like making hotel reservations or renting a car become difficult, if not impossible. Credit histories are used as a means of evaluating how reliable an individual has been about meeting obligations. Credit is a tool that can provide tremendous convenience and buying power to those who use it wisely.

Most Americans have embraced the notion of credit and use it responsibly. However, some have accumulated levels of debt that are overwhelming. Rearranging the debt in a manner that results in lower payments and interest charges is one way to make it more manageable.

One solution is to secure a debt consolidation loan. This is a loan designed to pay off a number of existing debts. The monthly loan payment is lower than what was being paid on the existing debt total. This is made possible through a longer repayment period and/or a lower interest rate.

Debt consolidation loans offer convenience and simplicity. With the typical U.S. consumer holding nine credit cards, affording access to approximately $19,000 in available credit according to myfico.com, bill paying is time consuming. Additionally, it can be easy to overlook a bill due to misplacing it. For most people, having fewer bills to pay—not to mention lower payments—is a major convenience.

HOW CONSOLIDATION LOANS WORK

WITHOUT A CONSOLIDATED LOAN			WITH A CONSOLIDATED LOAN	
Typical Bills	Balance	Monthly Payment	Loan Amount and Cash to You	Monthly Payment
Bank Credit Cards	$1,600	$54	$5,000	$129.68
Retail Store Credit Cards	$400	$40	$0	$0
Car Loan	$2,700	$240	$0	$0
TOTALS	$4,700	$334	Monthly Savings	$204.32

Source: www.citifinancial.com

A consolidation loan can solve payment problems before you become delinquent, or it can help get you back on track if you have fallen behind. A consolidation loan can be more than just a means to manage debts more efficiently and cost-effectively. Sometimes, it is a solution to a financial crisis.

Working Overtime Just to Stay Afloat

Serge seemed a little on edge as he approached the desk where Martine, an officer at his local consumer finance branch, was sitting. Awkwardly, he stated that he would like to see about borrowing some money. As Martine pulled his account up on her computer screen, Serge confided he'd had some problems making ends meet recently.

Serge, 60, was the sole means of support for his mother, who had just celebrated her 85th birthday. Up until 5 years earlier, his financial situation had been stable. But as his mother grew older, her physical and mental condition started to deteriorate. At first he ignored the obvious signs. Now, he couldn't leave her at home without hiring someone to watch over her. The day care program she'd been attending told him 2 months ago they couldn't have her come anymore. Her health had deteriorated to the point where she might soon become bedridden. Although she received a monthly disability check, the situation still put a strain on

Serge's finances. He had no siblings who might step in to help, and he was determined to keep her at home.

Serge's job with a printing company allowed him the opportunity to work extra hours for overtime pay, and he had been trying to make up the difference by adding up to 20 hours to his 37-hour work week. But every month he felt like he was slipping deeper and deeper into a financial morass, and he was now driving around in a car with an expired sticker on it because he hadn't been able to afford the monthly insurance payment since his mother became confined to the house. Without proof of insurance, he couldn't get his car inspected. "Every time I pass a policeman my heart sinks," he confessed. He knew well the consequences of being stopped and not having insurance—not to mention what would happen if he was involved in an accident.

Martine listened sympathetically as Serge told of his troubles. As Martine examined his account, she could see that Serge's credit bureau report was stellar. However, his income was simply not sufficient to meet his financial obligations. He took home $3,500 a month after taxes, but his expenses totaled almost $3,900 a month. His mother's check paid for the mortgage, and everything else was his responsibility. When Martine showed him the math, Serge suddenly understood why he could never seem to catch up. She also showed him that working overtime wasn't helping as much as he thought, given that now he had to hire someone to watch his mother while he was working the extra hours.

Martine worked with Serge for an hour or so, reviewing possible solutions. Serge had thought that taking out a new credit card or perhaps an overdraft on his checking account might be enough. But Martine didn't think that this would be a flexible solution. After making some calculations, Martine asked if saving $900 per month would help. Serge answered with a resounding "Yes."

Martine had figured out that by consolidating most of Serge's bills, his monthly payments would be lowered by $900 a month. Serge's credit score made him eligible for a debt consolidation loan with a lower interest rate than he was currently paying on most of his credit cards. The rate was fixed, too, so he would know exactly how much he needed every month to pay off the loan. The loan was approved for a larger amount than his existing debt load so that he could use the excess to catch up on his car insurance. Martine carefully explained that Serge should be careful to use the funds wisely and not run up new debts with it. Serge smiled and promised that all he really wanted was to spend valuable time with his mother, which now he could do instead of having to work overtime.

Commonsense Considerations

Although a debt consolidation loan can be a useful financial tool, it is counterproductive if it is used to take on new debts. Consider this example:

Jane Thrifty and John Spender each carry $30,000 in total credit card debt at an interest rate of 19 percent. Each obtains a home equity loan at 12.5 percent that lowers their interest payments from $900 per month to $320 per month.

Jane Thrifty borrows only the amount needed to pay off the credit card debt and then closes all her credit card accounts. See below:

Consolidation Loan Amount	$30,000
Interest Rate on CLA	12.5%
New Credit Card Debt	$0
Interest Rate on New Credit Card Debt	0%
Ending Debt	$30,000

John Spender takes the loan at $5,000 more than he needs and then continues to charge on his now-empty credit cards, eventually reaching his initial level of $30,000. See below:

Consolidation Loan Amount	$35,000
Interest Rate on CLA	12.5%
New Credit Card Debt	$30,000
Interest Rate on New Credit Card Debt	19%
Ending Debt	$65,000

Note the difference in ending debt levels. John Spender ends up with more than twice the amount of debt as Jane Thrifty: $65,000 versus $30,000!

A House Provides Peace of Mind

Becky lived in a neatly kept suburban neighborhood that had recently begun attracting young families, thanks to a new branch of the commuter rail system opening just a few minutes away.

Becky worked full-time at the headquarters of a chain of auto parts stores. She also held volunteer jobs at the local library and hospital. She felt she led a full and orderly life. However, recently, Becky started to feel pinched financially. Although she thought she had worked out the numbers correctly, she found that as her house grew older she was putting more into keeping it up than she had planned. Replacing the front steps alone cost more than $7,000 last year, and now it was looking like the roof might need to be replaced. She found that routine plumbing problems, which once cost under $100 to repair, were resulting in bills five times that amount. And now there was a rumor that property taxes were going to jump.

Dipping into her modest savings just to pay the monthly bills made Becky nervous. She saw this as money put away "just in case" and not for everyday expenses like electricity bills and payments on her revolving charge accounts. But she was forced to do this twice in the past year, and this year the last 2 months in a row she found herself transferring funds from savings to checking.

Meanwhile, Becky's neighborhood was clearly changing for the better. She enjoyed seeing children playing on the street and riding their bikes, and bright new gardens were being planted. Several houses were being remodeled, and she began to receive notices from real estate agents who wanted her business should she ever decide to sell her home. "The only way I'm leaving here is feet first," was what she always said. But secretly she was starting to worry that her house was looking a little shabby next to the spruced up ones. She wondered what it was going to take to maintain it properly.

Whenever one of her friends or work colleagues asked about the mortgage on the house, Becky would change the subject. She had grown up believing that paying off a mortgage was one of life's key goals. She had only a few years more to go, if she could just hold out. But the truth was, the mortgage was not the problem. The house needed a lot of work.

Coincidentally, while she was waiting in line at the coffee shop one day, skimming the local newspaper, she saw an advertisement for a financial services group explaining how much money could be saved each month by consolidating bills into a single loan with one monthly payment. She decided it might be worth her while to stop at the office of the firm that placed the ad. It was just a few doors up the street.

While informed that she certainly could apply for a personal loan, Becky was asked if, as an alternative, she had considered instead making use of the equity in her home. As usual, she bristled at the thought of refinancing her mortgage. However, the loan officer, Ken, explained that this was not her only option. While she certainly could refinance for a higher amount and possibly lower interest and use the extra money to pay down some of her personal debt, she could also get a home equity loan or consider a line of credit secured by her home. Ken pointed out that it was likely that the interest rate on her credit cards was higher than the current home equity rates and reminded her that, in many cases, mortgage interest is tax deductible (though he cautioned only her accountant could confirm that).

The main difference, so far as Becky could tell, between refinancing and taking out an additional home equity loan was that the latter would be an additional mortgage loan but she wouldn't have to pay for closing costs. The refinancing loans offered fixed rate interest options for varying lengths of times, so she could get a loan that would be longer than her current mortgage, or shorter, and rates were mostly lower than her present mortgage interest rate. The last option, the home equity line of credit, would give her the flexibility to use as much or as little as she needed. Becky thanked Ken and said she'd get back to him in a few days after she had given the matter some thought.

When Becky got home, she pulled out her bills, her checkbook, and her calculator. She called one of the real estate agents that had sent her a postcard and asked if she might venture a guess at a ballpark number on the value of the house. When Becky heard the number, she nearly dropped the phone. There was plenty of equity in her home to combine her current credit card debt and three other outstanding loans into one monthly payment, saving her almost $600 a month. Because this option offered a lower interest rate than she was currently paying, it made the most sense.

Becky became convinced that even though she had looked forward to the day when her mortgage would be paid off, taking out this loan was an economically sound step given her need for cash. She collected the necessary paperwork and made other arrangements, including asking other creditors for pay-off figures, and figured out how much extra she would need for home repairs. Then Ken called Becky with the good news. She had been approved for a home equity loan at the lowest possible rate, considerably lower than she was currently paying on any of her other loans or credit cards.

Within two weeks, all of Becky's bills were current. Becky's salary provided sufficient funds each month to pay living expenses and the debt obligation. There was even money left over to start putting money away again—rebuilding her savings account rather than drawing out of it. This extra cushion gave Becky peace of mind that she had a safety net—and she was able to fully enjoy the home that provided her the means to make ends meet.

Commonsense Considerations

If, like Becky, your home is your greatest financial asset, tapping the equity in it can be a sound money-management decision. Home equity loans are worth considering if you're looking to finance home improvements that increase the value of the home, pay for educational expenses, consolidate a number of debts from higher interest forms of credit, or cover the cost of an anticipated major purchase or expense. They have the following attributes:

- Your loan is secured by the residential real estate property.
- Interest rates are generally lower than for other types of personal loans.
- Interest payments may be tax deductible.
- The amount of equity in the home is the difference between the appraised value of the home and the principal balance of your mortgage. For example, if the appraised value of your home is $250,000 and the outstanding balance on your mortgage is $100,000, your equity is the difference, or $150,000.
- Another variable used to determine loan approval and interest rate is the loan-to-value (LTV) ratio, or the ratio between the outstanding

principal balance on a mortgage and the appraised value of the home. To calculate this, divide the value of your home into the balance of your mortgage and multiply by 100. If the appraised value of your home is $250,000 and you owe $185,000 on your mortgage, your LTV is 74 percent.

- Generally, the lower the LTV, the greater the amount of equity in the home and the more money available for borrowing.
- You may find your interest rates can be lower if the lender feels your creditworthiness is more secure.

It's important to remember that while a debt consolidation loan can help ease a financial strain, it is still a debt. Just because you can qualify for a larger loan, that doesn't mean you should accept the maximum amount available. Obviously, taking out a succession of home equity loans can also have a downside: When you sell the property you may end up with virtually no value if the house is heavily leveraged. You would have to first pay back the lender before you saw any profits.

Remember, too, that bankruptcy does not prevent a lender from foreclosing a property on which there is a home equity mortgage. If you fail to make home equity mortgage payments while a bankruptcy case is active, the lender may seek approval from the bankruptcy court to foreclose against the property while the bankruptcy is still in effect. If home equity mortgage payments have not been made, the borrower risks foreclosure even after final resolution of the bankruptcy case.

A home is an important asset well worth protecting. Use it to your advantage—but always balance the need to stabilize your financial situation against preserving your wealth.

For further suggestions, see Chapter 7, "Keeping Credit in Check."

PART 1 SUMMARY

The chapters in Part 1 of *The Citi Commonsense Money Guide* share common themes. They are all about how to get your financial house in order. To do this, a number of suggestions are offered.

Make a Financial Plan—And Make It Work

First of all, try not to run and hide from your financial responsibilities or circumstances, no matter how dire they may seem. It's much better to face up to them and then try to educate yourself, on your own or with the help of a professional, about your options. The sooner you can do this, the better off you will be. Financial problems don't just go away. Even if it seems like they have, they may come back to haunt you later when they may be a lot harder (or more expensive) to deal with.

Setting goals is important. Kay and Marc may have come from diverse economic backgrounds, but their story illustrates how open communications can make such differences recede. Forward planning is also critical. It is the most basic building block for individuals, couples, and even families to rely on. This is reiterated throughout the book.

George certainly learned about the importance of facing up to reality and planning in the first chapter. It is frightening to have your job threatened and to have to consider the many changes this might entail. But you should try to force yourself to think ahead. Making a plan is a positive step that can help counteract negative circumstances, no matter how ominous.

You Too Can Save

Luis and Angie learned something they didn't think was possible—how to save. Living from paycheck to paycheck is not an unbreakable pattern.

With a plan, you can find ways to cut your expenses and achieve your dreams. Sometimes it helps to have an outsider, in their case, a banking officer, help review your situation and make suggestions you might not have previously considered. Luis and Angie thought they were saving money by not opening a bank account, when it was actually costing them money in check cashing fees. It was also depriving them of a simple but valuable tool to analyze their situation—their monthly statement. Most people just review their bank statement in a cursory way, for errors, rather than use it as a planning tool that can help them track and evaluate how they have been spending their money.

You're never too old to learn new tricks. In the same chapter that Luis and Angie appeared in, we met Allan, who made good money but never was able to enjoy it. It was gone before he knew it. He learned the value of a financial education and how it can help you not only manage your money smarter, but give you a whole new lease on life.

Don't Drive Yourself Into Debt

The next chapter illustrated how major purchases—like a car—might literally drive you into debt. Diane and Roger wanted only the best and safest for their cross-country trip, an understandable desire. But they fell into the common trap of buying much more than they needed or were able to handle. All of a sudden, they were faced with one of those "What if" situations. You should always ask yourself "What if" questions when arranging a big purchase. "What if our income is suddenly cut in half?" is what they should have asked themselves. Because they didn't, the car they purchased cost them a far higher price than the sticker price on the window revealed. Whether it's a car, a house, or that antique dining room set, don't let a big purchase control your life.

On the other hand, even if it seems like you are in an unfavorable situation, there may be a reasonable way out. Skip was worried that he was going to be responsible for the unexpected repairs to his newly purchased truck. However, he didn't give up easily and started to ask questions at the dealership. This was a wise course of action because an examination of his purchase contract revealed that the document favored his rights. Skip learned the value of asking questions and reading the fine print before signing a contract.

Home Is Where the Heart Is—And Where Your Equity Is

When Kyle lost his job, he might have tried to make alternative arrangements for his mortgage payments, but instead he just hoped for the best. In doing so, he put his home in jeopardy. Luckily, he had two things going for him: his excellent history of previous payments and his willingness to sacrifice in the short-term in order to keep his home. Keeping your financial house in order today can pay off if unforeseen circumstances threaten disarray tomorrow.

Annie and Carl's story showed how important it is to stay on top of your financial situation as your life changes. In their case, their need for a large house had changed. But they knew that their decision had far-reaching consequences, not only for their own lives but also for family members who were financially or emotionally dependent on them. After considering numerous possibilities, they made a decision. It wasn't easy, but they could rest assured that they had not made their choice by default, or in a panic. Always try to take the time to consider all the options before making a significant financial decision. Sometimes the most obvious choice may not necessarily be the best one.

Higher Ed About Higher Ed

With college costs going up every year, even parents who have saved conscientiously may come up short. Understanding how to finance a college education doesn't require an advanced degree—but it helps to be able to differentiate between the pros and cons of loans and grants. Of course, if your child can get a scholarship, that's ideal, and this option should be thoroughly explored. There's no shame in having to borrow to pay for college, and in the end it should pay off in terms of a host of benefits, starting with greater long-term earnings potential.

Don't Overspend to Send Money

Sending money from the United States to other countries is something many are doing every day, sometimes at high cost. You want to make sure that the money you are sending is being used for the purpose you intend and, if it is to repay a financial obligation, that you have done everything you can to make sure this is documented. You may also want to be sure you have chosen the most economical way to convert funds into another currency and send them internationally. There are many different services for doing this, and you should try to find the safest way at the lowest cost.

Credit Yourself with Credit Smarts

Many readers may have found themselves in familiar territory in the chapter on credit. Len and Elaine had to turn to their credit cards to get through lean times and then discovered that the debt they'd run up was creating a whole new financial emergency for them. Instead of solving a cash-flow problem, credit can create one of its own. Working your way out takes a deliberate, committed effort. Paige, however, was in so deep she had to take on extra work to accelerate her climb out of the debt that resulted from her misuse of credit. And Jamie and Robert had not realized how severely their carefree spending actions would catch up to them.

All learned the hard way how easy it is to lose control, even unintentionally, of credit. Learning to use credit appropriately is an educational process that requires attention to the details of your credit agreements and monitoring your use of credit every month. You should familiarize yourself as to where the danger line is—and when you have crossed it.

Here's the thing about credit: It's not free. So every time you whip out your credit card to take advantage of that great discount and don't pay off the entire amount before your next billing cycle, that item you just bought got more expensive. Check out this chart:

COSTS OF CREDIT

BALANCE	APR	FIRST MONTH MINIMUM PAYMENT	TRUE COST	NUMBER OF YEARS TO PAY FOR THE ITEM
$500	15%	$20	$600	2.4
$1,000	15%	$22	$1,552	6.3
$2,500	15%	$55	$4,877	13.9
$12,000	15%	$270	$26,305	26.9

Assumptions: Minimum due is calculated at a 2.5% payment rate. Minimum due is the greater of: finance charges + late fee + 1% of balance, or $20, or 1.5% of balance.

Source: Citigroup Financial Education Curriculum, Credit Module

If you were to charge $500 worth of clothes on a brand new credit card with a 15 percent APR (annual percentage rate) and you only pay the minimum due and don't charge anything else to the card, it will take you 2.4 years to pay off that debt at a cost of $100. The more you spend, the more it's going to cost you. That $2,500 two-week vacation will take you 13.9 years to pay off and cost you $2,377 in interest, if you only pay the minimum.

Digging Out of Debt

The final chapter in the first part of the book examines the forms and uses of debt consolidation. This is a great idea for Serge, who is trying to cope with his mother's infirmity and has expenses that exceed his income. So long as he doesn't run out and run up his debt all over again, the debt consolidation loan will help get him back on track. Becky also found a solution in a consolidation loan, in this instance by tapping into equity in her home. Debt consolidation can be a useful financial tool, so long as it is used as a means of facing, rather than compounding, a debt dilemma.

In many instances in this part, an emergency savings fund might have at least alleviated, if not eliminated, many of the dire situations people found themselves in. George would have felt more confident that he could have made ends meet for several months had he lost his job. Luis and Angie could have used it to discipline themselves to save, and it would have given Allan a sense of security. Diane and Roger, as well as Skip, could have dipped into it for their legitimate "emergency" circumstances, and then replaced the funds over time. Kyle, too, would have been justified in using emergency money to pay his mortgage, and it might have kept Len and Elaine's business on track through lean times.

Remember, it's never too late to honestly assess the condition of your personal finances, and it's never too late to fix what's not working.

PART

Basic Training

Personal finance is really all about you—your past and your future. The next eight chapters focus on the various aspects of building a secure foundation for that future. They discuss the nuts and bolts of sharing a financial life with another person, who may be a spouse, a significant other, a roommate, or even a parent. Also covered are how to pay for your toddler's diapers, teaching your preteens about managing money through allowances, and how to introduce older children to credit. Home loans, insurance, college funds, investments, and retirement are also part of this section. These are all essential pieces of a stable financial life.

CHAPTER 9

Building a Budget

One of the most useful tools for educating yourself about how much money you have now, have had in the past, and will have in the future is a budget. Yes, it's hardly as exciting as house hunting or dreaming about starting a family (or about sending those hypothetical children off to college), or even planning your retirement. But it is a cornerstone of a personal money plan that, if undertaken in an accurate, disciplined way, will help keep you on track to achieve your financial goals.

There are lots of ways to approach budgeting, from the casual and informal to the complex and systematic. But the basic steps are tracking your expenses and writing down your projections of what your expenses will be for the year to come. Then, based on an analysis of your current and anticipated spending, you can track and analyze how you're doing versus your projections.

Out of the Rut

Twenty-five-year-old Carolina was in a financial rut. She made decent money as a civil engineer for the state. She paid all her bills on time. She always had just enough money to make do each month. She kept her costs manageable by sharing living space with a roommate. But she had no savings and no investments, and when her best friend announced she was buying a loft condo in a new building downtown near where she worked, Carolina found herself angry and jealous instead of happy for her friend. She joked with her mother that she might go see a fortune-teller to see if there was ever any hope that she would be able to get out from under and be in a position to buy herself a condo or a less utilitarian car. This time, rather than nag her about finding a nice husband to support her, Carolina's mother told her she had arranged for Carolina to have three 40-minute sessions with a financial planner. She called it an "early birthday present."

Carolina met with the planner, Adrienne, the following week. She told Adrienne about her desire to start saving some money so she might someday buy her own place to live, or perhaps even go back to school to change careers, get a fancier car, or maybe even travel a bit. Adrienne started by asking Carolina to describe her current lifestyle and to detail what she spent on a daily basis. Carolina replied that she led a pretty quiet life, but, truth be told, she had no idea what her daily expenditures were.

She did eat out a lot, as she wasn't a great cook. She usually paid cash, so she didn't have credit card receipts for her meals. And she did have a penchant for expensive shoes. Sometimes she bought two or even three pairs in a single month. Other than that, all her other expenditures were for basics, like her half of the rent and utilities, cable TV, and phone bills.

Adrienne suspected that once Carolina faced the actual numbers of what she was spending on restaurants and takeout food, she might be willing to pare this down. She asked Carolina to gather her financial information and bring it for an analysis they would do together. Carolina asked Adrienne if it would cost extra for the materials. Adrienne smiled as she pulled out a form from a file cabinet behind her desk. "This is all you need, and it won't cost you anything extra," she said. "Now let's get started."

Adrienne showed Carolina where on the budget form to record her fixed expenses, which included housing, transportation, and insurance costs. Then, the two of them reviewed the types of expenses that occur on a regular basis but may vary from month to month. To determine how much she was spending on her cell phone, for example, Carolina was to take the total amount she had spent the previous year and divide that amount by 12 to make a "guesstimate" of the monthly costs. Food, medical costs, clothing, personal grooming expenses, and entertainment all fell into this method of calculating the monthly cost. Then, Carolina was to put down her debts, which included her student loan and credit card balances.

The next week, Carolina returned with her forms filled out. Adrienne transferred the subtotals from each category of fixed expenses, variable expenses, debts, and savings to a separate chart. Then she showed Carolina how to compare these costs against suggested guidelines. Because she was sharing her apartment, Carolina's housing expenses were well below the 35 percent suggested guideline as compared to her net income. But this was offset by the amount of money Carolina was spending on food and clothing (specifically, shoes). Her debt levels seemed on a par with accepted norms, as were her transportation costs.

Adrienne suggested that Carolina take a "shoe inventory," in which she noted to the best of her recollection the date she purchased each pair, how much they cost, and whether she was wearing them rarely, regularly, or frequently. She also asked her to closely track her food costs. Here again, Adrienne saw an opportunity for Carolina to cut back.

Two weeks later, Carolina returned for her final session with her data. It turned out she was spending close to $25 on food every day during the workweek—and sometimes more on weekends. Carolina told Adrienne that tracking these expenses was one of the most helpful exercises she had ever done. Adrienne pointed out that if she saved just $8 dollars a day ($2 at breakfast, $2 at lunch, and $4 at dinner) for 4 weeks, she would be able to save $224 a month. Carolina thought she could do this—and more. She was even thinking of taking a basic cooking course offered at a local gourmet shop so she could learn to fend for herself. As for the shoes, she had decided to make some changes. She had several pairs that were still in their original boxes, never worn, that she thought she might sell through an ad in the local paper or on the Internet. This might yield enough to pay for her cooking course.

Adrienne told Carolina that she had advanced in her financial education farther, in just 3 weeks, than Adrienne had expected. Carolina was thrilled and felt she had finally gotten out of her rut. She figured by the time her birthday rolled around in 6 months, she would owe her mother a big thank you note for putting her on the road to financial success.

Commonsense Considerations

Sometimes, a minor tweaking of spending habits can have a huge impact. Unfortunately, most people, like Carolina, have never taken the time to figure out where their money goes. They pass their lives making money and paying it out with little thought to how much they actually spend, especially in discretionary areas where they don't receive a monthly bill (for example, food, clothing, and entertainment). Creating a budget is a great starting point for making a record of where your money actually goes.

There's no secret formula, and you don't need a PhD in math to put together a budget. But even before you sharpen your pencil or warm up your computer, you need to spend a few hours digging out all your financial records and organizing them in a way you can rationalize and understand. You may want to purchase a filing cabinet and file folders, or you may prefer the shoebox approach. There are numerous software packages on the market that will walk you through making a budget, and there are resources readily available on the Internet as well. Regardless of your system, you first have to gather the data. These include:

- Tax returns
- Personal insurance (medical, life, disability, long-term care)
- Investments
- Employment records
- Money borrowed (mortgage, auto, consolidation loans)
- Medical bills
- Income records
- Property insurance (home, auto)
- Household items inventory
- Credit cards
- Titles and deeds
- Bank statements
- Annual credit reports
- Retirement plans

- Employer benefits and policies
- Money loaned
- Childcare expenses
- Vacations and travel

Designating a storage place for all your paid bills and financial paper-work for the year is also helpful for creating and tracking progress on your budget. For this you can also maintain a file folder system, though, increasingly, paperless statements are offered online. While it's possible to print out these pages, you can also save these statements to an online filing system through your word-processing program. Don't forget to make regular backups of your data, though.

Once you've gathered these documents, you need to pull out that cal-culator or rev up your computer program to create a list of what you're currently spending in order to estimate (or guesstimate) what you will be spending.

The "Budget Worksheet" on page 285 will help you figure out your own spending plan.

Below are some guidelines for five major expense categories. Total up and compare what you spend.

EXPENSE CATEGORY GUIDELINES

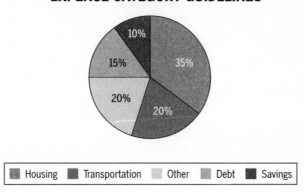

Source: How Money Works, *Primerica*, 2005

Housing includes mortgage or rent, utilities, insurance, taxes, and home maintenance. Transportation includes public transportation costs, taxis and car services, commuter tickets, car payments, auto insurance, licensing and registration fees, maintenance, gasoline, and parking. Debt is student loans, credit cards, personal loans, taxes, and medical debts. "Other" is everything else, such as food, clothing, entertainment, childcare, medical expenses, and charitable contributions.

These are, of course, only guidelines. You have to determine your personal tradeoffs. Where you live may be more important to you than what you drive. Or maybe it's just the other way around, in which case you may spend a little less on housing and more on transportation. Look at your percentages compared with the norms—is there any single category that stands out? Do you have significantly more debt and fewer savings?

Here's how one family learned to work with—and live by—their budget.

Shedding Light on the Family Budget

"He's doing it again," Jean whispered to her brother, J. J. (short for James Junior), as they worked on their homework at the kitchen table. J. J. looked up from his notebook and listened to their father asking their mother, who had left the upstairs bathroom light on, to please turn it off. The siblings suppressed a giggle. Their dad was a stickler about turning off lights. "Next he'll be asking who turned up the heat," J. J. whispered back. The teens knew their father's habits well.

"Who turned the heat up?" queried James Senior as he came into the kitchen. "Nobody, daddy," relayed Jean. "I'm baking brownies for the school bake sale." That seemed to satisfy him. James Senior loved his family, but it was frustrating how little they understood about the true costs of running a household. The electric bill had been $25 over budget the previous month and $20 over the month before that. If this kept up, he was going to have to start cutting back on the savings he'd planned to put away for the year. That was something he really didn't want to do.

James Senior asked the kids what their homework assignments were. J. J., a high school freshman, was working on history, and Jean, a junior, was poring over a math project that required her to make a computer spreadsheet. James Senior was an old-fashioned kind of guy who didn't have much use for computers. But he was glad his daughter was proficient in using one, because he recognized it as a necessary skill for getting a job these days. "Hey, Daddy," Jean said. "Maybe I can make a spreadsheet out of your famous family budget."

Every year on New Year's Day, James Senior sat down in his favorite lounge chair and wrote out the family budget on a yellow legal pad. Everyone knew not to disturb him. With a ruler, he made five vertical columns on a sheet of paper. He labeled the columns with the type of expense, the amount the family had spent in the previous year, and the amount he expected they would spend in the coming year. He left the fourth column blank so at the end of the year he could enter the amount the family actually had spent. The fifth was for calculating how much over, or under, the expected number the family's expenses were. He started out by filling in the numbers for the whole year and then wrote the names of each month on the following 12 pages, dividing each budgeted amount into 12 equal parts, for each month. It was a long, tedious and, in James Senior's opinion, necessary process.

James Senior had never shared his "famous" family budget with the children. He kept the sheets together in a file folder that he pulled out every month when he sat down to pay bills. That was when he entered the monthly numbers. The family knew about it only because of his grumbling when it seemed that things weren't going well. But his daughter's offer to make a computer spreadsheet wasn't unreasonable. James Senior thought that maybe if Jean saw how high expenses were, she might be a little more careful about things like turning off lights. So he told her that, yes, a spreadsheet would be an interesting idea. He went to the drawer where he kept the family financial information and withdrew the file folder.

Jean nodded her head as her father explained his budget system to her. She told him it was a perfect example for her math project. In a matter of just minutes, she had set up an electronic grid and was inputting numbers from the yellow pad. Then she realized she could make the spreadsheet program do most of the work for her. She added a few formulas and presto! The fifth column, showing the variance in the family's monthly expenses, was automatically calculated.

"Did you ever think of doing this?" Jean asked her father, as she cut and pasted some of the budget lines into a new position and created subtotals. "I've grouped expense lines by type. Here are all the sources of income, including yours and mom's salaries after deductions. Here are all our major regular expenses, like the mortgage, property taxes, and the car loans. These are pretty much fixed every month." She then showed him how she had rearranged his budget to put together the family expenses that could actually go up or down, like the phone bill, groceries, gas for the car, and, yes, the utility bills for light and heat. A final category showed all the pocket money the family required, including Jean's and J. J.'s allowances and money for eating out and going to the movies.

Jean's spreadsheet also displayed monthly totals of income plus outflows. It seemed that in January and March expenses were greater than income, so the number was negative. But in February, in spite of James Senior's grumbling about the electric bill, there was actually a small positive balance.

"Hey, maybe if there's money left over, you'll share it with us," J. J. suggested. He had been eavesdropping, because what his father and sister were doing seemed much more interesting than his own assignment. "Now that's a thought," his father said. "But not at the end of each month. How about we see if we have any left over at the end of the year and then use it to do something together as a family?"

"Sounds good to me," J. J. said. "Me, too," said Jean, not looking up from the spreadsheet. "Hey, Dad, let me show you something else about our budget." At that point, her mother appeared in the doorway. "What's going on here?" she asked. "We're helping Dad with the family budget," interjected J. J. "Will you please turn that light out behind you?" The whole family burst out laughing.

Jean got an A on her math project. James Senior felt like giving his whole family an A for their cooperative spirit in making the family budget work.

Commonsense Considerations

By involving family members, as James Senior learned, you not only gain a commitment from them to work with your family budget, but also teach them a valuable skill that will help them be financially responsible. Your budget is a fundamental tool that can be instrumental in helping you understand your personal financial status. If you are faithful about checking your actual expenses against what you budgeted, you should find your finances falling into place in short order.

Here are some further strategies to help you stay within your budget borders and improve your financial picture.

- Save unexpected windfalls, such as a bonus, that birthday check from Aunt Millie, or the net proceeds from your last garage sale.
- Use your budget to evaluate your true costs of such fundamental activities as the per-mile cost of driving your car, staying in your own home for one night, or shopping at the gourmet store for staples such as milk and butter.
- Eliminate expenses for items or services you never or rarely use.
- Before taking on a new pet, evaluate the impact on your budget, including the costs of food, training, medical care, grooming, and caring for the animal if nobody's around during the day or during a vacation.
- Know where you can skimp and save—and where you can't. Having a haircut every six weeks instead of every four probably won't hurt you. Seeing your dentist only once a year instead of twice might have some severe consequences down the road.

For additional information, see Chapter 2, "Making Do between Paychecks," and Chapter 17, "Saving Your (Financial) Life."

10

Sharing a Financial Life

Have you ever kept a secret about money from your spouse, partner, parents, or roommate? Have you ever fibbed about how much something costs? Money is a sensitive—sometimes even taboo—topic for many couples. People often sidestep discussions about money because they want to avoid conflict or they fear a partner's anger, disapproval, or berating. But for couples or, for that matter, any two adults cohabiting (parent and grown-up child, or even friends sharing an apartment and a refrigerator), talking openly and honestly about money is a necessary precursor to being able to manage it sensibly. Once the door is open to discussion and healthy debate, the rest will come easily.

Drawing the Big Picture

Ian had always wanted to be an artist. Janet had always wanted to be a dancer. They set aside these dreams when they married and realized that such ambitions would not pay the rent, so each of them would need to get "a real job." The couple hoped to start a family, and Janet was concerned about their financial stability. But she also recognized that she too needed to make a contribution, so she worked in a school as a dance instructor until their third child was born. By then, it made more economic sense for her to stay home and care for the kids.

Ian's artistic talents and desires were not tapped at all in his job as a payroll manager for a restaurant chain. Although he was a practical man, over time his resentment began to build. He blamed Janet, but mostly he blamed himself for acquiescing. He began to fantasize about quitting his job and trying to make a living as a painter—and not the kind that painted the outside of houses. Whenever he tried to articulate these desires, Janet reminded him that although his job didn't pay particularly well, it was secure.

One evening, Ian drove to an art supply store near the campus of the state university. There, he purchased a set of the finest acrylic paints available, a boxed set of brushes, several canvases, and other accessories considered necessary to professional artists. He had guessed the bill would come to a few hundred dollars, but it had been a while since he had purchased new supplies. The register showed more than $1,500 for the total. Even though Ian and Janet's joint checking account had almost no money in it, Ian decided it was now or never, so he calmly handed over his credit card to pay for his purchases.

On the way home, Ian decided to tell Janet that the paints had cost just a fraction of the actual total and then make sure he was the first to open the credit card bill when it arrived. He was sure he could cover up this purchase since he took care of the bills. Perhaps he could shift around some of their emergency funds to cover the cost. He also planned to tell her that he intended to find the time in his life to start painting regularly again, and if she didn't like that perhaps they ought to talk about separating.

Unfortunately Ian had miscalculated his wife's lack of attention to details. The minute he brought the bags in the front door, Janet knew that Ian had made a purchase far beyond the couple's financial reach. Ian braced himself for the explosion. It didn't come. Instead, that night, after the children were in bed, Janet quietly approached him and asked if they could talk.

She started the discussion by saying that, as much as possible, she'd like to see if they could review their situation without arguing. She said that some of it was about money, and some of it was about their relationship, and some of it was about their individual dreams. Ian nodded in agreement. She said she needed his help to work through these issues. But she also thought they needed some outside help too. She had given it a lot of thought and wasn't sure whether they needed to talk to a therapist, who would help them strengthen their relationship but might not be as skilled at dealing with their day-to-day budgetary problems. Or perhaps they should talk to a professional who would help them with their financial planning but might feel uncomfortable talking about their interpersonal relationship. What did Ian think?

Ian was definitely caught off guard. He listened to Janet and said he saw her point. Maybe they ought to see if they could find an individual who could do both jobs at once? He apologized for making such a large purchase and told Janet he'd see about returning the acrylics. Janet said that wasn't necessary. She recognized that Ian had made some sacrifices for their financial security, so she was prepared to make a sacrifice herself. She hoped that starting right then they could try to learn how to live happily within their budget—without crushing each other's dreams and aspirations.

Commonsense Considerations

For too many couples, money discussions only take place when there is a financial crisis. It's a time when the conversation is rarely calm or rational. That's why it's essential to lay out the parameters of your financial life before a big blowout.

Here are some rules of the road for married or cohabiting couples, or roommates.

- **Decide upon mutual goals and develop a plan to accomplish them jointly.** In some unions, one partner is designated as the chief financial officer who pays all the bills. In others, the fiscal duties are divided up. Do what works for you, but spell it out. No one wants to pay late charges because it wasn't clear who was supposed to pay the bill. A team approach means no unilateral decision-making.
- **Endeavor to be completely honest regarding your finances.** Ideally, this honesty occurs prior to cohabitation. For example, a negative credit rating may adversely impact a newly married couple's financial

life. Your ability as a couple to jointly qualify for credit at a low rate can be diminished by one partner's financial challenges. Additionally, a roommate who is carrying a large student loan will be less inclined to want to spend as freely as one who has finished paying for a college education.

- **Develop a spending plan (most commonly know as a budget).** Without a budget in place, you will have no idea where your money is going. A budget helps to create order in a household and cuts down on haphazard spending. Set ranges, rather than absolute limits, on certain expense categories. Once these are set, work as a team to stay within the parameters. For example, if you are approaching the upper limit of your "meals out" allowance for the month but are comfortably going to meet your "grocery" allotment, consider a steak at home instead of dining out.
- **Give some thought as to how your accounts will be organized.** There are several types of arrangements you can choose from. A joint account pools all your income together. Another option is to maintain separate accounts and assign bills based on income. This option gives each person the most autonomy. Some couples choose a combination of the two methods with a joint account for shared expenses like mortgage, day care, or groceries and separate accounts for expenditures that are individual, such as car payments, clothing, or hobbies. You may want to experiment with different organizational structures until you find the system that is the most compatible for your family.
- **Since couples may have differing ideas on the dollar amount that constitutes a "major purchase," you should set a limit.** Agree on a dollar amount where any purchases up to that limit can be made without consulting each other. Endeavor to be open about any instance when you deviate from this agreement. Hiding over-the-limit purchases made without consultation can only lead to trouble.
- **"Money talk" meetings should become a regularly scheduled family event.** Money discussions should be comprehensive and not only include a monthly budget review but also a review of the progress toward long-term goals. Your financial summits could coincide with bill paying or take place when your bank statement arrives. The first meetings may be difficult if you are not used to discussing money

matters, but after some time they will become routine, and sticking to the agenda will be more comfortable.

- **Decide upon financial goals that are challenging yet attainable.** For example, if you both agree that you want to start a college fund for your newborn, you need to decide on a set amount to go toward that account each month. Remember that this goal should not cause such hardship in your financial life that you decide it is impossible and abandon the goal.

- **Make it a habit to continually eliminate "wants" from your monthly budget.** Everyone has "creature comforts" they can't live without. But if you take a closer look at your finances, there are probably some areas you can eliminate without pain. Consider your monthly budget as your financial garden—plant it neatly and then go back and weed it regularly.

- **Maintain separate credit cards.** Even if you apply for joint credit cards, you should still have at least one credit card in your own name. Each partner needs a strong individual credit rating as insurance in case one of you gets into credit difficulties. If you do decide to part ways, you'll have an easier time obtaining credit with your own credit history versus a non-existent one or a negative joint history.

The Odd Couple

While he was still in college, a major international firm recruited Alex for its executive training program. The firm not only paid him a signing bonus and a great salary, but also helped him find a luxury two-bedroom apartment to share with another trainee. Both young professionals were so busy they were barely at home, ate most of their meals at their desks or in restaurants, and never really decorated the apartment. After two years, however, Alex's roommate was assigned to an office overseas. Although Alex could have moved to a smaller place, he decided to invite his brother Jim to live with him.

Jim was just about the polar opposite of Alex. You never would have guessed they grew up in the same household. Jim had no interest in establishing a career or earning a lot of money—and no temperament for these lofty aspirations, either. He was perfectly happy to float from job to job, working at coffee shops, electronics retailers, and bookstores that would always hire him because he was friendly and honest. Alex, by nature, was well organized and focused on achieving his goals. Jim's goals were a mystery to all. He was the sort of guy who saw no point in making his bed in the morning since he'd just be getting back into it in the evening.

A few days after Jim moved in, the boys' parents came to visit. They told the boys they wanted to have a talk with them. The boys both rolled their eyes—after all, they weren't teenagers anymore. They all sat together in the living room, parents on the couch and boys on the floor, since Alex had never gotten around to buying any chairs. The boys' mother spoke first.

She told them how happy she and their father were that the boys had chosen to live together. However, they were concerned that, because their sons had such opposite lifestyles and such different resources in terms of their paychecks, apartment sharing might create a problem between them. Their father said he didn't want the boys to part company under angry circumstances. It was very important to him, and to their mother, that the family respect and be committed to each other. They didn't care if the boys argued about sports or politics or movies, but they didn't want them arguing about money. So they felt it was essential that the boys work out a plan for sharing expenses and responsibilities. They would be happy to help Alex and Jim do this if they wanted.

Alex and Jim were completely surprised by their parents' concern. They hadn't really given much thought to how they would organize their household. Alex had assumed that since he earned the larger salary, he'd take care of the major expenses. Jim didn't really care how the apartment looked, though he was the one who spent the most time there and was in a better position to keep it up. At the same time, Jim didn't want Alex to feel justified in bossing him around or even telling him to move out simply because Alex was paying a greater share. Alex had already blown up at Jim for using up all the milk and not replacing it. Alex realized that there might be more scenes like that if he and Jim didn't figure out a plan.

Alex and Jim's parents left, and the boys sat down to discuss just how they would divide the finances. They figured they would try to agree on how they would split the rent and utilities, who would pay for groceries and how they'd shop for them, and how furnishing and cleaning the apartment would be handled. While as kids they used to arm wrestle to settle their differences, as adults, they could now use their brains instead of their brawn.

Commonsense Considerations

Alex and Jim made a financial plan for themselves that included the following general guidelines that they shared with their parents. These resolutions would work for any cohabiting adults.

- We won't be avoiders. We won't put off confronting any issues we have in the hope that they'll just go away.
- We will honestly disclose all money actions. If one of us doesn't stick to the budget, we'll bring it up rather than cover it up.
- We will bravely confront disagreements over money issues. We will try to rationally discuss areas where we don't see eye-to-eye.
- We will keep our debt under control. We will pay our bills in a timely fashion.
- We will monitor our credit score and continually try to improve it.
- We will plan for the unexpected by having a "slush" fund for emergencies.
- We will resist the tendency to be emotional about money issues. We will approach them in a business-like manner.
- We will keep working until we have a plan that works.

For further information, see Chapter 22, "Blending Finances in a Blended Family."

Raising and Educating Children—About Money

Chances are if couples stopped to figure out how much it really costs to raise a child—from the first diaper to the last law school textbook—there might be a significant drop in the birthrate in the United States. The price tag on rearing a child can be, in a word, astounding—well into six figures. According to the U.S. Department of Agriculture, a middle-income, two-parent family will spend on average $190,980 raising a child born in the year 2005 to the age of 18, or nearly 20 percent of their earnings. Single parents will spend an even larger portion. The essentials of a baby's first year alone almost reach $13,000—and that's just the basics like diapers, formula, furniture, and clothing. Childcare or medical expenses can double that figure.

A Pricey Bundle of Joy

Before their daughter Bethany was even born, Christine and Sean shelled out huge sums in preparation for her arrival. And while they thought their list of baby supplies was exhaustive, they had not anticipated that well-intentioned family members would pressure them to make further purchases they had not included in their budget.

For example, Christine's mother insisted they buy a new, "safer" car. In her opinion, their 8-year-old economy car was not adequate for transporting a baby. Christine and Sean were made to feel tremendously guilty for wanting to keep their old, reliable (and fully paid-off) car. Finally, they relented and purchased a new minivan that added $350 to their monthly expenses, as well as the increased cost of gas for this much larger vehicle.

Sean's older sister then told them they would live to regret it if they failed to visually document their baby's early years. She pressed on them the need to buy digital still and video cameras. She also strongly recommended a consultant who would baby-proof their apartment for "just" $500.

Conversion of a guest bedroom into a nursery cost Christine and Sean around $3,000. Had friends and relatives not been so generous at the baby shower, this would have been much higher.

After Bethany's birth, Christine continued to keep track of ongoing costs. These included a baby nurse for the first six weeks, a second car seat and stroller once Bethany outgrew her infant seat and baby carriage, clothing that had to be replaced every three months, and formula, diapers, and baby food. Baby entertainment included Mommy and Me classes, toys, books, DVDs, and CDs. And of course there were photo-printing expenses from their new camera. Because Christine and Sean felt it was important to spend time alone together, they hired a sitter once a week so they could go out to dinner. When Christine returned to work, they enrolled Bethany in a local day care center, layering on yet another expense.

When Christine and Sean totaled their monthly costs, they winced at how much their little bundle of joy was costing them. When they projected these costs over time, the magnitude really made them gasp. They realized they would be spending between $1,600 and $2,300 on diapers alone by the time Bethany was potty-trained.

But the biggest hit to their budget every month was day care. Because Bethany was under 18 months old, they paid the highest fee on the scale at the center. They understood the reason why: The infants and youngest children needed more hands-on care. But this meant their annualized day care costs would total $16,800. When their research revealed this was well above the national norm, they sought to reduce this cost.

Christine and Sean didn't have room for a live-in nanny and felt having a caregiver come in during the day was too unreliable. When making their initial decision about what center to take Bethany to, they had chosen a day care solely based on the recommendation of a friend, without considering the expense. After 9 months, however, they reconsidered their choice and pulled out their original notes. Their list of options included a facility at a nearby community center. It seemed to them Bethany would receive excellent care there—and at a cost of about $600 a month less. These savings were enough to bring their budget back on track.

In the end, Christine and Sean were glad that they had tracked their expenses. Although they could afford the more expensive day care, their analysis motivated them to seek a more economical solution. They chose to reroute the money they were saving to Bethany's college fund. They knew by the time she was heading off to college, they would be glad they did this. And that day was only about 17 years away!

Commonsense Considerations

Christine and Sean found caring for their baby thrilling—and daunting. From the start, they recognized that there would be not only physical and emotional demands but also financial changes. While they clearly wanted only the best for their child, they realized there are numerous ways to keep expenses under control without shortchanging Bethany's comfort and security. Here are a few pointers to consider:

- Any change in family headcount calls for a review of life insurance policies, wills, and retirement plans. You should also consider realigning savings goals to include a college fund and other big-ticket expenses, like summer camp.
- Babies call for budget realignment. Tracking expenses is useful for creating budgets, and budgets, in turn, help you keep expenses in check.
- Review your health insurance to determine if your current plan covers the majority of the family's needs—for both parents and children—completely and economically.

- One alternative to group day care or an individual nanny is nanny-sharing. It can reduce your costs and offer your child the benefits of a playmate. While it does require coordination with another family, it is worth considering for both its social and economical benefits.
- Make sure you take advantage of government programs designed to help ease the financial burdens of parenthood, such as the Dependent Care Tax Credit. Present-day tax law also awards parents a tax credit for each child under age 17, as long as family income is less than a certain level (with a lower limit for single filers). For up-to-date information, check with the IRS.
- Flexible spending accounts allow you to use pretax dollars from your paycheck to pay childcare expenses. This deduction lowers taxable earnings. (Note, though, that you become ineligible for the Dependent Care Tax Credit if you enroll in the flexible spending plan. Consult a financial advisor or your accountant to decide which option makes more economic sense.)
- Try to restrict shopping for baby clothes to outlet stores and sales, and establish hand-me-down chains with friends and family. You will be amazed at how fast your child grows! Be generous about offering your baby's outgrown clothing to other new parents, too.
- Join a warehouse club and buy in bulk, if possible. But be careful not to overbuy, or you may find yourself with supplies that you can't use or that have spoiled by the time you get to them.

Once your child begins walking and talking, new challenges appear. As your child matures from infant to toddler, toddler to preschooler, preschooler to elementary school student and on up through high school, it is in both the parents' and child's best interests to provide a solid, developmentally appropriate understanding about money and how it works in our society.

Parents today are being urged to take the financial training of their children seriously. This includes teaching kids how to handle money responsibly, develop and live within a budget, and learn to save, both to be prepared for emergencies and to learn important lessons about delayed gratification.

The Power of Positive Allowances

Julia, a single parent of three children ages 8, 10, and 13, had never received an allowance as a child. Her parents had felt that if Julia needed money, she should come to them and they would decide if her request was appropriate. When her own children were younger, Julia had tried to give them pocket money, but thought they dealt irresponsibly with it. They would spend it all at once or lose it or buy candy and cheap toys that she thought were a waste of money. When the kids made her mad, she'd dock their allowances. Lots of times she just simply forgot to give the money to them. Then one day while sitting in the pediatrician's waiting room, she read an article in a parenting magazine that inspired her to try again.

The article laid out a whole philosophy of allowances, the underlying principle being that an allowance can be used as a tool to teach children about money management. The article stated that an allowance should be given at the same time every week, with no strings attached to behavior, chores, or grades. The amount should be individually budgeted and should include enough so that the child (after "spending" money) can put aside a set amount every week for saving toward a short- or long-term, predetermined goal, and a second portion for "sharing," or charity. Periodically, parents should help the child sweep the savings funds from their piggy bank into a formal savings account that pays interest. Most important is for parents to not criticize what children chose to do with their money, even if they spend it foolishly.

Julia sat down with each of her children and determined an appropriate amount for their weekly allowance. Because her youngest attended an after-school program and needed money to purchase snacks, he actually would be getting a larger amount initially than his 10-year-old sister. Julia decided she would include lunch money for her 13-year-old in his allowance instead of prepaying for the school year. This way, she hoped, he might learn how to budget over the week and make good choices. Julia made it clear that if he ran out of money before the end of the week, that was tough. She wouldn't replenish or advance him money, though of course he was free to make a peanut butter and jelly sandwich at home.

Although Julia shuddered at the aggregate amount she was handing to the children each week, she noticed almost immediately that the children stopped "nickel and diming" her for money for snacks and candy on a daily basis. When they went to the movies, they had their own money to spend on popcorn. Her daughter bought small treats for her pet hamster—with her own money. When her younger son lost a $20 bill he had shoved in a coat pocket, he told his mother he'd learned it was important to keep better track of his money. Julia was proud of his response.

Within 6 months all three children had built up their savings and sharing, and Julia felt her eldest had shown such sound skills at managing his money that she decided to switch him to a monthly allocation—a hefty sum of $175. Rather than hand him this cash, however, she arranged to have the money transferred from her checking account to another account she opened at a local bank that had a branch near his middle school. She gave him an ATM card and explained that every month when the statements arrived, she would like to sit down and review them with him. Her son was thrilled with the new system, and her other children now can't wait until they can get accounts to manage, too.

Commonsense Considerations

Of course, the way in which a parent chooses to introduce children to money and money management is a highly personal matter. However there are some basic ground rules that are worth noting. Here are some ideas to help you form your own "family financial curriculum."

- **Provide a regular allowance that meets your child or children's needs.** Review and adjust the stipend at least twice a year. Resist the temptation to loan (if you do—charge them interest) or advance allowance money, and never borrow from your children, if you can at all help it.
- **Pay the allowance on the same day at the same time.** Do not use it as a means to bribe or elicit good behavior out of your children. And don't link it to responsibilities you expect them to shoulder as a member of the family, like pet care or keeping their room neat, or else you may find yourself in a predicament if they decide to deliberately shirk their duties. It is okay, however, to offer to pay for work outside their

daily duties, such as helping to paint a fence or baby-sitting for a visiting relative.

- **Help your children put away an agreed-upon amount for saving toward a specific goal and a separate amount for charity.** Keep these monies in separate envelopes or containers, and supervise periodic accounting to make sure the correct amounts have been accumulated over time. Set goals for both saving and sharing.
- **Open a savings account with your child.** Consider adding a "family supplement" to the interest rate paid by the bank at the time the deposit is made.
- **Keep the lines of communications open to discussing money with your children.** Ask if they are happy with the way they spent their money in the previous week (or several weeks) and if they are going to do anything differently in the week ahead, rather than lecture them on proper spending habits.
- **Above all else, lead by example.** Your children will learn more about healthy financial habits if you demonstrate for them by saving, spending, and sharing your money responsibly. Having organized financial records and workable budgets, paying your bills on time, and being prudent about credit will teach them as much, if not more, about sound money management than any textbook ever could.

Inevitably, as children reach their mid-teens, the issue of credit cards will come up. They will want to borrow yours or ask for their own. Teaching a child how to use credit wisely is an important lesson, and one that is preferably not learned through a bad experience.

Young adults are routinely listed as authorized users on their parents' credit cards. In this way, parents are assisting their children in establishing credit histories and learning how to use a credit card while under parental supervision.

Many parents discover unhappily that their children have not used credit cards as they might have hoped. Sometimes, the parents specify the card is for emergency use only. But the definition of an emergency may be something completely different from one generation to the next. This can come as a shock to parents—and a challenge to their finances and their credit report.

Giving Credit Where Credit Is Due

The summer before their children, Margot and Noah, left to start college, Warren and Debby decided they would feel better if their teens had some experience with credit cards. After all, they had been reading about how students on college campuses across the U.S. were bombarded with offers for credit every day and how many young people were graduating having to shoulder serious consumer debt in addition to loans for their education. Just to make it easier to track the kids' expenditures, they gave Margot a card on one of Warren's accounts and Noah a card linked to one of Debby's. This way, they could monitor their activity separately. However, before they handed them the cards, Warren sat them down in the living room. He had a few words of wisdom to impart.

"What is the most important type of history?" he asked the children.

"Ancient history?" Noah ventured.

"No," Warren said firmly. "Credit history." He then explained that nothing says more about their personal and financial future than their credit history. A good credit history means they'll have an easier time getting credit when they want it—for a new home, new car, or a credit card—and sometimes even with lower rates. Their credit history is publicly available information on how they have handled their past financial relationships.

"What's the purpose of a credit card?" was Warren's next question.

"I know that," Margot said, instinctively raising and waving her hand in the air. "It lets you buy now and pay later. It's like free money."

"You're half right," Warren told her. "Yes, it's a convenient way to carry money without carrying cash, and a good way to pay for larger purchases over time. But you are never, ever to think of a credit card as 'free money.'"

Warren continued. "I want you to think hard about each and every purchase you make with this or any credit card. Because as convenient as it is, it can get you in a whole heap of trouble."

"Like what?" Noah wanted to know. He was always one for specifics.

"OK, OK. Let me tell you about credit cards," his father replied. "Here are some rules for the road. First of all, never charge anything you can't afford—even if it looks good on you. Second, always pay your bills on time. Late charges can cost more than that pair of designer jeans, and they wreck your credit history to boot. Set a monthly spending limit and then stick to it. You want to make sure when you receive the bill that you can pay off the entire amount you spent in the month. Shop as carefully with your credit card as you would with cash—cash you earned the hard way, not just gifts from grandma. Charging the occasional dinner is okay, but make sure you pay it off right away at the end of the month, or the cost of that dinner will go up, up, up with interest charges added."

Warren caught Margot rolling her eyes. "Pay attention!" he barked at her. "There could be a pop quiz after this." She refocused.

"You need to know the terms of your credit card. Otherwise, it's like driving a car with a broken gas gauge. Anytime you apply for credit, make sure you know what the interest rate is, and how the finance charges are calculated."

Warren paused. "Any questions?"

Margot and Noah shook their heads. Warren handed each of them their credit card and said, "Class dismissed."

Both Margot and Noah had jobs that summer, Margot as a counselor at the town day camp and Noah as an intern in his uncle's law office. They were earning about the same amount of money, which their parents had indicated was theirs to spend as pocket money for the summer, or to put away to supplement their spending money at college in the fall.

Anticipating her first paycheck, Margot and two of her friends cruised the mall on the Monday night after her first day of work. She thought she sensed a little bit of jealousy when she whipped out her new credit card to pay for her purchases of some clothes and DVDs. But she felt that using the card was justified, since she would have spent cash on these items anyway, though probably not until she actually had the cash to spend, which wouldn't be until her biweekly paycheck.

Later that week, she forgot that she had clipped her cell phone to her bathing suit during free swim period at camp, and she dove into the pool with it still on. Fortunately, she didn't have to trouble her parents to order a replacement for her, since her father had the foresight to have the phone insured under the family plan. However, there was a $55 deductible, which Margot happily handed her credit card over to pay. It was truly convenient, she thought, not to have to carry cash around. She also generously filled the tank of the family car when it was running a little low, just to save her parents the bother. Before, she had always just put $5 or $10 worth of gas in, to get her where she wanted to go.

Margot found having the credit card was very convenient, particularly for ordering online. But as her father had cautioned, she was careful never to buy more than she could afford. Most of her purchases didn't amount to much more that $50—but she was making several a week. So when the bills arrived for the card, Warren summoned her to his study where he and Debby were waiting.

"So, your father and I have been going over your credit card bill," her mother said. "One thing we'd like to make sure is that you actually made all these purchases. There are 16 within the billing cycle, which is only one month. Do you have the receipts so we can compare them to the statement?"

"Whoops" was Margot's reply. That was what she usually said when she was trying to humor her parents.

"Do you have a plan for how you are going to cover this bill?" her father asked.

"Well, it isn't any more than $200 . . . is it?" asked Margot, suddenly concerned.

"Only about four times that," replied her mother.

"Yikes" was all Margot could manage. She wasn't making much more than that all summer.

"You are dismissed," her father said without further comment. "Send your brother in."

Noah entered the room. "What did I do now?"

It turned out that after his father's admonitions, Noah had decided it was simply too risky to use the credit card his father had provided, and he put it away in the top drawer of his dresser and promptly forgot about it. Although Noah was able to sidestep the situation his sister now found herself in, he also had failed to demonstrate to his parents that he knew how to use the card responsibly, even though not using the card had seemed to him to be the smart thing to do.

After Noah left the room, Warren and Debby discussed what they should do. They weren't angry at Margot—they felt she had done exactly what many teens do when they first get a credit card. And they knew she would be responsible for the charges. Nor could they be mad at Noah, though they felt like they had less information on his spending habits than if he had overcharged like his sister. With 6 weeks left before the kids shipped off to college, Warren and Debby decided they would continue to closely monitor their use of the cards before they left—and after.

Commonsense Considerations

Warren and Debby were glad they had taken the time to educate their children about credit cards before they went off on their own. Here are some additional ideas to help prepare your child for the world of credit.

- Explain to your child the difference between a credit card, where payments on purchases can be extended out over time; a charge card, where all charges must be paid at the end of the month; and an ATM card, which can be used in lieu of cash but is linked directly to "your money." Discuss the benefits and drawbacks of each.
- When your child seems ready, arrange for him or her to have an ATM card that deducts the amount "charged" from his or her bank account. Over several months or a year, you can then observe how carefully your child uses the card. Be sure to advise your child of the consequences of overdrawing the account.
- Teach your children that credit is not free—in fact, it can be quite expensive. Using a credit card to seize the opportunity to buy an expensive pair of jeans on sale may result in paying even more than retail if the bill isn't paid off immediately. Have them calculate the "real" cost of credit purchases.
- An important point to make is that credit cards are not created equal, either. The interest charged, stated as an annual percentage rate (APR), can be different for purchases, cash transactions, and balance transfers. Credit cards can have fixed or variable APRs and different lengths of grace periods before interest is charged.
- When your child is ready, open a credit card account with a low credit limit, clearly articulate proper and improper uses of the card, and closely monitor use for the first year or so. Don't let mistakes turn into battle zones, but rather see them as an opportunity for dialogue with your child.

CHAPTER 12

Home Sweet Home Loans

Choosing the right mortgage is a little like finding the ideal spouse or partner. Love at first sight, unfortunately, only happens with any regularity in the movies. Finding a mortgage that works for you involves research and analysis. One way to start is by estimating just how much you feel comfortable paying every month toward your mortgage debt. Your goal is to secure a loan that will result in this amount at the best possible interest rate.

You find this by tinkering with the many variables that a mortgage entails. How much down payment can you afford? If you increase the down payment, how does that decrease the monthly payment? Are you considering a fixed-rate or adjustable mortgage? Will the adjustable mortgage's different rates increase or decrease your monthly payment? Ten, 15-, or 30-year duration? Points or no points? Conventional or government insured? Bank-, mortgage company– or mortgage broker–provided? The options are legion. How you make these decisions can make all the difference.

Decisions, Decisions, Decisions

When it came to house ownership, Sam and Sally thought they were real pros. They'd bought their first home when they were first married with the help of Sally's parents, who provided the down payment as a wedding gift. It was an adorable house, but now, 5 years later, with business clients to entertain and a toddler in tow, they felt they wanted to expand their space. So they enlisted the help of a real estate agent, carefully scanned the Sunday real estate sections of the local newspaper, cruised neighborhoods they liked looking for open house signs, and even briefly considered new construction. After nearly a year of looking, they finally found what they wanted and placed a competitive bid on the table. After a bit of back and forth, their offer was accepted and the contract signed.

Next up on their list was selling their current house, because they would need the money for a down payment on the new house. They also needed to get moving on applying for a mortgage. Sally volunteered to spearhead the house-selling effort, and Sam took on responsibility for finding financing.

Sam knew that between his and Sally's earnings, they could conservatively afford a monthly mortgage payment of about $2,000. The new house was going to cost about $400,000, and Sam was sure he and Sally would be able to provide 25 percent of that, or $100,000, as a down payment. This money would come from the sale of their current house. Working backward and assuming a 7 percent interest rate over 30 years, this came to about $300,000 for a loan amount. Perfect, right?

Not so fast. Sally questioned Sam's assumptions about the mortgage. She pointed out that their previous mortgage had had a 30-year fixed rate and they had "paid through the nose" for it, as she put it. That's because it happened that there was a spike in interest rates on the day they locked in their rate 5 years earlier. They had signed forms guaranteeing a rate that was higher than the rates were on the day they closed on the house and, as it turned out, higher than the averages rates for the next 5 years. They might have refinanced, but since they assumed this was a "starter home" they wouldn't live in for too long, they decided it would be even more expensive to do this.

Still, they realized they would have been much better off taking an adjustable-rate mortgage back then, since rates progressively got lower and lower. Moreover, because they had stayed in that house only 5 years, they'd ended up paying a lot more for that mortgage in closing costs. Since closing costs, which include the fees to transfer the title and seal the deal, are paid up front, they can make the short-term use of a long mortgage an expensive proposition.

Sam agreed to explore their mortgage options a little further. He knew that the two basic decisions were the type of mortgage—fixed-rate or variable/adjustable—and the term of the mortgage, meaning how long it would take to pay it off in full. He had always assumed a fixed-rate mortgage was more desirable, since the criteria to qualify seemed harder to meet. He also preferred the idea of a fixed rate because he would always know what his payments would be every month, though experience had demonstrated that adjustable-rate mortgages have the potential to go not only up but also down, benefiting the homeowner. On the other hand, so far as he could tell, interest rates were now climbing again, which would make an adjustable-rate mortgage only more expensive over time.

Sam also looked more closely at the implications of obtaining a shorter-term mortgage than 30 years. It wasn't that he expected to sell the house earlier, but rather that he and Sally were interested in building equity faster. He made a chart of his options for his $300,000 mortgage, assuming the same 7 percent rate, even though he was aware that sometimes rates are slightly more favorable for shorter terms:

BORROWING $300,000 AT 7%

TERM (YRS)	MONTHLY PAYMENT	TOTAL INTEREST	PRINCIPAL BALANCE REMAINING AFTER 10 YEARS
10	$3,483	$117,990	$0
15	$2,696	$185,367	$136,823
30	$1,995	$418,527	$ 257,437

Note: For illustrative purposes only

This was really helpful in understanding the differences between shorter- and longer-term mortgages. While Sam didn't think the family could afford the $3,483 monthly payment on the 10-year mortgage, he realized that adding $700 a month to their initial budgeted amount of

$2,000 (the 15-year mortgage) substantially reduced the interest they would pay over the life of the loan and provided them with much more equity after 5 to 10 years than would the 30-year mortgage. If they went for the 30-year mortgage, they would be paying more in interest than the original price of the house!

Sam also looked into the issue of reducing the closing costs. He found out that most of these, which include loan origination, processing, and underwriting costs, as well as document preparation and tax-service fees, were unavoidable, as were the broker fees for selling the house. He did realize when he looked at rates that he should pay special attention to make sure that all fees were included by comparing annual percentage rates, or APRs, rather than the boldface advertised rates that might not include all the fees. This was the only way he'd be able to tell the true cost of his mortgage.

Sam was now prepared to revise his recommendation to Sally about the type of mortgage they should seek. Meanwhile, thanks to Sally's diligent effort at selling their present home, a small bidding war had taken place, and they accepted an offer that was greater than the selling price their real estate agent had helped them set. They decided to put the excess into their down payment, which would help lower the monthly payment and free up more of their cash flow for all those extra expenses associated with a new house, like remodeling and moving costs.

Commonsense Considerations

Like Sam, many people consider a fixed-rate, 30-year mortgage to be standard. However, there is no one-size-fits-all mortgage in today's lending market. Choosing the right mortgage is as critical to your future finances as choosing the right house is to your lifestyle. You should seek advice from trusted advisors and thoroughly investigate the variety of products available before making up your mind. Here are some questions that go into the equation.

- **How much do you plan to spend in total on a home?**
- **How much do you plan to spend on the down payment?** In considering your down payment approach, you have to determine whether

you care more about your monthly cost or your initial cost. Since the amount of your down payment directly affects your loan amount (purchase price - down payment = loan amount), it also affects the monthly payments on your loan. So the smaller your down payment, the larger your loan amount and, therefore, your monthly payments. Making a larger down payment can also lower your interest rate. This makes your monthly payments even smaller.

- **How long will it be before you move or refinance?** If you are moving from a rental to a home you own, time is one of the most important factors to consider. Unless you live in an area where property prices are shooting upward, it generally does not make sense to buy a house if you can't commit to owning it for at least four years. That's because there are many fees, charges, and deposits required in buying and selling a home. These transaction fees can cost you 10 percent or more of the selling price of the home. With costs like that, it generally makes sense to stay put for a while and wait for the property's appreciation to cover your transaction expense. If you are not sure how long you will own a house, make a conservative guess. The average American moves every 10 to 13 years. Most people move for lifestyle changes, not financial reasons. You may get transferred, or read a compelling article about the joys of life in rural South Carolina. In these cases, the last thing you want is to stay because of money concerns, but for others it can mean the difference between making a profit and taking a loss on housing.

- **What kind of mortgage payments do you want?** The three basic options are monthly fixed; payments that are initially fixed, then variable; and variable.

- **What type of property is it?** Single family, condominium or cooperative, or two-, three-, or four-family residence? This can affect both your rates and the types of mortgage you may be offered, and how much you can borrow.

- **How many points do you want?** Points can be either positive (discount points) or negative (rebate points). The more positive points you choose to pay up front, the lower your interest rate may be. For every point you pay, your rate will usually go down by about 0.25 percent. On the other hand, you can opt for a loan with a higher interest rate in exchange for a rebate, which will give you a credit toward paying some of your nonrecurring closing costs, such as title insurance, appraisal, and origination fee. You can't get any cash back from rebate points.

HOW POINTS AFFECT AN 8%, 30-YEAR TERM, $100,000 LOAN

POINTS	INTEREST RATE	YOU PAY/RECEIVE	MONTHLY PAYMENT
1.0	7.75%	You pay $1,000 for the lower rate	$716
0	8.00%	You pay nothing	$734
-1.0	8.25%	You receive up to $1,000 toward your closing costs	$751

Note: For illustrative purposes only

- **How long would you like to lock in the interest rate?** The lock-in period is the amount of time you're guaranteed a loan's interest rate. Once you've locked in an interest rate on a loan, you'll be guaranteed that rate for a certain period of time, usually for 30, 45, or 60 days. Normally, the longer the lock period, the more points that you have to pay up front, since the lender is taking a greater risk to guarantee a rate for a long time. You'll need to complete your home purchase or refinance within the lock period. If you need extra time, you may have to pay up to 1 point (1 percent of the loan amount) or more, and there's no guarantee that you can keep your original interest rate after the expiration date.

Any number of items can affect the rate you are ultimately offered, including your credit profile, the type of mortgage you are seeking, and the house itself. You may want to plan ahead and get your finances in order before sitting down to apply. You may even think you are ready when you're not. Take, for example, the following case.

Getting in Shape

Doug, a rising advertising executive who had enjoyed bachelorhood for several years, decided as he approached his 30s that it was nearing time to settle down. He felt he had spent enough money on rent, and the time was right to buy a house. He didn't have much saved up, but figured he could always throw some money from his next few paychecks into his savings account for a down payment. Once he made up his mind about things, Doug liked to act immediately. He was looking forward to moving into his new house by the end of the year, about three months away. He was already planning the housewarming party.

Doug's sister-in-law, Betsy, was a licensed real estate broker who offered to help him hunt for his new home. She raised her eyebrows when Doug told her his time line but didn't try to dissuade him. However, she did recommend that Doug set up a meeting with a mortgage broker or bank officer just to see what financing possibilities were available.

Doug figured he would be a highly desirable candidate for a mortgage because he had worked steadily at a number of jobs with increasing responsibility and had a wallet full of credit cards. His annual salary was more than adequate to support a couple, let alone a single guy, once he added in the substantial bonus he received in February of each year as part of his pay package.

Doug called to set up a meeting with a mortgage specialist at the bank where he had his checking and savings accounts. He figured he was a slam dunk to qualify for at least six figures at their best-advertised interest rate. Geoff, the loan officer who took his call, asked whether he'd come in to sign a form allowing the bank to order a full credit report on him. Doug signed the form and, the next week, returned to the bank for his appointment. Expecting the meeting to take all of five minutes, he had arranged to meet Betsy afterward to immediately start looking at some properties in his price range.

Geoff asked Doug to sit down and opened a file folder, scanning the contents of a paper on top. Geoff first complimented Doug on his prompt payment of his rent every month. He said that this was something that the bank specifically looked for in evaluating mortgage applicants. "I have a few questions I hope you don't mind answering," he told Doug. Doug shrugged and said, "Sure, no problem."

Geoff's first area of concern was Doug's work history and salary. Though Doug had thought his income was more than adequate to support a mortgage payment, he quickly learned otherwise. His career path, which had resulted in changing jobs four times in the previous 6 years, had placed him squarely in a high-risk category, and his bonuses, while hefty, weren't counted as part of his income, since they were tied to the profitability of his firm. Doug explained that in his industry, it is common to change jobs often, especially when an account is lost or moves to another firm. He also wanted Geoff to know that his bonuses over the previous 5 years had steadily increased and that he thought there was little chance of a decrease.

Next the subject of Doug's credit came up. It turned out that Doug's applying for—and receiving—numerous credit cards was a red flag to the bank. And although he kept low balances, the total amount of potential credit available to Doug signaled that he might be in a cash-flow crunch. He assured Geoff that he didn't need all those credit cards and would be happy to close out the balances on all but one or two if that would help assure the bank that he wouldn't overextend himself.

Then Geoff brought up two issues that caught Doug by surprise. The first was an open balance on a cell phone bill dating back more than 5 years. It was just $45, and Doug had completely forgotten about it. He had disputed the bill at the time but then never again heard from the wireless company and assumed they'd taken it off their books. Apparently, they hadn't. Geoff explained that many times, it's not worth the effort for a creditor to refer small amounts to collection agencies, but the balance can remain open on the consumer's credit record for 7 years. It was Doug's responsibility to clear this up, preferably before he formally applied for his mortgage loan, or the debt might adversely affect the outcome of his application. Doug thought that the wireless company had been bought out a while earlier, so he wasn't even sure if he could clear it up, but he said he'd try. Geoff made a note of that.

Geoff had saved the biggest bombshell for last. He asked Doug about his "other mortgage," the one that was currently in default for payments that were more than 30 days late. Doug laughed and said he had no other mortgage—and if he did have one, he certainly wouldn't be late in paying it. He asked to see the documentation that asserted this claim, and Geoff showed it to him. Puzzled, Doug saw that his credit report indeed showed an outstanding mortgage of $135,000, underwritten by a bank across the country. Was someone using his name perhaps? Geoff said this was entirely possible, though not necessarily in a criminal sense; it might be that the records of someone who actually had the same name were inadvertently mixed up with Doug's report. He recommended contacting the credit bureau and requesting an investigation.

Geoff explained to Doug that while he probably could secure a mortgage in spite of these factors, it wasn't likely he would be offered a preferred interest rate until his credit report had been cleaned up. He also suggested that the human resources department at Doug's company write a letter, to be submitted with the loan application, explaining the nature of the advertising industry and how its executives are typically compensated, so that more weight would be given to Doug's annual bonus. And he strongly recommended that over the next few months, Doug put aside as much money as he could to make a down payment that would lower the amount he'd need to borrow.

Doug left the bank knowing far more about what's important in getting a mortgage than he had realized on entering. When he met up with Betsy, he told her his timetable had changed and it might be longer than three months before he would move. Betsy just smiled.

Commonsense Considerations

As Doug learned, you need to get your finances in top shape before applying for a mortgage. Here is a program that you can follow to help get your profile in order before you apply.

- **Order a credit file disclosure.** These are generated by three consumer credit reporting agencies: Equifax, Experian, or TransUnion. You can easily order your credit report online through www.annualcreditreport.com (you're entitled to one free report annually at no charge, or you may opt to pay for more frequent reports or bells and whistles such as a calculation or analysis of your credit score). You can also order one through the toll-free number (877) 322-8228.

Scrutinize your report(s) closely for errors and "red flags."

- **Always pay your bills within 30 days of the due date.** Payments more than 30 days late are one of the measures creditors use to determine a borrower's credit unworthiness. Make yourself a payment schedule and post it in a prominent place, annotate your kitchen or personal calendar, or arrange for recurring bills to be paid automatically out of your bank account.

- **Pay off or negotiate current collection accounts to close them out.** Outstanding debts continue to be reported to the credit bureaus for 7 years from the date of nonpayment.

- **Work to reduce your debt-to-income ratio.** This is the total of all your debt payments every month divided by your monthly gross income (your income before subtracting taxes and any other deductions). Typically, lenders like to see a maximum debt ratio of no more than 40 percent of your gross monthly income. If your debt ratio exceeds the maximum, consider consolidating debts into a single lower payment.

- **Decrease your loan-to-value ratio.** If you borrow the full appraised value of the home, your loan-to-value ratio is 100 percent. You can decrease your loan-to-value ratio by offering a down payment. The higher the down payment, the lower your loan-to-value ratio will be. An additional incentive is that if you can offer a down payment of at least 20 percent of the purchase price of the home, you may be able to avoid private mortgage insurance, which is coverage from a private insurer that helps protect the mortgage lender against your mortgage default.

- **Call a moratorium on applying for additional credit.** Every time you fill out a credit application, it shows up on your credit report as an "inquiry." Numerous inquiries can indicate you are having a cash-flow problem and need access to open lines of credit. This can negatively affect your credit score.

- **Organize your documents.** Locate, sort, and file all your bank statements, pay stubs, W-2 forms, monthly credit statements, and tax returns. If any are missing, order duplicates.

- **Build savings.** You will need funds for your down payment and closing costs, as well as cash reserves in a bank account for two to three months before you apply for your loan. And don't forget those moving costs.

If you have recently experienced difficulty meeting your financial obligations, it just may not be the right time for you to buy a home. If you can hold out until your credit situation stabilizes, you may save yourself thousands of dollars—and diminish the risk of shouldering a high-interest loan that, in turn, might put you in further credit distress.

However, if you cannot wait, and you know your credit is less than perfect, your mortgage options may not necessarily be limited to subprime lenders who charge higher interest rates and fees. It all depends on a constellation of factors, some of which are within your power to affect and others that are not. Separating these two categories and focusing on improving what you can control will benefit your chances of getting the best rate possible, which, in turn, will benefit your wallet in the long run.

Grabbing the Brass Ring

After spending several years rebuilding her credit and many months pounding the pavement with the weekend real estate section of her local newspaper in hand, Lynda found a house that was perfect in every way. Because the owners were divorcing, they wanted to dispose of it as quickly as possible at a price well below market value. It was a once-in-a-lifetime opportunity for Lynda. Her real estate agent recommended a mortgage company that she knew from experience was willing to offer loans to applicants with a not-quite-perfect credit record.

Lynda's many years of steady employment strengthened her bargaining position. But unwilling to leave anything to chance, Lynda composed a detailed letter of explanation regarding her credit crunch. She explained that while in college she had been in an auto accident and found herself with insufficient insurance to cover significant medical costs. Eventually, though, she had been able to pay off the balances on those bills. Now she was able to provide proof of her commitment to her restored creditworthiness by contributing regularly to a savings account.

Lynda also had rent and utility receipts to verify a steady payment history and was able to demonstrate regular installment payments on her credit cards. Based on her credit score, the interest on the loan she was seeking was still higher than the rate available to individuals without her past problems. However, she was advised to consider refinancing in several years, after her credit score had had time to improve some more. This way, she wouldn't have to pass up the opportunity to buy this "perfect house."

Processing and approval of Lynda's loan application took somewhat longer than it would have if she'd had a better credit record. While it was nerve-wracking, in the end Lynda was granted an insured mortgage loan and became a proud first-time homeowner. This had been far out of the range of possibility several years earlier, when her financial situation was bleak. The passage of time, along with Lynda's concerted effort to improve her credit score, ultimately made all the difference.

Commonsense Considerations

When Lynda went to apply for her mortgage, she anticipated questions and took the extra step in providing a letter of explanation. When you are ready to complete an application, here is what you should know before you sharpen your pencils:

- **Obtain two applications.** Fill out one as a draft, and, if you make no mistakes, you can send it in. Otherwise, make all your corrections and then copy the accurate information to the clean form. Write as neatly as possible and try to avoid using correction fluid.
- **Fill out the application completely and precisely.** A lender cannot judge an application based on incomplete information and will return it to you with a request to provide the missing information, therefore prolonging the process.
- **Provide complete documentation.** You will typically need a month of pay stubs, 3 months of bank account statements, 2 years of W-2 forms, and 1 year of rent or mortgage history. You will also need proof for any source of income you are claiming on the application.
- **Be prompt in supplying additionally requested information.** Don't put yourself in a position to be turned down because too much time

has elapsed between a request for and delivery of additional information. If it's appropriate for a third party to provide or verify information, such as an employer or landlord, ask them to do so on your behalf.

- **Be prepared to explain any credit problems or late payments in detail.** "I forgot" won't cut it.
- **Make copies of everything you submit, and hand-deliver the documents or send them by certified mail.** Keep your copies handy until your mortgage loan is approved and closed, then file them carefully in a place where you can readily locate them if necessary. It will save you time if you apply for additional financing or for refinancing at a later date.

See also Chapter 4, "Mortgage Matters," for further information.

CHAPTER 13

Insuring Yourself, Your Family, and Your Property

Everyone needs insurance. Life is full of unanticipated occurrences that can have a high price tag (not to mention emotional burdens) attached. Most are horrific to consider: sudden death, automobile accidents, natural disasters, life-threatening or chronic health conditions, workplace injuries, theft, fire, and so on. Insurance provides financial support that can help you—or your loved ones—get through a difficult, often unexpected, experience. But it can be challenging to determine exactly what forms of insurance you need (or don't need) and how much coverage is adequate. Then there's the task of finding this at a reasonable price from a reliable source.

There are two broad categories of insurance. Insurance that covers your personal needs includes health, life, disability, and long-term care insurance. Insurance that covers your property includes automobile and homeowner's. You may not be able to purchase all your insurance policies from a single source. Health, life, and disability may be available from your workplace, but your employer probably is not going to help you insure your home or your car (unless it is a company-owned vehicle).

Expecting the Worst, Hoping for the Best

Bonnie and Henry felt truly blessed. They had been married for 5 years, had a healthy toddler son, fulfilling careers, a modest, well-kept home in a friendly neighborhood, and a late-model car that gave them no trouble. After watching a newsmagazine show about families struggling with healthcare costs, Bonnie and Henry began to question whether their own healthcare coverage was adequate. Because Henry was self-employed, Bonnie's policy covered the family.

Bonnie had never really read the materials given to her the first day she became eligible for coverage—she had just checked off a form for the cheapest option and sent it back. She wasn't even sure what the monthly premium was, since it was automatically deducted from her paycheck. When a member of the family needed to see a doctor, they picked one off a list of preferred providers and made an appointment. Now that his mother needed highly specialized care, Henry wondered if being in a HMO was what he and Bonnie really wanted. What if they decided to take their son to a pediatrician who wasn't on the list? What if the baby needed a specialist? Sure, they could always pay out of pocket, but why did they have insurance if it wasn't going to cover these costs?

As they began looking into their health insurance, Bonnie and Henry realized that now that they were parents, they also needed to obtain life insurance. They wanted to make sure that their son would be well cared for if something happened to one or both of them.

Bonnie made a deal with Henry to divide the labor. She would look into healthcare options if he would research life insurance policies. They set a deadline of one week to gather the information and agreed that they would use multiple sources: looking on the Internet, browsing in the bookstore, and asking friends and family about their coverage and recommendations.

The office manager at Bonnie's company was happy to help Bonnie navigate the different health insurance options available. There are two basic types, she told Bonnie: fee-for-service and managed care. With fee-for-service, Bonnie and Henry could pick their own doctors, and, after they met a specified deductible, their bill or a portion of it would be paid. Managed care programs, the other option, include health maintenance

organizations (commonly called HMOs), PPOs (preferred provider organizations), and POS (point-of-service plans). With HMOs, you are given
a list of doctors who participate and you must choose one of them, or pay
your own way. PPO and POS plans are a little more flexible; you may be
allowed to use a doctor outside the plan. Bonnie indicated that she and
Henry felt strongly about preventative coverage, especially after their
experience with Henry's mother. The office manager said to the best of
her knowledge, preventative coverage may not be covered by a fee-for-
service plan but typically is in a managed care policy.

The office manager also briefed Bonnie on some of the basic questions
she should consider in choosing a plan. Of course, expense is a major
consideration, but it should not be the sole determinant. Your medical
history and that of the other members of your family who will be covered
are also important, especially if there are pre-existing conditions that
require extensive and expensive treatment. Some plans make you wait a
certain period of time before covering these illnesses or conditions.

In fact, how healthy you and your family are can be another important
determining factor. Do you (or anyone who is to be covered) have any
chronic conditions that might make one plan more favorable over another?
What about medication? Do you care if prescriptions are paid for through
the plan or not? Do you have an accident-prone 7-year-old who is in and
out of emergency rooms? Are you a fan of alternative medicine, such as
homeopathic remedies or acupuncture? Some plans cover these treat-
ments; others don't. And what about family planning—obstetrics costs
are yet another consideration. The office manager emphasized that these
were just a few of the considerations for Bonnie to weigh.

A week later, Bonnie and Henry shared their findings while they sat
at their dining room table. Bonnie spread out the information package
on the family's current health insurance coverage and was able to outline
to Henry its advantages and disadvantages. She thought they should stay
with their same plan with a few minor adjustments, including one to the
deductible and another to allow them to be partially reimbursed for doctors outside the company's network. She had even investigated purchasing medical coverage outside of her employer and was horrified by how
expensive it would be to cover the family—thousands of dollars
monthly.

Henry had investigated both types of life insurance, term and permanent. He had made a chart explaining the differences:

TYPE	DEFINITION	ADVANTAGES	DISADVANTAGES
Term	Protection for a specific time period, usually 1–30 years, for a set amount at a set premium determined by age, gender, health, length of policy, and tobacco use.	Inexpensive and competitively priced Guaranteed rates May not require a medical exam Can start immediately	No savings or investment component Once the term ends you have to buy another policy, possibly at higher cost
Permanent (AKA Cash Value, Variable, or Universal Life)	Pays a benefit on death, but also accumulates cash value for every year you are alive. Available as Whole Life (fixed premium for a defined cash payout), Universal (flexible premium payments determining payout), or Variable (includes an investment component). Premiums are accumulated in a fund and paid out as dividends.	Premiums are set Cash value is a form of savings Doesn't have to be renewed	Value of the investment component of policy may lag the market and has to cover agent commissions and processing expenses More expensive than term Available only through licensed brokers and not online May incur a penalty for cashing out early

Together they concluded that for their present needs, term was a better fit. Henry could buy a 30-year policy relatively cheaply since he was in good health and not a smoker. He thought they should purchase a policy that would pay around eight to 10 times his annual salary. This was the amount recommended by industry experts. Then, he could add Bonnie to the policy so she wouldn't have to have a separate one. If somewhere later down the line they decided to switch to a whole life policy, they could revisit the issue. A client of Henry's had recommended a broker to write the term policy, and Henry said he would follow up if that was okay with Bonnie.

Henry's client had also suggested that Henry and Bonnie see whether they could find disability insurance at a reasonable price, perhaps from Bonnie's employer. In the event of a catastrophic illness, health insurance would not pay the everyday bills that Henry and Bonnie needed both salaries to cover. That was something they hadn't considered at all.

He additionally recommended long-term-care insurance in case an illness or accident resulted in the need for expensive long-term care. These costs also might not be covered by traditional health insurance. Although Bonnie and Harry thought this was important, they decided to postpone this purchase for a few more years.

Once Henry and Bonnie had educated themselves and made informed decisions about their personal insurance needs, they felt they could rest easier about what the future might hold.

Commonsense Considerations

Henry and Bonnie's research project helped them clarify the many options and determine a clear direction.

While health, life, disability, and long-term-care insurance offer distinctly different types of coverage, here are some common points to consider when purchasing insurance.

- **Your needs are unique.** You, your family, your financial situation, and a whole host of factors you can't control, such as your genetic predisposition to illness, make a difference. Don't let anyone talk you into general policies that don't take into account your particular circumstances.
- **Strive for enough coverage. But don't overinsure.** The point of insurance is to protect you and your family in the event of a tragedy. You need adequate coverage, but not so much that it is redundant or ties up valuable dollars that could be better invested elsewhere.
- **Try to find a provider that offers multiplan policies.** There may be substantial discounts if the same company issues your life, disability, auto, and home insurance.
- **Consolidate separate policies and maintain only one policy per family.** For life insurance, a policy with a rider for your spouse will save on processing fees. If you have access to two individual policies through work, analyze the costs versus a single family policy.
- **Life insurance on children is usually not necessary.** The coverage for their parents, however, is essential in providing for the children. If you are insistent upon life insurance for your children, include them as a "child rider" and only buy enough insurance to cover burial costs.
- **Stay away from adding on extra options.** These extra costs might keep you from affording the maximum protection. Do your homework:

Look up how much you spend on prescription drugs before you sign on for coverage. Compare the extra cost of this benefit with your out-of-pocket expenses. It may not be worth it.

- **Comparison shop.** Doing so is easier than ever, thanks to information readily available over the Internet.
- **Revisit all insurance decisions at least annually** or on the occasion of a "life event" such as a birth or death.
- **If you lose or leave your job, check out COBRA.** This is your federally mandated option to continue on your former employer's group policy (COBRA is short for Consolidated Omnibus Budget Reconciliation Act) for the first 18 months after you leave the job. You have to pay the premiums yourself, but it's a deal compared with paying for a policy on your own.

The other broad category of insurance you need to educate yourself about protects you from loss or damage to your property, mainly your automobile and your home.

Automobile insurance is required by law in nearly every state in the country. Components include:

- **Comprehensive coverage** that pays for vehicle theft or for damage that is not the result of an accident
- **Collision coverage** that pays for the repair or replacement of the policy owner's car in the event of an accident, regardless of who caused the accident
- **Liability coverage** that covers your legal responsibility to others for bodily damage or property damage
- **Medical coverage** that pays for the cost of treating injuries, rehabilitation, and, sometimes, lost wages or funeral costs
- **Uninsured motorists coverage** that pays for treating your injuries and repairing or replacing your property damaged as the result of an accident caused by an individual who does not have liability coverage

In the realm of home-related insurance, if you paid all cash for your home, you may be able to avoid mortgage lender–required homeowner's insurance, though it's a good idea to get this coverage anyway. Standard homeowner's policies exist primarily to protect you from catastrophic events like house fires and typically exclude damage caused by floods, earthquakes, sewer damage, and, in some cases, windstorms, hurricanes, and mold. Homeowner's policies may also include liability coverage in case someone is injured on your property. If you rent, you can purchase renter's insurance to cover damage or loss of your possessions, or injury to a guest or visitor. It's relatively inexpensive and definitely worth it.

Driving Down Insurance Costs

Patrick hated paying the monthly premiums on his auto insurance, but he knew he had to. It was part of the responsibility of owning a car. His uncle, who happened to be an insurance agent, had written the policy for him and made sure he was adequately covered. Patrick knew that his insurance rates were affected by a couple of factors over which he had no control—his age, for starters, and his gender and bachelorhood. His uncle had also advised him on a number of factors he could do something about—like where he lived, his occupation, and the kind of car he drove. It also made a difference that he had a clean driving record with no moving violations and no major claims.

One day, Patrick was driving to a meeting and heard a call-in talk show about car insurance rates. The show's guest host listed a number of additional items that Patrick hadn't realized could also affect his insurance rate, like how far he drove to work every day, the fact that he kept his car on the street instead of in a garage, and the car theft alarm. The host suggested that consumers looking to lower their auto insurance rates should definitely shop around and consider increasing their deductibles if they felt they had the financial resources to cover a larger amount in the event of an accident. And he revealed that an individual's credit report could have a positive or negative effect on rates.

That was news to Patrick. He resolved to give his uncle a call first thing in the morning to see whether he could update his policy so that it reflected those factors that might cause a decrease in his rates. Patrick was lucky to have been tuned to that radio station—it saved him $50 a month in the end.

Commonsense Considerations

While your insurance agent works with your best interests in mind, you should take responsibility, as Patrick did, for staying current on information that affects your wallet. These general guidelines can also help you make sure your property insurance—whether for your home or auto—is adequate and covers your property at the lowest cost possible.

- **Be a detective.** Compare your alternatives by researching and receiving at least three price quotes from different companies.
- **Consider a multiplan policy.** You may be able to reduce your rates if you buy both your homeowner's and automobile insurance from the same insurer. You might consider asking both companies to price the additional policy for you if you are presently buying your policies from different insurers.
- **Bump up your deductible.** This is the amount of money you will have to pay out-of-pocket before your insurance company's payment kicks in. Observe the relationship between your deductible and your rates. For example, if you can afford to raise it from $500 to $1,000 on our auto insurance, you can save significantly on your annual costs. (However, this means you should have at least this much on hand should you need to file a claim.)
- **Disaster-proof your home.** Ask your agent what actions you can take to prepare for natural disasters. Certain areas of the country are more prone to certain types of natural disaster such as tornados or hurricanes. Find out what protections you can install to minimize your risks.
- **Ask about discounts that may be available to you.** Every insurance company has a list of items that will qualify you for a discount—for example, a smoke detector or an alarm system may reduce your homeowner's rates, just as an alarm system on your car may do the same on your automobile policy. Safe-driver discounts and good-grades discounts (for students) should also be investigated.

- **Buy additional coverage when necessary.** Depending on where you live, you may need separate coverage, especially if you're in an area prone to natural disasters.
- **Try not to file claims if you don't have to.** Some experts recommend not filing claims for less than $1,000. If you file too many claims, your company may raise your premium or drop you altogether.

14

Being Smart about Saving for College

Like a house, a college education can be at once an expense and an investment. There can be economic, social, and even health benefits for college graduates. People with Bachelor's degrees tend to have higher incomes, have better jobs, travel more, and have improved access to health care compared to their counterparts who never went beyond high school.

Maybe you want to be able to provide higher education for your about-to-be-born child or grandchild, or maybe it's for your favorite 4-year-old nephew. Or maybe it's for yourself, so in another few years, when your preschooler is a little older and more self-sufficient, you can go back to school to get a law degree and start a new career as an attorney.

What are the options for funding a future college or graduate school degree, outside of borrowing heavily? One alternative can be a carefully crafted investment program. Even if you didn't start saving as early as you might have, if you have the resources and the motivation, you can begin now to put aside at least some money to help offset the staggering costs of a post-secondary education. This chapter suggests some strategies for doing so.

Setting It All Up

Ann and Mike were completely enchanted by their first child, Christy, who was just 6 months old. They felt strongly that it was their responsibility to give her the very best opportunities in life, even if it meant significant sacrifice for them. There was no question in their minds that Christy would go to college, and they wanted to make sure that she would not be financially burdened while in school or after she graduated. They were well aware of the rising cost of an undergraduate degree and realized they would have to save a significant sum to cover tuition and living expenses nearly two decades into the future for Christy. To help them figure all this out, they contacted a financial advisor.

The financial advisor, Maryann, helped them construct a preliminary educational funding analysis to determine how much they would need to save on an annual basis. The first figure she came up with was $600 per month. This was beyond what Ann and Mike felt they could come up with, even if they drastically reduced their expenses. The only way they could save this amount would be if they were to charge a lot more of their living expenses on their credit cards. It didn't make sense to them to increase their high-interest debt. Maryann agreed.

After further conversation, Ann and Mike told Maryann that at the present time they could afford to invest $400 a month. If they received any monetary gifts from their family or work bonuses, they would try to make up the $2,400 annual difference with it. They also vowed that they would increase the monthly amount once they were in a position to do so.

Maryann presented to Ann and Mike a plan that suggested they open a Coverdell Education Savings Account. Ann had read about Educational IRAs, which Maryann explained were what Coverdell ESAs were formerly called. These accounts are self-directed, allowing the investor to make investment and allocation decisions. A particularly attractive benefit of an ESA is that it may provide tax benefits if the funds are used for tuition at specifically designated schools. Maryann suggested the couple talk to their tax advisor or accountant regarding the tax implications. She did warn that if they were to take money out of the account without using it for the approved purposes, they might have to pay taxes as well as a penalty on the gains. But she felt confident that there was a low possibility of this happening, since Ann and Mike were so determined to use the funds for Christy's college education.

Ann and Mike decided that it made sense for them to invest in a diversified ESA portfolio structured for long-term growth. They would make the $2,000 annual maximum contribution allowed by law that year, so long as their income stayed below the maximums allowed by the IRS. Maryann gave them the following chart for guidance:

ELIGIBILITY FOR ESA

	ADJUSTED GROSS INCOME	CONTRIBUTIONS
Single Filer	$0–$95,000	$2,000
	$95,000–$110,000	Pro rata phaseout of contributions
	Over $110,000	Not eligibile to contribute
Married Filing Jointly	$0–$190,000	$2,000
	$190,000–$220,000	Pro rata phaseout of contributions
	Over $220,000	Not eligibile to contribute

Source: The Economic Growth and Tax Relief Act of 2001

Excerpted from Making the Grade, Smith Barney, 2005

If their income in any given year were to exceed the maximum allowed, they could keep the account open and benefit from the potential growth, but might not be able to make contributions for that year. Maryann emphasized how important it was for Ann and Mike to keep up with changes in the tax laws that might affect their investments. While they should feel confident that the professionals advising them would stay abreast of new developments, they, too, should make an effort to stay educated.

Since Mike and Ann's calculations about the approximate cost of college exceeded the amount that they would be able to accumulate in the ESA, they asked about how to invest the balance of the money needed for Christy's college fund. Would it make sense to put it into high-yielding certificates of deposit? Maryann said that that was one possibility, but she thought a better option would be to set up a Qualified Tuition

Account, commonly referred to as a 529 College Savings Plan, named for the section that addresses it in the Internal Revenue Code. Unlike the Coverdell ESA, a 529 Plan is professionally managed.

While there were certain risks that Ann and Mike would take on in opening a 529—namely, that investments in 529 Plans are not FDIC insured or bank guaranteed and may lose value—there were potential rewards as well. One of the most appealing qualities of a 529 is that the beneficiary of the plan can be changed. If, for instance, Ann and Mike decided to have another child and Christy was offered alternative financial support, such as a full or partial scholarship, or even decided not to go to college, her parents would be able to make her sibling the beneficiary of the account.

Maryann explained that most 529 Plans limit total contributions, so it is important to check the specific limitations on a plan-by-plan basis. In the event that Mike's income rises to the point where contributions to the Coverdell Education Savings Account are no longer allowed, the full amount could be invested in their 529.

Because there are various 529 College Savings Plans, Maryann said she would help Ann and Mike choose an appropriate plan that would take into account their state income tax situation, risk tolerance, and level of contributions. Some states have even set up plans that permit prepayment of tuition for state colleges, locking in the costs.

Maryann ended the meeting by stressing to Ann and Mike the importance of managing their finances responsibly throughout the process of building Christy's college fund. This entailed staying out of debt, continuing to save for their own retirement, and maintaining appropriate health, life, and other insurance needs. Ann and Mike left Maryann's office that day feeling like they themselves had gotten a college-level education—an early reward for their effort to fund a college education for their daughter.

Commonsense Considerations

Ann and Mike were lucky to find a good advisor who was well versed in the options for a college savings plan that was tailored to their particular needs, time frame, and risk tolerance. Here are some general guidelines that might help you plan for your child or children.

- **Build a budget.** Try to strike a balance between short-term expenses and long-term goals such as college and retirement. Ann and Mike had to compromise on the amount they were initially going to set aside so that they wouldn't have to compromise their current budget.
- **Involve trusted financial, tax, and legal advisors.** Although they may present different perspectives, this is a critical part of the information gathering necessary to make educated decisions.
- **Meet with advisors regularly.** Don't cancel meetings because the stock market is up. You need to constantly adjust your portfolio(s) in good and bad times, taking into account the current market environment, the time remaining until funds are needed, and current risk tolerance.
- **Do your research.** Before choosing a 529 Plan, carefully consider the plan's investment objectives, risks, charges, and expenses. Carefully read the offering statement before you invest or send money. Consider whether your home state (or the designated beneficiary's home state, if different from your own) offers its residents a plan with state-specific tax advantages or other benefits.
- **Stay flexible.** It's impossible to predict the future. The best you can do is make sure your current plan meets your future needs.
- **Don't discount "free money" opportunities.** If your child is eligible for a scholarship, do make sure your college savings funds aren't subject to penalties if you repurpose them.
- **Ask for cash.** Remind friends and family that gifts of cash or securities contributed to a child's college savings can be just as meaningful as the latest, greatest electronic gizmo—and have potentially longer-lasting benefits.

Filling the Gaps

Jack and Heather had been setting aside money for their grandson Brendan's college education since he was 11 years old. That was the year their daughter, Brendan's mother, was divorced. Brendan's father was an entrepreneur who had put himself through college at night and felt that Brendan should do the same. Even Brendan's mother was skeptical about college savings. Although Jack and Heather didn't expect they would be able to fully fund Brendan's college education, they wanted to do what they could for him.

Brendan was going to be a freshman in high school next year, and Jack and Heather felt it was time to reassess the savings they had set aside for him. They aimed for maximum flexibility, since Brendan's post high school plans were not yet firm. They had been contributing to a custodial account—also called a Uniform Transfers to Minors Act (UTMA) or Uniform Gifts to Minors Act (UGMA) account—with cash and securities. The assets were held in Brendan's name and would become his property at the age of majority (18 in their state). At that point, Brendan would be able to spend the money as he pleased. Unlike other college savings plans, there is no restriction on the amount of money that can be contributed, other than gift tax law allowances. However, custodial accounts can be subject to annual taxes.

In the past, Heather, as custodian, had set aside about 20 percent of the money in the account to buy government bonds. The rest was invested in stocks. While this mix may have been appropriate when Heather and Jack first set up the account, it seemed like it was time to reevaluate these allocations, given that Brendan was around 6 years away from entering college.

The first thing Heather found out was that the bonds she'd purchased were not due to mature until long after Brendan would graduate from college, assuming he entered right after high school. She felt terrible about this oversight. Although Brendan might be able to use the money to pay off student loans, Heather wished she had planned differently. She and Jack agreed that since college was becoming a near-term option, they should review the account as often as quarterly.

Jack called their accountant, and Heather consulted with a nephew who was a financial advisor. Both advised Jack and Heather to sell some of the equity assets and increase the percentage of bonds in the account. This would make available enough cash during Brendan's years in college, just in case the stock market made a downward correction in the next few years. The new allocation would be about equally divided between bonds and stocks.

This made Jack and Heather feel better about the money they'd saved for Brendan, and they promised each other they'd keep a closer eye on it. And most importantly, they chose short-term Treasury EE bonds with a 5-year term, which would thereby mature in time for Brendan to pay for his college tuition.

Commonsense Considerations

The length of time remaining until a child begins college is a strong determinant of how assets should be allocated within an education fund. The younger the child is, the more risk you can assume in a portfolio, since if there are losses, there will still be time to recoup them. Conversely, a shorter period until college requires you to be more conservative in your selections.

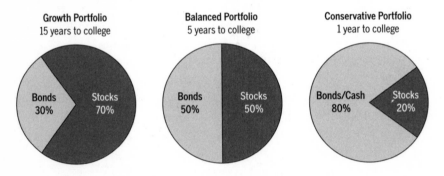

Growth Portfolio
15 years to college

Bonds 30%   Stocks 70%

Balanced Portfolio
5 years to college

Bonds 50%   Stocks 50%

Conservative Portfolio
1 year to college

Bonds/Cash 80%   Stocks 20%

Source: Making the Grade, *Smith Barney, 2005*

Jack and Heather might also have considered starting, even at this late date, a 529 Plan for Brendan. A 529 Plan provides an accelerated gift option that allows you to average certain gifts over $12,000 per beneficiary ($24,000 for married couples) over a 5-year period without incurring the federal gift tax. So an individual can contribute up to $60,000 per beneficiary in 1 year, and a couple up to $120,000 per beneficiary, without incurring the gift tax. An added advantage to a 529 Plan is that if Jack and Heather were to pass away before Brendan completed college, as long as their contribution was below the annual gift tax threshold, the contribution would not revert back to their estate.

For additional information, see Chapter 5, "Covering College Costs," and Chapter 15, "Investing in Learning about Investments."

Investing in Learning about Investments

Investing in the stock market has become as American as Mom and apple pie. Three times as many households today are investing in the markets as were two decades ago. That means even if you don't own stocks (directly or indirectly through mutual funds), your next-door neighbors on either side of you probably do.

The reason you (or your neighbors) may choose to invest money (assuming you have accumulated funds above and beyond what you need to cover living expenses) is because the potential for higher returns is much greater than if you put that money in a traditional savings account. Savings accounts generally pay lower percentage points in interest—earnings that may be eroded, if not outright negated, by inflation and taxes. For example, assume that the inflation rate will be around 3 percent and that taxes will claim about 25 percent of your interest earnings. Even if you manage to find a savings plan that will pay you 5 percent interest (2 to 3 percent is more typical), you can expect to pocket only 1.5 percent of that after inflation and taxes.

The stock market, on the other hand, has historically offered a much better shot at pulling ahead. Over the past 10 years, the stock market, as represented by the Wilshire Dow Jones 5000 (a compilation of just about every U.S. stock traded on the major exchanges) has increased in market value approximately 9 percent a year. That has given investors a big advantage, in terms of higher returns, over savings accounts. If you are investing to meet long-term goals, such as retirement or paying for a college education, you want to make sure that you will have enough to cover these future, escalating costs. Investing in the market could more quickly bring you closer to meeting your financial goals. Keep in mind, however, that past performance is not a guarantee of future results.

Another way to illustrate this is through the "Rule of 72." You can readily calculate how long it will take your money to double by dividing the number 72 by the interest rate. For example, at 2 percent interest, it will take approximately 36 years for invested money to double. But it will only take 9 years at an 8 percent rate of return.

HOW LONG WILL IT TAKE FOR YOUR SAVINGS TO DOUBLE?

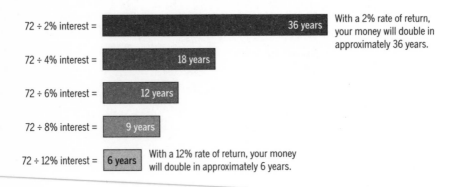

72 ÷ 2% interest =   36 years   With a 2% rate of return, your money will double in approximately 36 years.

72 ÷ 4% interest =   18 years

72 ÷ 6% interest =   12 years

72 ÷ 8% interest =   9 years

72 ÷ 12% interest =   6 years   With a 12% rate of return, your money will double in approximately 6 years.

Source: How Money Works, Primerica, 2005

You may be currently investing through a 401(k) plan at work. The advent of defined-contribution retirement plans has been a major factor in the growth of individual ownership of securities. Fueling this growth was the technology boom, with its gold-rush mind-set (and 20 percent rates of return), the widespread availability of business news through global media sources, and, of course, the Internet. While stories abound about investors losing their shirts, the evidence suggests that equity ownership has grown even when the market has been down (a circumstance known as a bear market), as well as when the market has been up (known as a bull market).

Company 401(k) plans have proven to be a gateway for first-time investors, some of whom may then graduate to explore the market outside employer-sponsored plans. This pattern is particularly pronounced in investors under 35, who have had more experience with 401(k) plans (which were first established in 1981). This has created a generation gap between older and younger investors, with the former group more likely to own taxable individual stocks and the latter more attracted to mutual funds in tax-deferred accounts.

Eric's Big Secret

If asked to describe his investment approach, Eric might mumble something that sounded vaguely intelligent. In truth, Eric had no idea what he was doing in the market. Worse, Eric was a 42-year-old successful computer programmer at a multinational investment bank with a significant brokerage business. He knew that just a few floors below his office, there were 24-year-olds who knew more about stocks and bonds and buying and trading than he did. He was too embarrassed to reveal his lack of investment savvy.

Stocks: Ownership shares in a corporation. Stockholders share a portion of the profit the company may make, as well as a portion of the loss a company may take. If the company grows, the stockholder may benefit from the rise in the company's stock price.

Bond: A security issued by a corporation or a government body. A buyer (the investor) is lending money to a seller (a corporation or a government body) in return for regular interest payments and the eventual repayment of the loan.

Mutual Fund: A company that pools money to invest in stocks, bonds, or other securities on behalf of a group of investors. The fund is managed by a professional investment manager. Mutual funds offer investors greater diversification because their portfolios consist of many different securities.

Eric was completely overwhelmed by the sheer quantity of investment products. Stocks, bonds, and mutual funds were just the tip of the iceberg.

Every day he heard financial advisors gossiping about the opportunities they put together for their clients, with "puts" and "calls," "selling short," "going long," and other lingo permeating their conversation. The market seemed to him like an enormous candy store, and he had no idea where to start.

But because he thought it was something he ought to be doing, Eric continued to add to his portfolio. He bought shares of the hot stock his dentist recommended, then more shares in a software company where his cousin worked. He even bought some corporate bonds from the company that manufactured the car tires he used.

Eric also had several different accounts holding his securities. His firm offered him an account at a slight discount, just for being an employee. He barely used it, though, because he hated paying for trades at top dollar. It had just three stocks in it. He had another account at a discount brokerage and two separate accounts with discount online financial advisors.

The online advisors had offered him special bonuses for signing up. One sent him a newsletter he never read, and the other gave him two free trades he used right away. Then there were the mutual funds he owned in his 401(k) plan. Trying to reconcile so many statements was a nightmare every month—not to mention at tax time. Eric could never tell whether he was winning or losing in the market.

The uncertainty and anxiety Eric was feeling about investing added to the stress of managing a career and being the sole income provider for his family. With a child just entering high school, Eric was acutely aware that the first college tuition payment was 4 short years away. He knew his portfolio should be able to help with this, but already he was looking into taking out loans.

It wasn't as if Eric was living from paycheck to paycheck. His earnings provided him with the ability to meet household expenses, add to his investments, and contribute to the family's short-term savings account. However, his investment illiteracy severely limited his financial security. He had no idea how to use his investments to provide returns sufficient to pay for college and attain his retirement goals.

What Eric needed was an investment strategy he could believe in, something that would give him a point of view and sense of direction and allow his investment dollars the opportunity to grow while working to reduce risk.

One night while he was surfing the Internet, Eric stumbled across an article about asset allocation. Asset allocation is the distribution of investments across broad categories of asset classes, such as stocks, bonds, and cash. Then, within each asset class, it is important to further mix the holdings. Eric figured out this meant he should be holding some stocks in large companies and some in small companies, as well as stocks representing several different types of industries. He felt he should also own both government and corporate bonds.

Reading the article, Eric realized how misguided he was about his approach to investing and how much basic education he needed. He decided to enroll in a class at the local community college, where he was unlikely to run into anyone from work. This would allow him to build his confidence while he rebuilt his portfolio.

Commonsense Considerations

Among the first suggestions Eric's instructor is likely to offer is for Eric to determine how he would like to buy securities and where he would like his portfolio held. Then Eric could go about consolidating his various accounts into one. Individual investors have choices that include:

- **Full-service financial advisors,** where you may designate an individual advisor who helps you manage your account and offers ideas, with the opportunity to have a one-on-one relationship.
- **Discount financial advisors,** where it's up to you to come up with ideas, keep an eye on the market and your portfolio, and place the orders to buy or sell via a Web site or over the phone, sometimes without ever speaking to the same person twice. Within the discount category, there are several different levels of service with, as the names suggest, a difference in the cost of each type of advisor.

Here is a breakdown of your options.

TYPE OF BROKERAGE	FUNCTION	COST	ADVANTAGES	DISADVANTAGES
Full Service	You have personalized service from a financial advisor who works with you on your portfolio holdings.	Commissions based on a percentage of buy or sell price	Personal relationship; access to firm research; someone helping you "mind the store"	Expense and quality of ideas and service can vary from advisor to advisor
Premium Discount	You place orders over the phone or online; they maintain your records and give you access to research.	Per trade	More service than the discount advisors at less cost than full service; add-on services for a fee	You have to do all the legwork. They may be available to consult, but will not approach you with ideas
Discount	You place your orders over the phone or online; may offer access to research, but less than the premium discount advisors.	Per trade	Lowest price	It's up to you to keep your eye on the market

Here Today, Gone Tomorrow—Back Saturday?

Jillian had dabbled in the stock market for several years, with excellent results. She was lucky to get in on the ground floor of several fast-moving stocks when the market was heating up, and she succeeded in turning a relatively modest initial investment into a sizable sum. Recognizing that nothing lasts forever, she cashed out and spent about half of her profits on creature comforts that she otherwise might not have been able to afford: a sports car, a luxury spa vacation, and a collection of antique furniture, which was her passion. She reinvested the balance of the proceeds, after taxes, in government bonds that seemed insulated from the difficulties of the market.

To her dismay, Jillian watched the market continue to climb even higher than she had ever imagined, with her new investments trailing far behind. Had she left her money in her original investments, they would have returned well over four times the amount she received when she cashed out. Frustrated, Jillian called her financial advisor and asked him to move all her money back into her original purchases.

Seth, her advisor, strongly advised her against this action. He questioned Jillian as to what, exactly, her investment goals were. "What do you mean?" Jillian shot back. "My goal is to make more money, of course!" Seth laughed and said he had never met a client who didn't have this goal, but she needed to be more specific. He explained that it had been clear to him a few years earlier that Jillian was willing to invest aggressively, taking on risk in order to gain high returns. In fact, he would classify several of the stocks in her former portfolio as speculative, and she had been fortunate in receiving higher-than-average gains for assuming higher-than-normal risk.

It then seemed to him that Jillian swung abruptly in the opposite direction. She became a conservative investor by putting her money in financial instruments that emphasize the safety and preservation of original investment over returns. No wonder she was frustrated by the slow growth of her money, especially in the face of a bull market.

Seth assured Jillian that if she wanted to jump back in with both feet, he would execute the orders—she was his client, after all. But he suggested that perhaps she might like to consider a middle ground that would protect her if the market fell, as she had once thought it might, while still offering some growth potential.

Jillian didn't have to think long before telling Seth she agreed with him about her haphazard strategies. She also had forgotten that her accountant had suggested she look into investments that were more tax-efficient than some of the high-flyers she had owned in the past. She asked Seth if he would help her create this "middle ground," by positioning her investments into a diversified portfolio, thereby combining growth stocks that could appreciate in value over time with fixed-income investments. She admitted that her earlier gains had gone to her head, and now it was time to acknowledge that her needs and her philosophy had changed.

Jillian's portfolio gained some momentum and weathered the stock market downturn that finally arrived. Instead of regretting the money she could have made if she had stayed in her go-go stocks, she now appreciated how much she had not lost.

Commonsense Considerations

Jillian's financial advisor was smart to suggest that she look before she leap. When setting up your first portfolio or realigning an existing one, you should first figure out what it is, in a general sense, that you want to get out of it. Here are some guidelines.

- **Establish a clear goal.** Be specific about your objective—the better defined it is, the more likely it is that you might obtain it. For Jillian, this meant supplementing her company-sponsored retirement fund with an individual portfolio and having some immediate resources to indulge in her collection.
- **Set a time frame.** Jillian's was dual: In 2 years, she would like to receive some money to update her antique collection, and she anticipated retiring in 20 years.
- **Commit to regular contributions toward your goals.** Jillian already had a portion of her paycheck automatically deposited in her investment account and was making the maximum permissible contributions to her 401(k) plan.
- **Consider dollar-cost averaging.** This means investing a certain fixed amount each month, regardless of what's happening in the stock market. The price you pay—your "dollar cost"—can average out over time. When the market falls and share prices go down, your monthly investment can buy more shares than when the market is up and share prices are higher. Over time, as the market rises again, shares bought in a down market can dramatically increase the value of your portfolio. Remember this strategy does not guarantee a profit or protect against a loss.
- **Calculate the annual investment return needed to reach your goals.** For example, if Jillian hoped to receive an annual return of 8 percent and long-term stock returns are only 5 percent, she might need to increase her contribution level or lower her target to meet her goal.

- **Be disciplined, yet flexible.** With her short-term goals so close, any drop in portfolio value might cause Jillian to miss the mark. Seth suggested that anytime there was a 3 percent loss in value in the portfolio during any 3-month period, he would consult Jillian about realigning to a more conservative allocation.
- **Map out asset allocation.** The appropriate investment mix is determined by your circumstances, needs, and goals. The charts below are hypothetical examples of how different types of investments might be combined in a portfolio according to your goals. The investments include bonds, which are the most secure, large-cap stocks (stocks of a company with a market capitalization of more than $10 billion, with market capitalization arrived at by multiplying the number of shares outstanding times the current stock price), international stocks (stocks of non-U.S. companies), and small-cap stocks (stocks with a market capitalization of under $1 billion). Small-cap and mid-cap companies often experience sharper price fluctuations than stocks of large-cap companies. Jillian's new portfolio would be modeled on the Moderate Growth chart.

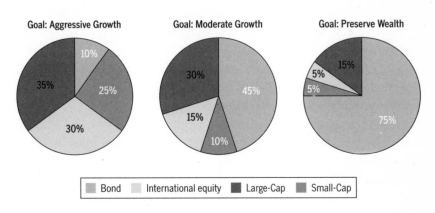

Note: For illustrative purposes only

Source: CitiStreet Building Your Future, 2002

There are many lessons to be learned about investing. The more informed you are about how the markets work, the better positioned you will be to get them to work better for you. The worst-kept secret of successful investing in the market is to buy low, sell high. It's also no secret that diversification is critical.

Learning Diversification

The unexpected passing of his grandmother was sad for Ben, though he knew she had lived a good life as the wife and then widow of the founder of a small but profitable pharmaceutical company. Well into her 90s, she had managed the money his grandfather had left her. Ben's grandmother Evelyn was a wonderfully warm, smart, and sometimes stubborn woman. Ben and his six cousins were now going to inherit her money. A state-employed social worker, Ben had devoted his life to the well-being of others, without planning much for his own future. This now seemed like a good opportunity to make up for lost time.

Evelyn's portfolio was composed exclusively of the stock of her late husband's company. "I will never sell this stock," she had told Ben many times after his grandfather died. "It took your grandfather years to accumulate it. He called it our security blanket. He tried buying other stocks and always lost money. He said that this was the one stock he knew was worth the paper it was printed on." She then always added, "And you should never sell it, either." In the years after her husband's death, Evelyn had managed to live comfortably on the dividends from the stock, along with his pension and other retirement benefits.

About a year after her death, Evelyn's estate was settled. Her executor, an attorney who was a close family friend, notified Ben that he would shortly receive one-seventh of the portfolio—several thousand shares of the company stock. Ben asked the executor what it was worth and was informed of the current price and dividend-per-share amount. The executor also recommended that Ben have the shares transferred to his own account rather than keep the certificates in a safe deposit box as his grandmother had insisted on doing.

On the recommendation of a colleague at work, Ben opened an account at a local brokerage firm, directing the executor to have his stock sent there. The transaction went through smoothly. A day after the stock arrived, Ben received a call from a young woman who identified herself as a member of his financial advisory team. She invited him to come in to discuss his investment options. Ben was surprised—he hadn't been aware that he had any options. Since he had to stop by the firm to sign some papers anyway, he made an appointment.

When he arrived at the meeting, there were two professionals in the office: Susan, the woman who had called him, and an associate. He immediately thanked the women for arranging the meeting but said it was hardly worth their time. In accordance with his grandmother's wishes, he had no intention of ever selling the stock.

Susan agreed that the stock in his grandfather's company had been good to Ben's family over the years. However, she explained that continuing to hold it now was not the best approach. There was simply too much risk in holding just the one stock. Diversifying the portfolio might reduce that risk. For a start, diversification should increase dividend income. While the dividends from the pharmaceuticals company had been adequate for his grandmother, Ben was receiving only one-seventh of that amount, since his grandmother's stock had been divided among her seven grandchildren.

More importantly, the risk level of the portfolio would be greatly reduced. As Susan explained to Ben, there are three kinds of risk associated with holding just one stock. There is the risk connected to the specific company: Will there be an accounting scandal or a lawsuit? What if the latest product is a bust? Then there is industry risk: Will prices go down, or will the company's product or service become obsolete? Lastly, there is market risk: Will the market as a whole fall due to world events, economic issues, or other factors? There's not much you can do about market risk. However, the two other categories, company and industry risk, can be addressed through proper diversification.

Susan estimated that the benefit of diversifying the portfolio of stocks and allocating 40 percent of the portfolio to bonds could help bring the concentration risk level down to about one-quarter of that of holding just a single stock.

Ben was hesitant. Shouldn't he follow his grandmother's wishes? He wondered whether he was under some legal obligation to do so. And even if he wasn't, he felt that selling the stock would almost constitute a betrayal. But he promised to go home and think about it.

When Ben got home, he telephoned several of his cousins to ask what they were going to do. It seemed to him that the ones who were most knowledgeable about investing were reconfiguring their portfolios. One cousin was selling the stock outright to buy a home. He told Ben that he believed Evelyn wouldn't have minded so long as he didn't gamble away the money or use it for some other purpose that would upset her. And if something were to happen to the company that made the stock price fall drastically, she would be even more upset that the money was lost.

Ben called Susan and told her he'd like to come back in—this time to talk about what new stocks should be in his account. He did want to make sure that he kept some of the original stock, if only a token amount, out of respect for his grandmother.

Susan said she was sure that could be arranged.

Commonsense Considerations

A diversified portfolio consisting of many different types of securities can help reduce the risk to your wealth when a single stock drops in value. For example, if you own stocks in a variety of industries, the risk could be reduced even further. It only makes sense: If you held all your assets in one stock and it fell by 50 percent, you would lose half of your asset value. If you owned 50 stocks and one of the stocks dropped 50 percent, you would lose just 1 percent of your value. That's the effect of diversification. A properly diversified portfolio of 50 stocks can help to reduce nearly 60 percent of the total risk. Again, remember this strategy does not guarantee a profit, or protect against loss.

In the world of investing, risk is seen as the unpredictability of the future value of an investment. Return is the increase or decrease in the value of the investment. Studies have established that there is a trade-off between risk and return. When taking on higher risk, investors will demand greater potential returns to compensate for the risk. Markets tend to price investments to reflect expectations of return and perceived risk.

Risk and return are balanced out through diversification. The value of stocks and bonds often exhibit an inverse relationship. Smaller-company (or small-cap) stocks and larger-company (large-cap) stocks behave differently from each other. Similarly, stocks chosen using a value approach differ in performance from growth stocks.

By combining small-, midsize-, and large-company stocks with growth and value styles of investing, as well as foreign stocks, you can produce a portfolio with different risks for the level of return you desire. Alternatively, you can seek a higher expected return if you can tolerate a higher level of risk.

Knowing your investment objectives, matching your investments to them, and diversifying are three of the most fundamental rules of the road in investing. Here are a few more tips to keep in mind as you learn about this challenging—and rewarding—area.

Investors can classify stocks in many different ways: by company size, by products or industry, by geography, or as growth, value, or income stocks. **Growth stocks** are those of companies that are well established and have demonstrated they can sustain profitable growth. **Value stocks** carry somewhat more risk, and their prices reflect this. Investors hope that value stocks will prove to be profitable in time, thus raising their stock price in the market. **Income stocks** are often chosen by investors for dividends.

- **Maintain realistic expectations.** There is no magic formula for investing. Remember that there are no stupid questions. You should continuously review your portfolio's performance and make adjustments as appropriate. The more you learn about investing fundamentals, the better prepared you will be to reach your goals. The necessary ingredients are patience, discipline, and developing a sound financial plan.

- **Invest with complete understanding.** Knowing the relationship of risk to return will help you to gauge your anticipated returns, in addition to making sure your investment choices fit your risk tolerance. Also important is the need to compare similar securities so that your choices have the greatest income return potential.

- **Clarify your investment objectives.** Determine first what it is that you would like to accomplish. For example, do you have a preference for your investments to generate income now or do you prefer to build wealth over the long run? Having a plan will help you to generate the best investment strategy for your personal needs.

- **Remember the time value of money.** Compound interest works in your favor over time. In simple terms, it allows your money to make you more money. If you earn interest and dividends and reinvest them, your portfolio can grow exponentially. It is important to pay particular attention to the role of inflation in eroding your purchasing power. If your investment returns are not keeping up with inflation, you may want to re-examine your portfolio's composition and adjust it to increase your rate of return above the current inflation level.

- **Make sure you are appropriately diversified.** It is not wise to be on either end of the spectrum regarding diversification. You want to avoid having a portfolio with too many diverse types of securities. Likewise, if you don't have enough diversification in your portfolio, you run the risk of having "all your eggs in one basket." This will put a disproportionate risk on any one type of investment.

- **Keep an eye on market conditions.** Keep in mind that, over time, most market fluctuations will balance out. One should not be overly concerned about short-term dips or upswings. However, if trends in the market are identified, you may want to re-evaluate your portfolio composition.

- **Be mindful of tax laws.** When making investment decisions, ask: What is the most opportune time to realize capital gains and losses? Are tax-free bonds appropriate for me? How should I save for retirement? How should I borrow money?

- **Don't allow losses to run.** Although this book has been counseling you to not overreact to the short-term movements of the market, many investors become paralyzed when faced with confronting investments that have been performing poorly. If there is evidence of a negative performance trend, you may be better off realizing your losses instead of waiting for an upswing that may never materialize.

- **Take profits at the right time.** The difference between investing and trading is an important distinction. Investing should be considered a long-term activity. However, when it is approached as a means for short-term gains, it is actually not investing but *trading*. Investing should be viewed with the eye on the future and not the day's closing bell.

16

Gliding through the Golden Years

You may not be looking forward to getting older, but there's a lot you can and should do to help make the latter years of your life the best ones. Planning, if you haven't already started it, should begin today and not a minute later. Retirement planning involves more that just saving money. It is an ongoing process that requires you to envision and articulate the kind of lifestyle you might like to lead once you are retired, a discussion that must necessarily include your spouse or life partner and perhaps other members of your family as well. Then you can work to estimate the financial requirements of that lifestyle.

You should also consider your options in the event your health declines. Revisiting these plans regularly and making adjustments as appropriate is important, too. A passion for fly fishing may give way to a love of golf, prompting you to cancel your plans to build a retirement cabin in Montana and start looking for, instead, a country club condo in Southern California.

You are undoubtedly already aware of your need to accumulate capital in order to supplement any benefits you may receive from Social Security. You also will need to learn how to live on a fixed income, a skill requiring different money-management tactics than when you had cash flow from a salary with potential for increasing over time. Retirement planning is sometimes described as a "three-legged stool," comprising contributions from pensions, government benefits, and personal savings. Increasingly, individuals are recognizing the shortcomings of both the government and the pension legs of the stool. However, there are many options for making up these deficiencies. Moreover, long-term-care insurance can also help bridge potential gaps.

Over the past century, improvements in healthcare and lifestyle have helped increase life expectancy by almost 30 years, according to the National Center for Health Statistics. Developing an elder-care plan will help protect you and your family from the financial burdens of caring for you when you can no longer care for yourself. Unfortunately, many people do not think about these issues until they are faced with them. By then, many options may have closed.

Lastly, having an up-to-date will is the best way for you to communicate your wishes for the disposition of your hard-earned (and carefully saved) assets. Don't leave them to chance—or to the government.

Laughing All the Way to Retirement

Even though she was only 32, Rebecca was already looking ahead four decades. Her parents, who were both retired, lived almost exclusively on Social Security, giving her a bird's-eye view into a way of life she did not want to live. It seemed that they spent all their time scrimping and saving to get through each month. It made Rebecca realize she had to do something that would provide her with a comfortable income during her retirement years.

Rebecca worked as a manager of a computer sales and service store that did not offer a retirement plan. While she wanted to buy a new car or even her own house someday, her first priority, she decided, was to set up a way to save for retirement. Her friends made fun of her when she mentioned this one night when they were hanging out. They thought they were way too young to worry about retirement. Rebecca shrugged them off.

Rebecca suspected that just putting money away in a savings account was not an efficient way to start her retirement fund. She was worried that she might be tempted to raid the account if she came up short, and interest rates seemed pretty low compared with the stock market. She decided she needed some professional help. Right next door to the store where she worked was a branch office of a national investment firm. One day, she wandered in and saw a display shelf of brochures that seemed to be about planning for retirement. She asked the receptionist if she could take a few. The receptionist said of course, as the brochures were free.

A week later, Rebecca approached the receptionist again and asked if she might make an appointment with someone about establishing a retirement account. The receptionist said that if Rebecca was free now, she could speak with Paul, the resident retirement specialist, right away. She led Rebecca to an office in the rear.

Rebecca explained to Paul that she was interested in opening a Roth IRA. Paul asked if she had considered the benefits of a traditional IRA and Rebecca said she had. One of the differences between the two was that her contributions to a traditional IRA might be tax-deductible on her income taxes. But Rebecca didn't feel she needed the deduction. She said she knew that both types of IRAs were a popular way for individuals to accumulate retirement savings tax-free, and that she could contribute up to $4,000 a year presently, though that amount would change in the future.

She also knew that if she held on to the Roth IRA account for at least 5 years, under certain circumstances she would be able to draw from it with no penalty or tax consequences. For example, if she wanted to purchase a house, her status as a first-time buyer would mean she could take up to $10,000 out of the Roth account to use as a down payment. This would not be possible with a traditional IRA plan. Furthermore, if she leaves her money in a Roth account until she turns 59½, she may be able to withdraw it with no penalty or tax consequences. Rebecca even knew that although everyone refers to these types of tax-protected accounts as "individual retirement *accounts*," the official name is "individual retirement *arrangements*."

While Paul was impressed with Rebecca's knowledge, he felt it was his job to make sure that she was fully aware of the difference between the two basic types of IRAs. So he pulled out a brochure that Rebecca recognized immediately and opened it to display the following chart.

	TRADITIONAL IRA	ROTH IRA
Annual Contribution through 2007	Up to $4,000	Up to $4,000
Annual Contribution through 2008	Up to $5,000	Up to $5,000
Earnings	Tax-deferred	Tax-deferred
Retirement Withdrawals	Taxable	Tax-free if the Roth IRA is held at least 5 years
Distributions	Required at age 70½	No age requirement

Source: IRAs: Building Blocks for Your Retirement, Smith Barney, 2006

Rebecca assured Paul that she understood that saving for retirement in an IRA had more restrictions than if she were to just put money into a regular savings account. But the benefits more than compensated for the restrictions. Any interest she might earn in a savings account would be considered taxable.

Rebecca said her income was well below the maximum limits for the Roth IRA, which is an adjusted gross income of $110,000 for a single filer. (For married couples filing jointly, it is $160,000.) Now confident that Rebecca fully understood her options, Paul asked how she would like her money invested. Rebecca replied that she had been thinking of a goal of an average annual yield that was neither overly conservative nor too risky. With that information, Paul would be able to help her create a portfolio of stocks, bonds, mutual funds, and certificates of deposit.

It was Rebecca's goal to contribute $4,000 a year over the next 10 years. After that, she might consider other types of retirement vehicles, such as a regular investment account, in addition to her IRA. There might even be some new types of tax-protected products available. Or perhaps she would have a job that offered a pension, profit share, 401(k), or other retirement plan.

The next time Rebecca went out with her friends, they started teasing her about her "old-age money." She retorted that by the time she was 65 she planned to have close to a half million dollars from her Roth IRA alone. In fact, she didn't even miss the money she was investing, since

she had arranged to have an automatic monthly transfer from her checking account to the IRA. It came to only a little more than $10 a day—not
much more than the cost of one of those fancy coffee drinks they were
each enjoying. And if her friends didn't wake up and smell the coffee
soon, she warned, she'd be the only one of them who could afford to buy
that coffee when they all retired.

Commonsense Considerations

Procrastination is one of the biggest obstacles to achieving an adequately
funded retirement. The earlier you can start, the easier it is to accumulate funds. The closer you are to retirement, the more you'll have to put
away each month. Those who start later rather than earlier may be able
to get a leg up through such features as "catch-up" provisions for IRAs
that allow individuals 50 or older to make additional contributions.

Many people are lucky enough to be employed by companies that
offer structured retirement plan options. The following summarizes
some of the different retirement plans that may be offered by an
employer.

- **401(k) plan.** These popular plans allow you to make contributions
  with pretax dollars, typically through payroll deductions. Participa-
  tion is optional and often matched by your employer. You assume
  responsibility for your retirement income by determining how much
  you will contribute (limited by rules set by your employer) and also
  through directing the investment of these funds if this option is made
  available to you.
- **Profit-sharing or Stock Bonus plan.** An employer may contribute up
  to 25 percent of an employee's compensation (subject to certain limits) into individual accounts set up for that employee through a profit-
  sharing plan. The decision to contribute is made by the employer each
  year, allocated according to a set formula, and may be linked to the
  profitability of the business.
- **Savings Incentive Match Plans.** These are designed to make employee-
  retirement plans more accessible to small businesses. They are available in two formats, SIMPLE IRAs and SIMPLE 401(k) plans. They are
  also known as Simplified Employee Pension (SEP) plans. Both types

are available to employers that have 100 or fewer employees and no other qualified retirements plans.

- **Defined-benefit pension plans.** These plans provide for a specific amount or percentage of annual income during retirement. Contributions to the plan are mandatory. Prior years of service and salary level may be used to calculate the current benefit. Benefits are protected in many plans through federal insurance provided by the Pension Benefit Guaranty Corporation.

Planning versus Saving

Hal and Dorothy were both in their early 60s with grown children and a comfortable life in the suburbs. They had earned a good living over the years, and they planned to retire in the next 2 or 3 years and begin enjoying the next chapter of their life together.

Hal, who took charge of the family finances the day he and Dorothy were married, felt it was time to talk with a professional about the couple's current and future needs. He decided that the family's personal accountant, Ron, was in the best position to advise him, as Ron had been preparing Hal's financial statements for more than 20 years. When Hal called to make an appointment, Ron suggested that perhaps Dorothy might want to be included in the discussion.

When Hal and Dorothy arrived at the meeting, Ron handed each of them a summary of their financial resources. Hal immediately turned to the cash flow chart—and he was shocked. It had been his hope that when he retired, he and Dorothy might travel a bit, join a private golf club, maybe even buy a ski condo. If Ron's numbers were right, Hal and Dorothy would barely be able to afford a can of soda from the machine at the public golf course.

Ron explained that the cash flow projections he had worked up were based on Hal and Dorothy living for two more decades and included a safety net for an illness or disability that would require medical care not covered by insurance.

Dorothy, meanwhile, was looking at the numbers herself. She then spoke up, pointing out that throughout their married life, she and Hal had always spent freely, buying expensive cars and taking first-class trips abroad. She said she had always assumed that retirement would mean a slowing down of their lifestyle—that they would stay home, baby-sit for their grandchildren, get involved in some charitable endeavors, or even start a small, home-based business. For this, the amount of money they had saved was probably adequate.

Ron asked the couple if they had ever sat down together to talk about what they had envisioned for retirement. They both shook their heads and admitted they hadn't. Dorothy had figured that Hal shared her vision, and Hal had never really thought in concrete terms about life after his career ended—until now.

Ron explained to Hal and Dorothy that at this point in their lives, they still had alternatives. If they still wanted to retire sooner rather than later, they could significantly scale back their lifestyle to match their available cash flow. Or they could continue working and try to accumulate more assets to support the type of life that Hal envisioned. In hindsight, they probably ought to have sought advice earlier in their working lives, but it was not too late to try to set up a plan.

Then Ron pulled his chair close to Hal and Dorothy's. He said he had known the two of them a long time and what he was going to tell them was very important. He said that even before a couple makes a plan to save, it is critical that they have serious discussions about how they envision their retirement together. Planning for retirement should not be confused with saving for retirement. Once they worked out their plan, he said, they should come back to see him, and he would figure out a way to make their plan work financially.

Hal and Dorothy left Ron's office with a new appreciation for what work they would have to do to prepare for retirement, as well as new appreciation for Ron and his ability to see "the big picture."

Commonsense Considerations

Over a lifetime, domestic situations may compel you to consider liquidating assets in order to have access to cash. The composition of your retirement investment portfolio will need adjustments to accommodate different cash-flow needs and changes in income and living expenses, as well as your changing vision of life after retirement. Your portfolio needs regular review as your life situation changes.

If you are heading into retirement with a spouse or partner, you need to open an ongoing dialogue that can then be communicated to your advisor. Hal and Dorothy neglected to do this, but were prepared to make up for lost time. Some of the main points of their dialogue should include:

- Where will you live once you and your partner have given up your jobs? Is downsizing a possibility?
- How will you live? What activities do you think you might enjoy doing? Are you interested in a second career or working to keep busy, or do you envision retirement as a time to give up a paycheck altogether?
- Are there dependents to consider, either children or grandchildren or your parents?
- What are your anticipated healthcare needs over the long term? How would a serious illness or the death of one spouse affect the retirement plan of the other?
- How much money do you think you'll need to support the lifestyle you envision?

Increasingly, forward-thinking individuals are formulating an elder-care plan as part of their retirement-planning process. Some have decided to do this after direct experience with caring for their own elderly relatives. Others recognize, and are seeking to mitigate, the risk of an illness or infirmity obliterating even the most disciplined retirement plans. Open discussions with your parents, your partner, and your children are a first order of business here. Educating yourself as to the options is the next step, and then designing a plan and putting it in place is the third.

Taking Care of Mom—And Me

Sandra and her husband, Larry, were good financial planners. They had worked hard to save for their children's educations, their own retirement, and a vacation home. Now they were faced with an unanticipated situation and were not sure what they should do.

Sandra had just returned from spending a week at her mother Shirley's house. Sandra's father had died years earlier, and her mother still lived at the home where Sandra was raised. In recent years, Sandra noticed her mother's memory and other mental abilities start to decline. Because of this, she employed a part-time caregiver to help her mother around the house.

The recent trip to visit her mother was precipitated by a call from the caregiver, who told of a recent rapid decline in her mother's state. Sandra's hastily prepared visit had verified that indeed her mother's condition had deteriorated.

For Sandra, this experience was a wake-up call. Her mother, now in her late 80s, had always been self-sufficient until recently. However, it was clear that one day very soon she would not be able to take care of herself, even with the assistance of a part-time caregiver. Sandra feared that her mother was experiencing early signs of Alzheimer's. Sandra, as an only child, felt she would then be responsible for her mother, even though she lived on the other side of the country. Sandra felt uncomfortable about being uninformed about both the financial and practical aspects of developing an elder-care plan for her mother. At the same time, she realized she herself had nothing in place to inform her own children about her vision for her later years or to financially support that vision.

Sandra and Larry decided they should speak with an attorney specializing in elder care. They realized this might involve some fees, but felt it was one way they could protect themselves from further costs down the road. The attorney recommended that Sandra gather up important information about her mother's daily life, including the name, hospital affiliation, address, and phone number of her mother's primary doctor and her pharmacy, a list of her mother's medications, phone numbers for her mother's neighbors, and contact information for a local grocery delivery service to ensure an adequate supply of food. Sandra thought she knew the name of a neighbor who had a key to her mother's house and said she would confirm this too. The attorney also advised that Sandra investigate options offered by the local agency on aging in her mother's county, for information on available care options, including full-time adult day-care services and nursing homes in the community.

In addition, the attorney recommended that Sandra talk with her mother about some important legal documents, including:

- **Health Insurance Portability and Accountability Act (HIPAA) Release.** This form is often required for a doctor's office to authorize release of health records. At her next doctor's visit, Shirley might specifically name Sandra as a person who could receive medical information about her.
- **Power of attorney.** This document would allow Sandra to act on her mother's behalf to handle financial and legal affairs. If, for example, her mother was unable to pay her bills, Sandra might be able to pay them directly out of her mother's bank account.
- **Healthcare proxy.** Such a document would allow Sandra to make medical decisions for her mother if Shirley were to become incapacitated.
- **Living will.** A living will would express Shirley's wishes in the event that she should find herself in a terminal condition with no hope for recovery.

Sandra understood the importance of these documents, but was concerned that her independent and self-sufficient mother would think she was meddling and would not be open to a discussion. Sandra's attorney suggested that she approach the subject by presenting the case that her mother would be more in control by talking about these issues now and making her wishes known, as opposed to being in a medical condition where she would be unable to verbalize her desires. If Shirley failed to plan, decisions might be made for her that she did not agree with.

Sandra followed this advice and, to her surprise, found that her mother was open to speaking about these issues. She had also realized that her memory was not as good as it used to be and that she was needing more assistance than usual. Shirley had already given some thought as to what type of care she would want should she not be able to take care of herself. Ironically, she admitted she had not initiated a conversation with Sandra about this matter because she thought Sandra might get upset.

Sandra was surprised to find out that her assumptions about her mother's care-giving preferences were not correct. Shirley did not want to move in with Sandra. Nor did she want to be cared for in her own home any longer—she felt it was just too expensive an option. It turned out that some of her lifelong friends had recently relocated to a local assisted living complex. This was where Shirley wanted to move. Between the sale of her house and her own savings, she felt she could manage it financially without any assistance from Sandra.

Having this open and honest conversation with her mother prompted Sandra to discuss her own plans with Larry. She did not want to put him or their children through the emotional or financial stress that caring for her might cause. What seemed to make the most sense was to investigate some form of long-term-care insurance. Sandra's initial impression was that this would be very expensive. After researching various policies, she realized how much sense it made to purchase such insurance. The annual premium she would pay on a policy covering both herself and Larry was less than what a one-month stay in a nursing home would cost.

Sandra also learned that long-term-care insurance could be applied to more than just nursing home costs. It can cover services provided in a community facility, including adult day care. It may even cover emergency medical response systems or the temporary services of a medical professional for at-home convalescent care.

At the end of the process, Sandra confided to Larry that although she had started this journey because of an unfortunate occurrence—her mother's deteriorating mental abilities—she felt that something good had come out of it. Issues like death and aging were something she hadn't actively sought to confront. Now she felt the family could look forward to a secure future, no matter what it held in store.

Commonsense Considerations

Like Sandra, many people do not consider care-giving issues until directly faced with them. Others assume that Medicare coverage will provide for care-giving needs. However, Medicare pays only limited amounts for skilled care following a hospital stay and does not cover extended, long-term care at home or in a nursing home beyond certain specific periods. On the other hand, depending on the policy chosen, long-term-care insurance can pay nursing home and home health care costs that would otherwise be only partially covered through Medicare and Medicaid or paid out of pocket. These costs can be devastating to your financial nest egg.

Certain long-term-care insurance policies might pay a daily benefit, depending on your policy, and cover a period ranging from one year to a lifetime. A policy might be designed to take effect when you can't manage daily activities, such as bathing, feeding yourself, dressing, or even just walking. Most financial experts recommend buying long-term-care insurance while you are in your 50s, when the premiums are still low.

Long-term-care insurance is not for everyone. For example, certain health conditions may prevent you from being able to receive a policy. Long-term-care insurance is medically underwritten. As such, your premiums are not guaranteed and may vary from any initial quote you receive. You should not cancel your current coverage until your new coverage is approved and in force. A policy change may incur fees and costs and may also require a medical exam.

To determine whether long-term-care insurance makes sense for you, here are some of the important points to consider.

- **Daily benefit amount.** What is the amount that the policy will pay for daily costs?
- **Elimination period.** Are there a certain number of days in a nursing home you would have to pay for out-of-pocket before benefits begin?
- **Exceptions to elimination period.** What are the circumstances, if any, when the elimination period is waived? For example, does hospitalization time count as part of the elimination period?
- **Benefit period.** How long would you be covered, and does that time frame make sense?
- **Tax status of the policy.** Is the policy tax-qualified, meaning you would receive the benefits tax-free?
- **Inflation protection.** Does the policy include inflation protection to keep pace with the escalating costs of long-term care?
- **Survivorship benefit.** If your insured spouse or partner dies and you want the insurance coverage to continue for yourself, will you have to

pay additional premiums, or would the policy be paid up? If a policy has a survivorship benefit, the surviving spouse would not pay premiums as long as they meet the conditions of the survivorship benefit, which might include the policy's being in force for a certain number of years. Without a survivorship benefit, the survivor would need to pay premiums on the policy to continue coverage.

- **Extent of coverage.** Does the policy include such items as purchase and rental of equipment, such as a special bed or bathroom grab bars?
- **Care coordination.** Is the care coordinator an independent health expert or a company representative? Are they available locally, or through a toll-free phone number?
- **Underwriter stability.** What is the strength of the insurance company that is offering the policy? How big is the company, how long has it been selling long-term-care insurance, and what is its rating according to worldwide insurance rating agencies such as A.M. Best, Standard & Poor's, or Moody's Investors Service?

Expecting the best but preparing for the worst is a sound policy in planning your elder care. This way, should things turn out less than ideally, you can devote your emotional resources to making sound decisions, rather than having to divert your energy to deal with financial matters.

For further information, see Chapter 13, "Insuring Yourself, Your Family, and Your Property," Chapter 15, "Investing in Learning about Investments," and Chapter 17, "Saving Your (Financial) Life."

PART 2 SUMMARY

This middle part of *The Citi Commonsense Money Guide* takes a look at some of the fundamental building blocks of a stable financial life, starting with creating a budget and moving on to consider such topics as sharing household expenses, affording children and financially educating them, home loans, insurance, college savings, investments, and retirement.

Budgeting ABCs

Budgets can take many forms. If you're young, single, and just starting out, you might be able to track in your head how much you make and how much you spend. Once you've acquired responsibilities, such as a home, a spouse, children, two cars, a mortgage, a retirement fund, you may find the budgeting process easier if you put it on paper or even computerize it using a spreadsheet program or a special software program. At any stage of your life, it does require commitment. You have to create your budget, track against it, make adjustments, and analyze your data on a regular basis. Are you spending too much and saving too little? Or vice versa?

Carolina was just starting to learn about how to use a budget to monitor and control expenses. But even experienced budgeters, like James Senior, should be open to learning new tricks. And it is important to consider including the entire family in the budgeting process, to get not only their valuable input, but also their even more essential cooperation.

Caring and Sharing

Money management is tough enough for an individual. Adding another person to the picture further complicates the situation. Even siblings raised under the same roof can have different spending styles and philosophies. Perhaps the most important money management tool for married or cohabiting couples, or roommates (which might include parents and adult children living together), is communication. It should be practiced early and often. That's what Janet and Ian should have known before they were married and, fortunately, discovered before it was too late. Even siblings sharing an apartment might wish to sit down and work out formal financial arrangements.

Financial Management Is Not Child's Play

Most couples planning a family have an inkling about how expensive it is to raise a child. But to see the numbers in black and white (and maybe red) on paper is another matter altogether. A new baby can require much more than just budgeting to redecorate an extra room in the house. It can even demand a complete reevaluation and revamping of your finances, above and beyond adding diapers to the budget. You may also need to consider your insurance needs and your estate plan. Anticipating expenses as best you can is one of the best ways to keep them under control. Finding ways to economize without sacrificing quality is illustrated by Christine and Sean's story. The "big ticket" expenses of raising a child, such as day care, summer camps, extracurricular programs, and, of course, college, should also be carefully evaluated in terms of competitive options and on a cost-benefit basis.

Financial education is a parental imperative of keen interest lately. Teaching your children their money ABCs—how to budget, spend, save, and share—will serve them well throughout their lives. Practice makes perfect, and financial experts today advocate an allowance as a teaching tool. Because credit is so easily acquired on college campuses today, experts advise you to thoroughly indoctrinate your children, before they leave home, on the appropriate and inappropriate uses of credit.

Home Financing Basics

Purchasing a home is a true test of a financial education. It requires attention to detail, as Sam and Sally discovered. Matching your needs to the market's offerings can be key. Doug thought he had it all down, only to discover otherwise. Your credit history can be very important when you're applying for a mortgage, and you would do well to check it out before your lender does. There are a number of steps that can help you get your financial profile in shape to help you put your best foot forward when you apply for financing. Because a few extra points in interest on your mortgage can mean thousands of dollars, it may be worth delaying your application until you are assured of the best rate possible.

Still, nobody's perfect, and even a responsible person like Lynda might have a few skeletons in the closet. Being upfront about previous financial trouble and building a strong credit history should, in the end, pay off.

Covering against Catastrophe

Insurance is yet another area where you may stand to benefit from being financially educated. Whether it's personal insurance, which includes health, life, disability, or long-term-care insurance, or insurance on your property, encompassing auto and homeowner's, figuring out what type of coverage and how much you need is an important part of your money profile.

Bonnie and Henry didn't wake up to this until they saw Henry's mother struggling with healthcare costs. And Patrick's story underscored the importance of educating yourself about the factors that go into a premium payment and how you can find ways to reduce your payments without denying yourself adequate coverage.

College Saving 101

Saving for a child's college education today requires that you yourself become educated about the many options available. While it's challenging to stay apace of the rapidly increasing costs of higher education, a disciplined and informed approach is imperative.

When Ann and Mike couldn't come up with the monthly payment calculated by their advisor, they didn't walk away, but instead offered as much as they thought they could afford and promised to try to make up the difference over time. How college fund money is invested depends on a number of factors, including risk tolerance, age of the child, tax considerations, and level of contribution. In the case of Jack and Heather, they discovered they'd made a mistake in their investments on behalf of their grandson, so they learned to keep a closer eye on the accounts, especially as the college years grew near.

Investing for the Long Haul

While investing is a topic that has spawned whole libraries of books, success in investing can still be summarized by the four words of the age-old advice, "buy low; sell high." This is, however, easier said than done. Non-professionals depend on investing as a means to protect and grow funds they are hoping to use in the future, perhaps for college tuition for a child or for their own retirement.

For those who are just starting to invest, there are a few basic principles that should be kept in mind. Asset allocation is one. Eric learned about this only after several years of haphazardly throwing money into the market. Asset allocation means you divide your investments across asset classes, such as stocks, bonds, and cash.

Jillian, another investor, needed to more accurately define her investment goals after having had success in the market. Her earlier success blinded her to how important planning is to the investment process. And after Ben's grandmother died, he came to understand the importance of diversification to reduce risk. This is one of the best ways to protect your money in the market.

Life after Work

The final chapter in Part Two considers life in the golden years. While it's difficult to look ahead 30, 40, or 50 years when you are just starting out, this is an ideal time to commence planning. Rebecca was acutely conscious of her need to save for retirement because she saw her cash-strapped retired parents struggling. She educated herself financially about her options and consulted an expert. Because of this, she will have an easier time reaching her goals than her peers who might prefer to put extra cash into material purchases. There are numerous employer-sponsored retirement plans that are painless to participate in, and if you have this option, you should take advantage of it. If you don't, as Rebecca didn't, you may have to fashion a plan for yourself.

Hal and Dorothy thought they had planned adequately for their retirement, but came up short. Critically, they had neglected to reconcile their individual visions for their retirement years. Yet again, the importance of open and ongoing communications about finances is underscored. Once you agree on the kind of life you'd like to lead in retirement, you can go about translating it into dollars and cents.

Then there's the question of long-term care. If you plan ahead like Sandra and Larry, you will be in much better shape to deal with critical lifestyle choices than if you wait for a crisis to occur.

In each of these important areas discussed in Part 2, having a budget can help support financial goals and keep expenses on track. Couples and roommates sharing expenses can use it as a means to decide how to split up household expenses and as a valuable way to organize record-keeping of how money has been spent. Parents need budgets to be able to analyze the costs of child rearing and should help their children, when they are old enough, to learn to budget their money. Budgeting is one of the best ways to understand where your money is coming from and where it is going, which in turn supports your progress toward your financial goals. Once you have accommodated the financial necessities in your budget, you can then use it to help you plan for major lifetime goals, such as owning a home, paying for your children's college education, and setting aside money for your golden years.

PART

Curveballs

Wouldn't it be great if life were a straight road that allowed you to see miles ahead? Unfortunately, it's not. It's full of bumps and curves. You may have worked hard to get out of debt, fund that college education, and make up for missed car or mortgage payments. You figured out how to make your paycheck cover all your expenses, and then some. You may have put together a reasonable budget and started saving for retirement or your children's college tuition, and then suddenly found yourself facing one of those bumps. You lose your job. Your credit card is stolen and someone has charged thousands of dollars of merchandise on it. You get divorced, or maybe you remarry and now have a whole new family to assimilate. That's what the next eight chapters are all about.

This part also underscores the importance of savings, particularly in an emergency account. Yes, it's hard. Throughout the chapters in this book, you have read how people who didn't think they had a penny to spare were able to find ways to save money. You can save, too.

Why an emergency fund? The answer, short and simple, is so an emergency won't catapult you into a financial crisis. So you don't have to miss a car or mortgage payment, so you don't have to load up on costly debt if something interferes with your ability to earn a living. Emergency savings are, in effect, a form of insurance. You get to decide how big the premiums should be, and you get to decide when to file a claim.

CHAPTER 17

Saving Your (Financial) Life

Many Americans are living from paycheck to paycheck, unable to put any money aside for savings. In fact, while Americans' personal savings rate in the 1980s averaged 9 percent, that rate had declined to slightly below 1 percent in 2005, according to the Department of Commerce. This is the lowest personal savings rate since the Great Depression.

Saving requires you to analyze, plan, organize, and evaluate. But first, you need to educate yourself about what you will be saving for and what your savings goals are. You need to slice and dice your savings needs, first into long-term and short-term goals. Examples of long-term savings goals are retirement and college. Examples of short-term savings goals might be a vacation or home repairs that you anticipate requiring sooner rather than later.

While savings toward a purchase like a car or vacation are easy to estimate, it's trickier to put the numbers together for an emergency fund. There are a number of factors to take into consideration. You need to set a goal. How much does it actually cost you to live in your house or apartment, eat, travel, and pay your bills every month? How many people are you responsible for? Do you have other resources (e.g., generous parents, insurance policies) you could turn to if your source of income was suddenly cut off?

It has been generally recommended that up until you are in your mid- to late-40s, your emergency savings account should have enough to cover 3 months of your living expenses. Three to 6 months of expense money is advised from your 40s to your 60s, and, after that, a full year's worth. If you currently have no emergency savings set aside, it might take you several months, even years, to build up to this amount. You also need to determine where you are going to keep this money and your ground rules for accessing it. Decide as a household what is the definition of an "emergency."

Louise's Savings Plan

Louise had worked for more than a decade as an administrator in the federal courts system. She had no dependents. She had managed to save enough money to make a down payment on a two-bedroom house in a suburban neighborhood, where she had lived for 5 years. Because of the tax deduction she received for the interest payments on her mortgage, she was able to take two allowances. This meant that she got more money in her paycheck every month and less of a refund after she filed her federal income taxes.

Louise was not a great saver, and she knew it. She had a small savings account and took advantage of her employer's retirement plans, but she really didn't have much of a cushion if an emergency arose. In order to buy her house, she had completely emptied out her savings account to make the down payment and pay for the various closing costs that took her by surprise. She knew it would take several years to build the account back up, especially with all the new purchases she wanted to make for the house. So she decided to rent out the second bedroom until she got caught up.

After 2 years, her financial situation had stabilized and she had rebuilt her savings. But now she realized that every year she had a few thousand dollars' worth of work that needed to be done in order to keep the house in good shape. One year, it was the gutters. The next she had to have the house painted. And this year it looked like the basement was going to need some sort of waterproofing work. So she kept emptying out her emergency fund and never could build it back up to a point where she was comfortable.

One day at lunch, she was discussing with her work colleagues how hard it was to deal with the costs of home ownership. Her friend Barb said that she had discovered the theory of "paying yourself first." As soon as she got her paycheck, she automatically put a set percentage of it into a money market deposit account. Sal, the court clerk, said his savings plan was to bank one whole paycheck every 12 weeks. It was easier, he thought, to go cold turkey once every third month than to try to scrimp and save all the time. He also put his tax refund, a few hundred dollars, into savings every year.

Louise wondered aloud about her refund. Maybe she could discipline herself to save more consistently by reducing her two withholding allowances on her paycheck to zero. That way, she would get a larger refund and—voila!—instant savings.

Barb said she had heard that this was exactly what you were *not* supposed to do—use the government as your piggy bank. Why let the government use your money interest free? But Louise thought it might be worth a try. She calculated it would mean she'd receive about a $4,000 tax refund to apply toward whatever project she needed to do on the house. If there was any left over, she promised herself she'd add it to her emergency funds.

Although her friends told her this was not a good way to save, Louise found it worked perfectly for her needs. She was able to stop pillaging her emergency funds for house repairs and could plan ahead every year, knowing exactly how much she had "saved," thanks to the government. And she was just about the only person she knew who actually looked forward to filing her taxes—and doing it as early as possible.

Commonsense Considerations

An emergency fund may be easier to calculate than accrue. Louise found a way to save for hers—here are some more tips that might help you.

- It doesn't make much sense to scrimp and scrape to put money into emergency savings if you are carrying a lot of high-interest debt. You are much better off concentrating the majority of your money on paying down debt first, while still adding a lesser amount to your emergency fund. To totally neglect your emergency fund is not wise either.

- If you are making investments in the stock market, you should consider detouring some of the money you have invested, or are planning to invest, into your savings.

- Your monthly expenses can be divided into "fixed" and "variable." When looking for ways to cut your expenses and begin to save, start with your variable expenses first. You have more control over your grocery bill, your clothing allowance, even your gasoline bills than over your mortgage, rent, or car payment. But don't overlook opportunities to lower your fixed expenses. Make sure you have the lowest mortgage rate, the most cost-effective insurance plans, and a car that isn't costing you more than it's worth.

- Make a "savings sacrifice" that will give your fund a boost. Can you give up spending that end-of-year bonus or the birthday check from your Great-aunt Matilda? Forgo the monthly full-service car wash or decide that next summer you'll use the public tennis courts instead of joining the racquet club? Cut that week-long ski vacation to a long weekend?

- Remember, you are your own emergency fund insurance adjuster. Think through what is a true emergency and what can and should be accommodated through other means. Having a car that won't start is probably an emergency. Having a car that's not this year's model probably is not.

- Teach your children the importance of saving in general. Offer them matching grants or scholarships to encourage them in saving toward a special goal.

Savings for emergencies should, by definition, be kept available—but not too available. Typical places to stash your cash include high-yield savings accounts, or money market deposit accounts or money market mutual funds. However, you might prefer to keep this money in a higher-interest-bearing instrument, like a certificate of deposit, with the understanding that if you have to cash out for an emergency, you may lose interest or pay a penalty if it is before the CD's time limit, such as 6 months or a year.

Earning to Save; Saving to Earn

Ray and Meg were creatures of habit. When they were still newlyweds, they had established an annual "checkup" routine. Every year, in February, they scheduled appointments with their internists for their annual physicals, followed by an appointment with their accountant to give him the information he would need to prepare their taxes and to undergo a general review of their finances. Then, they would always take a week's vacation in a warm climate.

The couple's accountant, Dave, had helped them financially navigate through their 20s and 30s, when they were building their careers, buying their first house, and starting their family. He encouraged them to save as much as they could, even above and beyond the recommended 10 percent of their gross income. His motto was "Be prepared." He impressed upon Ray and Meg the importance of purchasing adequate insurance and, after helping them establish an adequate emergency fund, taught them the fundamentals of investing.

At their annual meeting the year that Ray turned 55, Dave suggested that the couple might want to think about making some retirement income projections. He encouraged them to review their wills and make sure all their estate paperwork was in order. At that point, the couple was 20 years into a 30-year mortgage, and Dave said they might consider paying it off in its entirety in the next few years, so that they could retire mortgage-free.

He checked that they were investing for growth, with an eye toward gradually reducing their level of risk as they approached retirement. And he strongly urged them to think about increasing their emergency savings fund to cover a minimum of 6 months of expenses. Meg asked why, and Dave explained that the sad reality is that if one or the other of them was to lose their job, it might take longer to find another because of their age and specialized experience. Presently, the couple had enough funds in a savings account to cover 3 to 4 months of living expenses.

The thought of increasing these emergency savings funds didn't sit well with Ray. He was used to earning a solid return on his investments and to put away 6 months' of living expenses in a low-yielding emergency account struck him as foolish. Dave agreed that there was a trade-off: Keeping their emergency funds relatively liquid, or accessible, did mean that they might lose out on some money that they might have made by investing in the stock market. On the other hand, he noted, Ray and Meg didn't necessarily have to keep their emergency funds in a low-interest savings account. There were a variety of money-market account investments that they might consider, so long as they were willing to actively manage their assets. That's because a number of these investments are for very short terms, even just one month, so they'd have to pay attention and continually reinvest the money.

Meg said she had heard the term "money market" before but was never quite sure what it meant. Ray replied that he thought it referred to checking accounts that paid higher interest. Actually, the money market is part of the fixed income market, Dave told him. The fixed income market includes both the bond market and the money market. The difference is that the money market encompasses short-term debt securities that mature typically in less than a year (though you can buy a certificate of deposit for as long as 5 years).

One example is T-bills, or treasury bills, and T-notes, or treasury notes, sold and backed by the U.S. government. You can buy T-bills with various maturities of under a year. You buy T-bills at a discount to their face value, and when they mature, you cash them in for their full value. The difference between the price you paid and the amount you receive at maturity is your interest. They are issued in denominations as low as $1,000 and as high as $1 million. You can sell a T-bill before maturity, but you can lose some of your investment if you do.

T-bills are just one type of money market investment. Ray and Meg could choose from a variety available to individual investors. Dave reviewed the options as Meg took notes.

Ray and Meg thanked Dave for the information and said they would go home and discuss where to keep their emergency funds—right after they made a stop at their travel agent's office.

Commonsense Considerations

Now that Ray and Meg were armed with all the information about the various types of money markets, they needed to comparison shop. Here are points of comparison to consider when making a decision.

- **What is the interest rate?** Obviously, the higher the better, though always take into account any additional risks higher rates may carry.
- **What is the risk?** Money market investments range from lower-risk U.S. government instruments to those that carry greater industry and issuer risk (such as corporate bonds) and market risk on any resale. Consider also what the risk is in terms of your having to make an emergency withdrawal, for those instruments that carry a withdrawal penalty.
- **How do yields compare?** You have to consider identical time periods, the price you paid, and whether or not interest is assumed to be reinvested, among other things.
- **How much does it cost to purchase?** Some short-term debt instruments, like some types of bonds, may even have a charge to own them.
- **What is the minimum investment required?** You may decide to divide up your emergency funds, putting some money in higher-yielding, longer-term money market investments that require larger minimums and keeping the balance in more liquid accounts or instruments.
- **What are the penalties for selling before maturity?** You might compare the cost of the penalty against the increase in yield. Proceeds from the sale may be more or less than originally invested, due to changes in market conditions, issuer credit, or interest rates.

Further information can be found in Chapter 2, "Making Do between Paychecks."

18

Budget Busters: Holidays and Special Events

Everyone is well aware of the inverse relationship between waistlines and wallets around the holidays: As one expands, the other contracts. Americans love holidays, and their shopping patterns reflect it. In 2006, they spent some $5 billion on Halloween alone, and $13 billion on Valentine's Day, according to the National Retail Foundation. More than a whopping $438 billion was spent on the 2006 winter holidays (Thanksgiving, Christmas, Hanukkah, and Kwanzaa).

Then there are the more personal events, like housewarmings, anniversary parties, big- (or little-) number birthdays, or the grandmamma of them all, weddings. All of these are stressful on the budget. But you can avoid the financial equivalent of overeating. It just requires some sensible planning, organization, and discipline.

Establishing New Traditions

Several months before the holiday season began, Stephanie accompanied her friend Nicole to the bank where Nicole was making a deposit to her holiday account. Nicole had been contributing to this account on a weekly basis and already had enough money to pay for gifts for her extended family. Stephanie sat down with Michelle, a customer service representative at the bank, to discuss her own needs. Stephanie explained that her husband had just started a new job after being out of work for several months. During this period of unemployment, their savings had been depleted. Now they were trying to catch up. Paying bills on time was still a challenge. Seeing Nicole contributing to her holiday fund made Stephanie wonder how she was going to be able to afford gifts for her two small children.

Michelle suggested that Stephanie bring her husband to the bank to evaluate their financial picture. Michelle viewed holiday spending as secondary to the broader problem of corralling the couple's debt and reestablishing an emergency savings fund.

A few weeks later, Stephanie and her husband, John, met with Michelle. Michelle compared the couple's available income with their bills and other debt obligations to establish a picture of their cash flow. There wasn't much they could do to lower the rent, gas, and electricity bills, but credit card interest was high. If they transferred their balances to a lower-rate credit card or an installment loan, they would save money through lower interest charges and smaller monthly payments. Additionally, by opening a checking account, they could eliminate the check-cashing and money order fees they had been paying. This saved $15 a week. By making other small changes in their day-to-day spending, they were able to free up a further $75. Michelle suggested that they set up a weekly automatic transfer of $50 into an investment account for long-term goals and $25 a week into a short-term fund earmarked for the holidays.

That first holiday season was bound to be difficult for the family, since Stephanie and John had only a few months to accumulate money in their holiday fund. Ever resourceful, Stephanie figured out a way to make the season joyful nonetheless. She went to her local library to research community events that she then marked on a calendar with colorful pens. She told the children that starting this year, the family's holidays would last a whole month instead of just one day.

For the next 4 weeks, they attended a different community event each weekend. These outings included visits to a downtown ice-skating rink, a tree-lighting ceremony, a multicultural caroling evening, and a holiday book reading at the library. Stephanie enlisted the children to help her bake cookies and festive breads that they then wrapped and delivered as gifts to friends and family.

Meanwhile, Stephanie and John made a private pact to not exchange gifts this one time. They would make it up to each other when their finances had stabilized. In a break with the past, when they each had purchased separate gifts for the children, they collaborated this year, which kept costs under control.

The week after the holidays, Stephanie stopped by the bank with her children and introduced them to Michelle. The kids excitedly told Michelle about their month-long celebrations and how they had enjoyed this special time with their parents as much as the presents they received. Michelle helped Stephanie open a full-year holiday account as well as individual savings accounts for the children.

Michelle was inspired by Stephanie's creative approach to making the holidays affordable. She decided to put together a list to share with other clients who may not have a lot of money to spend on holiday gifts each year. For this, she solicited ideas from her workmates that resulted in quite a long list full of creative and helpful tips.

Commonsense Considerations

Michelle's list can work for you, too. Here are the tips she gave her clients.

- **Start planning early.** Review cash flow and set up a savings plan. Look for ways to cut your spending so that each week you can save a little bit that will add up by year's end.
- **Determine how much you have to spend, then spend only the money you have.** Don't base your holiday budget on an expected raise or bonus that may not materialize. Increasing balances on your credit cards by charging gifts that you cannot immediately pay off will only add to the cost of each item. Before you charge anything, mentally calculate the true cost as roughly 20 percent more than the price tag if you are tempted to put it on your credit card. Can you afford it now? Is it worth it?
- **Create a multiyear holidays-notes binder or file.** Use it to store lists

of gifts you have given and to whom and notes about future gifts. File holiday card lists and recipes, guest lists, and budgets for parties. Keep it handy throughout the year so you can add ideas. Maintain holiday gift receipts and expense totals in order to track your expenses year after year.

- **Before you purchase anything, window (or catalog or online) shop and comparison shop.** That means look—don't touch. Write down ideas (and prices) for everyone. Then go home and organize your list. Are there stores where you can purchase the same items for less money? Resolving to stick to the list should help you avoid impulse purchases. Take the list with you every time you go shopping, and don't buy anything that isn't on it.

- **Remember, you are shopping for your family and friends only.** Did you include your name on your shopping list? If you see something you'd like, make a note so you can ask your family for it.

- **Avoid procrastinating.** This will keep you from succumbing to panic shopping, where you just scoop up presents for the sake of buying something for someone, without giving sufficient thought to your actions (or their consequences). But don't go out so early that you end up overbuying because you have lengthened the buying season.

- **Take lots of quarters when you go shopping, and don't let your parking meter run out.** One parking ticket can easily negate that great discount you went out of your way to track down.

- **Remember, quality trumps quantity. Stacks of gifts can readily overwhelm small children.** Coordinate purchases, whether for toddlers, teens, or even adults. If you plan to buy a dollhouse for your daughter, ask relatives to supply furniture for it. If your husband has a hankering for a DVD player, ask his friends to buy him DVDs. For tweens and teens, purchase gift cards for bookstores, music, or clothing shops. It's hard to guess what kids want, and by the time you figure it out, they want something else. And for hard-to-buy-for adults, consider charitable donations.

- **Six to eight weeks before the holidays, stop buying all but the most essential family purchases.** Sneakers, calculators, teapots, books, athletic equipment, and even non-essential toiletries make great gifts.

- **Enjoy holiday traditions together as a family, but establish new ones too.** Sometimes it's just time for a change. Find a way to participate in a cultural or religious event that is not your own, to add variety and broaden your family's understanding of others. Consider creative gift-giving alternatives such as "Secret Santa," a regifting exchange, a dollar-limit challenge, or a pooling of funds to skip the presents and take a trip. (Warning: may be difficult if children are involved.)
- **Once you've completed your shopping, take stock.** Shut yourself in a room and lay out all your gifts. Have you overbought? Are there some items you could put away for a future birthday or for next year?
- **If you distribute cash tips, keep a list.** This will help ensure that you don't over- or under-tip from year to year people like the newspaper delivery person or your parking attendant. If your budget is tight, tip what you can, include a personal note, and make up the difference midyear.
- **Take advantage of post-holiday sales.** Purchase wrapping paper, ribbon, cards, and other supplies that you will need next year, and store them where you will be able to find them. Peruse stores for nonperishables that will be "evergreen" in a year: holiday-themed books, games, decorations, etc. Keep a list of everything you have bought (and who it is for) in your holiday notebook.
- **During the year, entertain yourself with a hobby that might result in gifts.** Baking, canning, winemaking, crafts, gardening, photography, and compiling CDs might all be meaningful to friends and family.

Holidays are tough on the budget, and so are celebrations. Costs associated with the latter have risen steadily over the years. Major birthdays, anniversary parties, quinceañeras, sweet 16s, bar and bat mitzvahs, and housewarmings can run to several thousands of dollars. These days, the average cost of a wedding, including the ceremony and a formal reception, tops $25,000. Usually, these events can be foreseen in time to set aside specific savings for them. But sometimes this just isn't enough, or an unexpected event comes along. What's the best way to handle this situation?

A Year to Remember

It was the first week of December. For Carlos and Belkis, a working couple in their 40s with two children, the year ahead was promising to be a good one. In March, Carlos and Belkis would celebrate their 25th wedding anniversary. They were hoping to take a second honeymoon over spring break, accompanied by their 14-year-old son Ernesto and his older sister, Guadelupe. Then in May, Ernesto would be graduating from the school he had attended since kindergarten and moving on to high school. They were looking forward to throwing a large party for his classmates and their families after the graduation ceremony. Just as they had begun to think about how they were going to budget for these events, Guadelupe called with great news. Her longtime boyfriend had proposed marriage, and she had said yes.

Both 22, Guadelupe and her fiancé had met at the state college, where they had both been accounting majors. Carlos and Belkis were thrilled about the engagement. Then Guadelupe mentioned that she had her heart set on a June wedding. Not a year from next June—this June, just six months away.

Whereas Carlos and Belkis had been married without much fuss or bother, at a time when big, expensive weddings had gone out of style, Guadelupe was of another generation and mind-set altogether. Ever since she was a little girl, she had fantasized about a dream wedding: the perfect dress, the perfect cake, and the perfect pictures. Now she had the opportunity to live her dream. Although they hated saying no to Guadelupe, Carlos and Belkis knew they had to tell her that they thought her date was unrealistic and hoped to persuade her of a more realistic date, perhaps 6 or 8 months in the future.

Carlos and Belkis also felt strongly that they wanted to take full responsibility for the costs of the wedding. Guadelupe and her fiancé were just starting out and had significant student loans to pay off. Her parents felt it would be a bad beginning to a marriage for the newlyweds to be deeply in debt.

While considering how to finance the wedding, they noted that they had some money put away to help pay for their wedding anniversary trip. They considered telling Ernesto that they just couldn't swing a graduation party for his class—not if they were going to have to foot the bill for the wedding and take the trip. Of course, they didn't feel this was really fair, since Ernesto's graduation party had been talked about long before Guadelupe's engagement. They also wanted to plan and take their trip. How were they going to manage all of this?

Carlos and Belkis decided they should start by trying to organize the information about all three events. They wrote down each one and discussed reasonable budget numbers. For their anniversary celebration, Carlos and Belkis had been thinking about a cruise, maybe a week long, to the Caribbean. They called a local travel agent and found this would have cost about $2,000 for just the two of them; plus airfare to Florida, where the boat embarked; and incidentals. Since their original thought had been to take Ernesto and Guadelupe, they would have been prepared to spend double that, assuming the children had shared a stateroom. Of course, now there was a new wrinkle. Should they now offer to take Guadelupe and her fiancé, in which case they might need a third stateroom? If they took only Ernesto, there could be a surcharge on his fare for a single room. They set these issues aside to research at a later date and just put down $5,000 as their cost estimate for the anniversary trip.

Ernesto had about 70 classmates, and Carlos and Belkis agreed that before having the wedding to consider, they probably would have planned on spending about $5,000 on his party, including renting a party space, hiring a disk jockey, and arranging a catered buffet dinner. They estimated that each classmate would bring at least one parent or a sibling.

For the wedding, they budgeted $20,000. They knew they were being very optimistic with this number. They were aware that a wedding during the prime months of May through October often costs more. But perhaps by keeping the guest list to a minimum, they could stay within budget. They hoped this would pay for the ceremony, a dinner reception, a live band, limousine service, flowers, photography, and invitations, though they suspected this would take extreme discipline.

So now they had some basic data. Before factoring in the wedding, they were looking at spending $10,000 on two celebrations. With the anticipated wedding costs included, they were looking at $30,000. This was far beyond any amount they would be able to come up with in a single year. The estimating was the easy part—now they would have to make some tough choices.

First, they checked the status of their savings accounts. They had about $7,000 in excess of what they considered their "dire emergency" funds that they didn't want to touch. The "dire emergency" money was 3 months of living expenses, in case the unthinkable happened to either or both of them and they were unable to support the family. The extra $7,000, however, would not make much of a dent in their consolidated celebration estimate.

So they started suggesting various solutions that would make everyone happy. They wrote them down as they came up with them, and then discussed them one by one.

1. Postpone the anniversary cruise for a year or until they felt they could afford it. This would save them $5,000. After counting in their savings, they would have to find $18,000 to pay for the wedding and graduation party.
2. Ask their daughter to postpone her wedding until the following June. It would buy them some time—a full year—to save for it.
3. Suggest to Guadelupe that they combine the wedding and anniversary trip into a single event, perhaps a destination wedding in the late fall. This would probably save about $10,000, since most resorts provide many of the wedding festivities as part of the package. This might bring their out-of-pocket costs down to $15,000 for all three events. However, this would shift the financial burden of the wedding to the guests, who would have to pay to travel and stay at the resort, which was another consideration.
4. Ask that everyone in the family pitch in to cut back on all the events, across the board. The graduation party would be scaled down to a backyard barbeque, with Carlos's buddies working the grill. For the wedding, all the pomp and circumstance would still be arranged, but instead of a sit-down dinner, a cocktail reception with hors d'oeuvres would be substituted. And Carlos and Belkis would celebrate their anniversary not *on* the high seas but *near* the high seas, spending a week at a rented seaside cottage in a resort town they could readily reach by car.

For Carlos and Belkis, these seemed like reasonable options to present to their children. They felt confident that whatever solution was chosen, they would all be happy with it—and they could all look forward to this special year of celebrations.

Commonsense Considerations

Sharing your special times with friends and family creates indelible memories—and debts that live on long after the last balloon has popped. Carlos and Belkis sought to avoid the debt part from the start. With creativity and planning, you, too, can have a celebration to remember while minimizing any additional debt. Here are some general guidelines.

- **Create a budget.** This helps keep your expenses foremost in your planning. Start with the total amount you wish to spend and then allocate numbers to anticipated expenses by category, such as venue rental, food and drink, entertainment, decoration, and service. Now go back through and create ranges for each expense by adding 15 percent to each category. How much does this expand your bottom line? The "Event Budgeting Form" on page 291 will help you create your budget.
- **Fill in your budget as you start to spend.** Compare actual costs with those estimated and adjust accordingly. If you choose to go over in one category, find another category in which you can scale back.
- **Set a date and time for your event.** This can have an impact on how much it costs, especially if your party involves a rental space or a catered meal.
- **Comparison shop before you commit.** Even if your event is a simple pizza party for your child, there will be differences in costs for the food and other factors to consider, like whether it is delivered or not. Is it less expensive to order balloons from a party store or to rent a tank and inflate them yourself? Focus not only on the cheapest option but on the best one for your circumstances.
- **Educate yourself and be creative.** To find out more about planning an event like yours, check out magazine articles, Web sites, and library books. Also brainstorm with your co-planners. Your goal is to have a good time and create a memorable event.

- **Ask for help or subsidies within reason.** A potluck Valentine's Day party with a "bring something red" theme could be a lot of fun. Asking wedding guests to BYOB may make the event memorable for all the wrong reasons. Hiring your teenagers and their friends as waiters and waitresses for a formal event could be a huge money saver—or a disaster waiting to happen.
- **Keep track of everything.** It will help you plan more accurately and confidently the next time around.

19

Balancing the Books between Jobs

At some point during your working life, you may find yourself between jobs. Sometimes leaving a job is your decision. Maybe you no longer find the job satisfying, or you feel the commute or the hours are too stressful, or you just need a change. Sometimes it's not your decision—perhaps you have been downsized, or didn't see eye to eye with your superiors. Or maybe your job was temporary.

Whatever the reason for unemployment, being without a job and a steady source of income can be traumatic, especially if the job loss was sudden and unplanned. If you leave voluntarily, you have the advantage of being able to make financial arrangements in advance to tide you over. You should plan on being out of work longer than you might hope you will be. Statistically, only one out of three unemployed workers finds a job in 5 weeks, and one in five takes almost 7 months, according to the Bureau of Labor Statistics.

Maybe there are hints that you may soon be out of work: a new supervisor takes over and wants to reorganize the division, sales have been steadily declining and your company has not met revenue targets, or your company has been the target of a take-over. Sometimes, that pink slip comes out of the blue. If you are prepared for any contingency, you will be in a better position to handle it if it occurs.

Preparing for the Worst

Jessica was a sales professional for a highly competitive pharmaceutical company. The company had a pattern of building up and then scaling back drastically, but somehow Jessica had always survived the cutbacks. Over the years, Jessica observed how some of her colleagues coped well with being laid off and others suffered terribly. She tried to keep a mental list of what seemed to work—and what did not. Now, once again, rumors were swirling. Two new products that had seemed promising just a few months ago appeared to be having problems in testing, and Jessica sensed that she may be included in the next wave of lay-offs. It turned out she was correct.

Before, however, Jessica's boss gave her the bad news, Jessica was busy lining up her ducks. She had always been conservative with her personal finances, and as soon as the buzz started that the company would once again be handing out pink slips, she took the opportunity to review her current situation. She started by updating her monthly budget so she could figure out exactly how much it cost her each month for rent, utilities, food, transportation, and other necessities of life.

In the course of doing this she realized she had acquired several new ongoing expenses that added to her monthly outflows. For example, she had signed up for a gym membership option that permitted her to visit associated health clubs in other cities while she was "on the road," at a cost of an extra $50 a month. She realized that in the year that she had been paying for this option, she had only used it once. Another discovery was that 6 months earlier, Jessica found a new hairdresser who gave her a great short haircut, but she now needed monthly trims. These were $80 a visit. And the rent at the storage place where she had stashed her winter clothing, extra furniture, and mementos from her childhood had just increased significantly.

Jessica knew that the last thing in the world she wanted to do if she became unemployed was live off her credit cards, so she decided to create an emergency fund to cover her living expenses. She figured this would not be a wasted exercise if, in fact, she was not laid off; she'd been meaning to start one anyway. She called and had her gym membership put on hold, which required a small monthly fee but would save her money when she decided to reinstate it. She decided to tell her hair-dresser that she'd like to grow her hair out so she could go longer between appointments, and finally she decided to clean out the storage space and either give the stuff to charity or find room in her current house.

Jessica's sister worked for an insurance company and advised Jessica to make sure she got set up with medical insurance through COBRA, the Consolidated Omnibus Budget Reconciliation Act. COBRA was meant to provide short-term medical insurance between jobs. Although she would have to make the premium payments out-of-pocket, the rates would be much lower than if she were to purchase an individual policy to cover any period between jobs. Her sister also suggested that there was nothing untoward about Jessica taking care of her annual checkup now, if she anticipated being out of work, and following up with any specialists her doctor recommended.

Jessica then decided to get creative. She invited four business colleagues, formerly employed by her company but now working elsewhere, to a reunion at her house, explaining that she wanted to pick their brains for their best ideas about surviving unemployment. All of them had had first-hand experience with this unfortunate state. All enthusiastically accepted, eager to share what they had learned—and maybe pick up a pointer or two along the way.

One friend, Penelope, urged Jessica to fight for the best severance package she could obtain. Penelope said it took her two lay-offs to realize that the terms of a separation agreement are completely negotiable. She found out, for example, that it is fair game to request a larger amount of severance pay than may be offered if you can make the case for it. For example, if as a salaried employee you regularly worked over weekends or holidays, this might be considered extra time to add to your tenure. Penelope also reminded Jessica not to forget to claim unused vacation and sick days.

Celia brought up the issue of benefits such as stock options and pension plan benefits. She had the experience of being laid off once when she was only a few months away from being fully vested and was able to convince a sympathetic human resources executive that she was entitled to her full due. She said it was merely a question of keeping her on the books for 4 months after she had left so she would become eligible for pension benefits. She also had inquired if she could keep the company car she had been assigned, but this request was turned down. Still, she wasn't embarrassed and had thought it was worth a shot—nothing ventured, nothing gained. Everyone admired her gumption.

Jessica asked if anyone had used an outplacement or career counseling service, and everyone agreed these were valuable. If nothing else, they provide a place to go every day for free access to a phone, fax, and computer. The former employer can, and should, pick up the tab for these services as part of a package agreement. Penelope's résumé was written by one of these services, and Celia had worked with an employment coach.

Larissa chimed in that although she had only had one experience with being out of work "involuntarily," as she put it, she found the most important thing was to have a solid cushion of living expenses to fall back on. That made Jessica feel good that she had already stashed away nearly 4 months' worth. Larissa said she was out of work a lot longer than she had anticipated but actually found there were some aspects of unemployment that made life less expensive, like lower dry cleaning bills and no need for doggy day care. She also reminded Jessica that every little bit helps, so not to forget to apply for unemployment insurance.

The last of the four friends, Shubha, urged the group not to forget to consider the long-term as well. She made the mistake of cashing out her 401(k) when she left the company, unaware of the tax consequences of receiving such a payout. If she ever had to do it again (and she hoped she didn't), she thought she would request a rollover, in order to avoid the penalty for early withdrawal, in addition to the fact that this income was considered as taxable.

The dishes from supper were barely put away when Jessica received notice that her entire department was being eliminated. Instead of panicking, Jessica knew exactly what to do. Although she hoped she would be able to find work in just a few weeks, she was well prepared to stick it out if it took longer.

Commonsense Considerations

Jessica learned a lot about preparing for her period of unemployment. You can, too, following her plan:

- **Be prepared.** Have an emergency fund equal to 3 to 6 months of living expenses.
- **Live below your means.**
- **Have a disciplined savings strategy.**
- **Create a budget.** Take a close look at discretionary spending to think about what you can reasonably cut.
- **Cut down credit card debt.** This will also reduce the interest charges that go along with any revolving balances.
- **Apply for a home equity line of credit.** This is an option if you think you might be unemployed for an extended period of time.
- **Understand your company's policies and benefits.** This way you will be in the best possible position to negotiate a severance package.
- **Don't be afraid to negotiate.** Even if you can't gain a greater severance package, you may pick up "non-cash" benefits, such as outplacement services.
- **Apply for unemployment benefits.** Do this as soon as you can.
- **Don't raid your retirement accounts.** If you take a distribution before the set retirement age, you will pay a penalty, in addition to increasing your taxable income.
- **Stay calm and focused.** An anxious state doesn't help you plan or act rationally, or make a good impression during job interviews.

The Morning After

When her boss called an all-hands-on-deck meeting one Monday morning, Sharon had little idea that within the hour, she and her co-workers at the import-export concern would be out of work. The business had been sold and everyone was instructed to pack up and leave the premises that afternoon. What a nightmare! Even worse, the new owners weren't offering severance checks. Sharon placed her personal effects in a cardboard box and headed home right to bed.

Sharon had no idea what she was going to do. She felt like she had been hit by a truck that she hadn't seen coming. She had a pile of unpaid bills sitting on her kitchen table, plans to meet a friend in Northern California and travel the wine country for a week in June, and had just been starting to think about finding a way to save some money. This news paralyzed her with fear.

Even if she found a new job right away, she realized, she would be in a deep, deep hole that would take a long time to climb out of if she missed even just a few paychecks. She shuddered to think about what state her finances would be in if she missed a month—or more. Instinctively, she pulled the covers up over her head, as if she could hide from her creditors that way. She could envision the unopened bills, stacked high, and hear the messages on her answering machine from the collection agencies. But she knew full well that ignoring her situation would not make it go away.

Eventually, Sharon had to get out of bed. She fixed a cup of tea and sat down to look at the bills. She took a deep breath and started opening the envelopes. On several accounts, late fees had already started accumulating—and she had only been unemployed less than a day! She realized how much she took her weekly paycheck for granted and how casual she had been about due dates. If she didn't do something now, her creditors might start to threaten legal action. Sharon decided to stop procrastinating and take action.

First, she made a list of all her creditors, their toll-free contact numbers, the amount she owed, and the minimum payment due. This was a revealing exercise, as it showed the full extent of her debt. The list was daunting. However, for the first time Sharon knew exactly how much she owed. Although it was painful, it was an essential starting point. Like many people, Sharon had underestimated the combined level of her debt. She'd known that she owed a lot of money, but she had no idea that she owed as much as she did. But as depressing as it seemed, it was also inspiring her to think about finding a better-paying job that might help her clear this debt away.

Sharon then filled out a net worth form for herself. This gave her a more positive outlook on her options because she knew not only what she "owed," but also what she "owned." The positive side of her net worth sheet listed assets that she had forgotten about, including some antique rugs from her grandmother and her 401(k) plan. She realized that she could sell some of the rugs in order to pay off some of her creditors. Additionally, she remembered she owned savings bonds her godmother had given her as birthday presents every year until she was an adult. The bonds were sitting in her safe-deposit box and had matured, so she might be able to cash them out and use the money to pay off more debts, or, if necessary, pay her living expenses until she found a job.

Next, Sharon listed these living expenses. Rent, bus fares (she didn't own a car), food, utilities, and entertainment were all included. She had already made a deposit on her vacation and another payment would be due soon. She decided she would have to call and see if she could get out of the trip. It was a painful decision, but she just couldn't justify the expense. Once she got back on her feet she would try to reschedule.

With her debt list in hand, Sharon started calling each creditor to ask if payment arrangements could be worked out. She was surprised at how sympathetic and helpful the creditors were due to the fact that she had a hardship situation. Without her asking, the second one she called offered to reduce the interest rate on her credit card in addition to suspending the late-payment fees currently on the card. This agreement was valid so long as Sharon would pay the minimum on time and not go over her credit limit, which she was hovering close to. Sharon made note of the offer, as well as the name of the customer service representative. Using this offer as a model, she then made the same request of each of the other creditors she called.

By the early afternoon, Sharon felt that she had stabilized her financial situation and was ready to move on to face up to her career crisis. She decided that as an interim measure she would try and pick up a job in retail or maybe waitressing, just to keep the cash flow coming. She decided to head into town to pick up a copy of the local paper to check the ads. She felt a lot better, having confronted her situation instead of hiding from it. In fact, she felt like a new day was dawning.

Commonsense Considerations

If you find yourself falling behind on debt payments, you can count on hearing from the lender's collection department. Ignoring past-due notices or phone calls will eventually result in your account being turned over to an independent debt collector.

Once an outside collection agency takes over, the original creditor loses almost all control over possible payment arrangements. Moreover, collection agencies are usually more aggressive and less willing to compromise. They may choose to bring a lawsuit against you to collect money. They may also be more willing to go to court than the original creditor may have been. You have a much better negotiating position with the original creditor. So don't wait until the debt is turned over to a collection agency to discuss your concerns.

As a first step, you should make a list of both secured and unsecured creditors. Secured creditors should be contacted first. If you are not sure whether a creditor is secured, ask yourself this question: "If I don't pay the bill, can they take the item away from me?" Commonly secured debts are your auto loan and home mortgage. Adding up the total balance column will give you the full picture.

The "Debt Total Worksheet" on page 283 will help you figure out your debt level.

Once you know how much you owe, you need to figure out whether you have any resources available to pay your obligations.

The "Net Worth Worksheet" on page 292 will show you both the pros (assets) and cons (liabilities) in your financial portfolio.

Have all this information on hand when you call each creditor. The net worth sheet will indicate any assets that may be used to free up some cash. Assets can be liquidated (savings accounts or stocks), sold (real estate or collections), or borrowed against (securities or retirement accounts) in order to access cash that then can be used to pay bills until you catch up or find employment.

Having the full list of creditors will remind you of everyone you need to contact. By having a list of all your creditors in front of you, you will be less inclined to promise to pay any one creditor more than you had budgeted. If you overpay one creditor, you may not have enough money left over to pay the others.

Bill collectors will almost always be friendlier if you take the initiative to call them before they call you. It is also important to realize that you do have protections under the Fair Debt Collection Practices Act (FDCPA).

It covers third-party or outside collectors (though not original creditors with collection departments of their own). The FDCPA requires that debt collectors treat you fairly and prohibits the following practices:

- Use of threats of violence or harm.
- Publishing lists of consumers who refuse to pay their debts (except to a credit bureau).
- Use of obscene or profane language, or repeated use of the telephone to annoy you.
- Use of any false or misleading statements when collecting a debt.
- Stating that you will be arrested if you do not pay your debt; or that they will seize, garnish, attach, or sell your property or wages, unless the collection agency or creditor intends to do so and it is legal to do so.
- Sending you anything that looks like an official document from a court or government agency when it is not.
- Engaging in unfair practices when they try to collect a debt. For example, collectors may not collect any amount greater than your debt, unless your state law permits such a charge.

If you feel you have been treated unfairly according to the law, you may report the collection agency to your state Attorney General's office or the Federal Trade Commission office that oversees your region.

CHAPTER 20

Fighting Credit Fraud and Identity Theft

Every year, millions of consumers discover that their credit or debit cards have been used without their permission. According to the Federal Trade Commission, approximately 10 million Americans a year experience the vexing crime of identity theft.

Credit fraud occurs, for example, when credit card information is stolen and used for unauthorized charges. Identity theft involves the use of another person's name, address, Social Security number, or other personal information to take over or tap into existing bank, credit card, or other financial accounts and/or establish new ones.

While the advent of the Internet has certainly increased opportunities for credit card number or identity information to be stolen, these crimes long predate the digital age. Most identity theft does not, in fact, involve the Internet but is perpetrated by individuals known to the victim or by thieves who physically obtain the documents or information they target.

Identity theft can be a federal crime and, in many states, a state crime. Individuals and businesses suffer huge losses every year due to it, on the order of $5 billion and $48 billion respectively, reports the Federal Trade Commission. Victims also must spend much time—on average 30 hours—dealing with illicit uses of their names and other personal information. The crime may be as minor as a few low charges on a credit card bill or as major as applying and getting approval for taking on huge debts, or even acquiring a criminal record under the assumed name.

This is just one more reason that you should stay on top of your finances at all times, balancing your checkbook when statements arrive, reviewing all credit card bills scrupulously, and checking your credit bureau reports at least annually. Credit card and identity theft scams are also regularly reported in newspapers; familiarize yourself with new forms of deception so you won't fall victim to them.

Sheila's Saga

Sheila had lived her entire life in a small southern town in Alabama. She graduated from the local high school, worked in the town five-and-dime store, married a local dairy farmer, and stayed in her beloved farmhouse even after her husband died. Alone in her house, her eyesight starting to fail, Sheila found it harder and harder to get around. It was difficult to read and driving became out of the question.

A friend read to her an ad posted on the bulletin board of the grocery store where Sheila shopped, and through it she contacted Virginia, an experienced home health aid. They agreed that Virginia would help maintain Sheila's home so that Sheila could continue to live independently. For an entire year, Virginia helped Sheila with all the details of everyday life. Virginia drove her to doctor appointments, helped her shop for food, read the newspaper out loud to her, and accompanied her to church every Sunday. Sheila came to trust Virginia as she would a member of her own family.

One day while Virginia was out running errands, Sheila received a phone call from a representative of the credit card company where she had long had an account. The representative told Sheila the company had not received her last three payments. Caught off guard, Sheila was shocked. She always prided herself on keeping up to date on all her bills. Now that Virginia had taken over bill paying as part of her duties, Sheila had assumed all payments were being made in a timely fashion. "I'm sure my aide has just overlooked these bills. I'll talk to her when she gets back," Sheila informed the credit card representative.

The representative reported that Sheila's credit card had been used to make dozens of purchases outside of her usual spending pattern, including charges at liquor stores, big chain stores, car repair shops, and for digital cable TV service. Confused and concerned, but certain she had never made those charges, Sheila said she wanted to dispute them. "I don't even have a television anymore," she told the representative.

The representative referred Sheila to Patricia, a case review representative in the security department. Patricia, a 20-year veteran of her job, was very familiar with Sheila's scenario. To rule out a robbery, Patricia first asked Sheila to retrieve her card. Sheila groped around and found it in the back of her drawer, just where she always kept it. Patricia asked her to move it to a different place, promising to call her back in a few days.

Patricia then went to work checking each of the card charges. She obtained copies of the signed credit card receipts and had them sent by express service to Sheila. Patricia asked Sheila to verify the scribbled signature. Examining it carefully with a magnifying glass, Sheila recognized the handwriting: It was Virginia's. She called to report this to Patricia. By then, it seemed clear to both Sheila and Patricia that Virginia had fraudulently used Sheila's credit card. Sheila was quite distraught.

Patricia proposed that Sheila consider the following plan. First, Sheila needed to put a stop to the fraudulent use of the card. Second, there was the matter of confronting Virginia if, Patricia warned, Sheila felt she could do so without jeopardizing her own safety. Finally, there was the issue of what this would mean for Sheila going forward. Patricia suggested that Sheila have her mail rerouted to a neighbor's house. Patricia also obtained Virginia's phone number so that the aide could be contacted directly by the credit card company's investigations department. Given the nature of the women's relationship, Patricia did not want Sheila to have to confront Virginia directly.

The credit card company's security operations left Virginia several phone messages asking her to please call back about an important matter. Virginia finally returned the call but denied she had ever used Sheila's card. She blamed a medical van driver who picked up Sheila to take her to therapy once a week. Following established procedure, the security unit requested that Virginia mail a copy of her driver's license with a signed, notarized letter stating that she had not made the charges. A week later, Patricia called Sheila to tell her she had not received these papers. She advised Sheila to file a police report.

Before Sheila had an opportunity to do this, though, she got a call from her bank, advising her that her checking account was overdrawn. Sheila told the bank that she hadn't written any checks recently and that her checks must have been stolen and her signature forged. The bank advised Sheila to immediately file a police report. Now recognizing that the situation had gotten out of hand, Sheila did just that.

Faced with the facts, Virginia finally admitted to making the credit card charges and writing the checks. She agreed to sign an acknowledgement-of-responsibility document and to pay back, within a specified amount of time, the amounts she had charged and taken from the checking account. Needless to say, Virginia now needed to find a new job.

Commonsense Considerations

When Patricia called to check on Sheila, she suggested some simple ways to help reduce her vulnerability to credit card fraud and debit card theft in the future. Here are some tips from Citi Cards's *Use Credit Wisely Guide*.

- Purchase a paper shredder. Use it before discarding old credit card receipts, solicitations, cancelled checks, ATM receipts, and any other financial documents that might have personal information on them.
- Whenever you receive a new credit card, sign it right away. Call your credit card company immediately if your credit card has expired and a new one has not arrived.
- If you decide to cancel a credit card, call the company to inform them. Don't just put away the card or cut it up and throw it out.
- Don't sign blank charge slips. If you aren't tipping on a restaurant bill, draw a line through the tip space. Don't leave receipts around at work, in your car, or in pockets of clothing that you might send out to be dry cleaned or laundered. Make sure you have been handed a receipt after every purchase, and tuck it away securely.

- Never lend your card to anyone, under any circumstance.
- Notify your bank and other credit grantors and financial institutions when you change your address or phone number.
- Report lost or stolen cards immediately. Most credit card companies have a 24-hour toll-free number.
- Record card numbers, expiration dates, and phone numbers. Keep this record in a safe place, separate from your cards. One easy way to do this is to take all your cards to a photocopy center and place them face down on the copying machine. Make two copies and put them in a safe place. Update your card inventory at least once a year.
- Don't carry around any more cards than you need or use regularly.
- Don't give your account number over the phone unless you know the company and you made the call.
- Take advantage of security features, like photo cards.
- Always check receipts against monthly statements. Errors must be reported within 60 days of the statement mailing date.

Who Is That Person?

Gary had just arrived home after a long day. As he ran in from the rain, the phone rang and he yelled to his wife, who was busily preparing dinner, to answer it. She said it was for him. Gary shook out his umbrella and grabbed the phone. On the other end was a representative from the business department of a credit card company. The representative explained that he was doing a routine check in connection with Gary's application for a credit card with an electronics specialty chain store in a mall some 50 miles away.

There was just one problem. Gary was sure that he had never filled out an application for this card. He explained there must be some mistake. Maybe his son, Gerald, had been the applicant? It didn't make sense, though, since his son was in the army, stationed abroad. And the personal information on the application matched Gary's—name, address, and phone number.

As soon as Gary denied applying for the card, the representative pulled and flagged the credit application. He transferred Gary to a specialist in the investigations department. Here, personnel were trained to deal with issues related to identity theft.

Immediately, the office opened a case file on Gary and ordered his credit report online. Through this, Gary discovered other accounts fraudulently established in his name. It took only minutes for the investigator to reach these creditors and arrange for those accounts to be immediately canceled to prevent further financial loss. The investigator also placed a special alert with the credit bureaus.

Gary was advised to file a police report. He did, and the local police began a formal investigation. The detective on the case contacted the credit card companies directly to review specific details of the identity theft. They were able to supply the police with information that helped solve the case: the P.O. box number that the imposter had used to create the fraudulent accounts. Tracing the post office box to its owner, the police discovered it belonged to a man who lived right in Gary's hometown.

Three weeks after the first call from the credit card company, the criminal brazenly tried to buy a hunting rifle while posing as Gary. The local police arrested him on the spot for identity theft.

It turned out that Gary wasn't the only victim. The forger had at least half a dozen fake IDs in his wallet. His modus operandi could not have been simpler. He intercepted his victims' mail, stealing it from their mailboxes (commonly called "dumpster diving") and searching personal correspondence and credit card statements for the vital information he needed to commit identity theft. Authorities filed both state and federal charges against him.

Gary was glad the matter was over and resolved and promised himself that he would be more aware of the basic precautions he could use to protect his most valuable asset—his good name.

Commonsense Considerations

Gary was fortunate that his case was solved in a relatively short time. A substantial amount of damage can be done if an identity theft is not detected in short order.

Here is a checklist to follow if you think you've become a victim of identity theft. Make sure you keep careful notes of when you called, the name of the individual you spoke to, and any follow-up that may be necessary.

- **File a police report.** Start with your local police or with the police department in the community where the identity theft took place. You may also want to contact your state law enforcement authorities. If you're told that identity theft is not a crime under your state law, ask to file a "Miscellaneous Incident Report" instead. Get a copy of the report in case you need proof of the crime.
- **File a complaint with the Federal Trade Commission.** Contact the FTC's Identity Theft Hotline by calling (877) 438-4338 or via www.ftc.gov/idtheft. The FTC enters complaints into a secure consumer fraud database that is accessible to law enforcement agencies for use in pursuing criminal investigations.
- **Check all credit or debit card accounts.** Obtain a copy of your credit report from one or all three of the major credit reporting companies through www.annualcreditreport.com or by calling (877) 322-8228. Explain that you're an identity theft victim and ask that a fraud alert and a victim statement be placed in your file. This way, creditors must call you before changing existing accounts or opening new ones. Once you receive your report, check personal information for any fraudulent accounts opened in your name and for unauthorized charges. Also review the section of your report that lists "inquiries." If the report notes inquiries from the companies that opened the fraudulent accounts, ask that those inquiries be removed from your report. In a few months, order a new copy of your credit report to verify that your corrections and changes have been made.
- **Contact your bank.** If you have reason to believe that an identity thief has tampered with your bank accounts, checks, or credit or ATM cards, close the accounts immediately. When you open new accounts, insist on password-only access. In addition, if your checks have been stolen or misused, contact your bank to obtain stop-payment instructions. Also contact the major check verification companies to request that they notify retailers using their databases not to accept these checks, or ask your bank to notify the check verification service with which it does business.

- **Protect your investments.** If you believe that an identity thief has tampered with your securities investment or brokerage accounts, immediately report it to your financial advisor or account manager and to the Securities and Exchange Commission at (800) 732-0330.
- **Phone service fraud.** If an identity thief has established new phone service in your name, is making unauthorized calls that seem to come from—and are billed to—your cellular phone, or is using your calling card and personal identification number (PIN), contact your service provider immediately to cancel the account and/or calling card. Open new accounts and choose new PINs. If you are having difficulty removing fraudulent phone charges from your account, contact your state Public Utility Commission for local service providers or the Federal Communications Commission for long-distance service providers and cellular providers.
- **Secure your Social Security number.** It is a crime for someone else to use your Social Security number to apply for a job or to work. Report it to the Social Security Administration's Fraud Hotline at (800) 269-0271. Then contact the Social Security Administration at (800) 772-1213 to verify the accuracy of the earnings reported on your Social Security number and to request a copy of your Social Security statement.
- **Check your driver's license.** If you suspect that your name or Social Security number is being used by an identity thief to obtain a driver's license or a non-driver's ID card, contact the local Department of Motor Vehicles. If your state uses your Social Security number as your driver's license number, ask that they substitute another number.
- **Investigate bankruptcy proceedings.** If you believe someone has filed for bankruptcy using your name, write to the U.S. Trustee in the region where the bankruptcy was filed. A listing of the U.S. Trustee Program's regions can be found at www.usdoj.gov/ust/ or in your phone book under U.S. Government-Bankruptcy Administration. Your letter should describe the situation and provide proof of identity, such as a copy of your birth certificate, driver's license, or passport. The U.S. Trustee will, if appropriate, make a referral to criminal law enforcement authorities if you provide appropriate documentation to substantiate your claim. You also may want to file a complaint with

the U.S. Attorney and/or the Federal Bureau of Investigation in the state where the bankruptcy was filed.

- **Dispute criminal records or arrests.** In rare instances, an identity thief may establish a criminal record under your name. An imposter may give your name when being arrested. If this happens to you, you may need to hire an attorney to help resolve the problem. The procedures for clearing your name may vary by city or state.

Because credit card usage is rampant during the holiday shopping season, this time of the year presents particular opportunity for thieves. You should be particularly vigilant during this period, monitoring your accounts carefully.

Stolen Holiday Joy

Cynthia, a college recruiter for a local consulting firm, was an enthusiastic supporter of the power and convenience of online banking technology. She had been managing her checking, savings, and credit card accounts online for more than 5 years. Her job required frequent travel to recruiting fairs at colleges around the country, so she felt that nothing could replace the efficiency of managing her accounts from anywhere, anytime via the Internet.

One December morning shortly before Christmas, Cynthia was on the road when she got a call on her cell phone. The woman on the other end of the line identified herself as Robin, a customer service representative from Cynthia's credit card company. Cynthia got nervous, wondering whether she had somehow gone over her credit limit. She had, after all, been spending more than usual that month, buying presents for her friends and family.

Robin had indeed called to inquire about unusual activity on Cynthia's credit card. She wanted to discuss some recent charges that seemed suspicious. Robin ran through a list of numerous purchases from a variety of stores—expensive women's clothing and shoes, cases of wine, and even some jewelry. While Cynthia had, in fact, purchased some clothing and jewelry as gifts for her mother and sister, the items Robin was calling about were bought from a store in Naples, Italy. Cynthia immediately informed Robin that she had most definitely not made those purchases. She hadn't been to Italy since her honeymoon 15 years earlier, and even then she hadn't visited Naples.

Together, Robin and Cynthia identified six purchases made with Cynthia's credit card information at the store in Italy. Cynthia was shocked but also relieved that the unauthorized purchases had been spotted so quickly. The most recent transaction had been posted to her account just that morning. Robin was able to immediately cancel Cynthia's card and send her a new one in the mail, as well as remove the fraudulent charges from Cynthia's account.

Cynthia asked Robin how the thief might have obtained her credit card information in the first place. While it was impossible to know for sure, Robin suggested that it may have been obtained off the Internet, especially since Cynthia had recently been making a lot of purchases online. Robin reminded Cynthia to be careful when making online purchases. She recommended buying items only from reputable vendors with secure servers. Cynthia admitted to Robin that, while she did make many purchases online, she was not always diligent in verifying the authenticity of the vendor—a mistake that she would not make again.

Commonsense Considerations

Cynthia was fortunate to have the oversight of her credit card company reviewing her charges. During the holiday season especially, so many charges may be placed that it can be easy for a thief to slip a few more on the card unnoticed.

You can reduce your risk of credit card and identity theft by safeguarding your identifying information using these simple guidelines from Citi Cards's *Use Credit Wisely Guide*.

Protect Your Mailbox
- Remove mail from your mailbox as soon as possible after delivery, especially if mail is left in a box or basket outside your door.
- Deposit outgoing mail in post office collection boxes or at your local post office rather than leaving it on a desk or in an open mailbox for pickup.

- Never put your account number on the outside of an envelope or post-card.
- If you are traveling, have your mail held at the post office, unless you can arrange for a relative or trusted friend to pick it up at your house daily.
- Investigate the possibility of having a mail slot cut in your front door so mail will not be left out in plain sight.

Protect Your Wallet
- Regularly purge your wallet of credit cards that you don't use, as well as old receipts.
- Keep items with personal information in a safe place at home, and do not share this information with friends or acquaintances.
- Don't carry your Social Security card in your wallet or purse. Memorize your Social Security number, and never write it down on anything you carry.
- Memorize your PIN numbers.
- Conceal your credit or debit card while waiting to pay for purchases. Someone in line behind you may be able to memorize or copy your account number. Make sure the cashier promptly gives the card back to you, and be sure to put it back in your wallet and/or purse rather than slipping it into a pocket or other place from which it could fall out or be easily stolen.

Shop on the Phone and Online Safely
- Try to deal only with companies that have a physical address and, if you are shopping online, a phone number you can call for additional information. Check that the vendors have secure ordering. To determine if a Web site uses security software, look for a locked padlock, an unbroken key, or a lock icon (displayed on the status bar or at the bottom of the screen). Carefully read the company's privacy and security policies.
- Don't disclose personal information online or over the telephone. The only information a merchant needs to process an order is the name on the credit card, the account number, the security code, and the expiration date.

- Be careful about information you are asked to supply either over the telephone, online, or via an e-mail solicitation. Don't fall for phone scams offering free goods or prizes. Say no and hang up if you are asked for personal data, such as your Social Security number or a credit card number. Read commercial e-mail solicitations carefully if they are from institutions where you have an account; often these emails are "phishing" campaigns directing you to a false Web site where you are asked to type in account data.
- When your billing statements arrive, compare them to your receipts to spot any unauthorized charges.

21

Untying the Knot

According to a 2004 National Center for Health Statistics report, nearly half of all marriages end in divorce. Suffice it to say that many marriages in the United States do not survive. Most of us have personal familiarity with divorce in some way—if not the end of our own (or our parents') marriages, then that of a friend, family member, neighbor, or colleague. It's rarely a pleasant experience.

In addition to the emotional stress a divorce can bring, there is more often than not financial stress involved. In many cases, money is at least a contributing factor to the breakup of the marriage. And adjusting to single life again can feel like moving in reverse. You spent years accumulating a home, cars, furniture, and investments with a spouse, and now you are selling or splitting up those assets. That's why, as soon as you can, it's essential to take control of your finances. Many have found that the more financially savvy they are, the more in control, both financially and emotionally, they will be.

For Richer or Poorer

Claire felt like a walking cliché. The year she turned 50, her husband, Donald, told her he had been unhappy for many years and wanted a divorce. He was moving out that day, and his lawyer would contact her in the near future. Within 6 months, they were divorced, and a month later, Donald married a young woman he had met through an online dating service.

It was ironic to Claire that she hadn't seen this coming, since she was Donald's second wife. Twenty years earlier, she had been branded "the other woman" and called his "trophy wife." His first wife, with whom he had two children, took him to the cleaners in that divorce. After witnessing the bickering and pettiness that accompanied that experience, she'd secretly sworn to herself that if she and Donald ever separated (not that this was something she'd thought would ever happen), she would try to be as civil and fair as possible. Now, this would be put to the test.

Claire worked as the executive director of a nonprofit children's rights organization. The position paid an honorarium, rather than a salary, which had been fine with Claire—so long as Donald was supporting her. Now she wasn't quite sure what she would do. That she and Donald had no children of their own may have seemed on the surface to simplify matters, but she now felt resentful that Donald had pressured her on the issue of not starting a family.

Claire's friends rallied around her when the divorce was announced. Several had been through the experience themselves, and they formed an informal support group that helped Claire get through the shock and stress that can occur in the early days of a divorce. In addition to offering emotional support, her friends encouraged Claire to think through some of the more long-term practical and financial issues. As one friend put it, she should learn from their *inexperience*.

For example, one friend had neglected to make sure that her name was put on any of the deeds for the property she and her husband had bought during the marriage, and she found he had quietly transferred these assets to his sister during their so-called trial separation. Another had prolonged philosophical and financial disagreements with her ex-husband about financial responsibility for her mother, who lived with them at her ex's invitation. Claire's pal Erica reminded her about the out-and-out war she and her ex-husband had over the family pets, a spunky cat and an ailing dog. Her husband thought it was perfectly fair to give her the dog and take the cat.

Claire realized it was important to discuss financial and property issues with Donald and, if possible, have specific financial commitments spelled out in the divorce agreement. For example, what if he refused to continue to support her? Would she have to leave her current job for a salaried position? This thought saddened her, since she enjoyed her current position and felt she was good at it.

Although she had been responsible for handling most of the household bills during the marriage, Claire had only involved herself superficially in long-term investment decisions. It was clear that she would need to understand those matters now. Realizing that she needed professional advice to help her navigate the financial issues she would face during and after the divorce, she took the time to interview three financial advisors recommended to her by her friends. She wanted to make sure the professional she signed on with understood her specific situation and would be able to give her the time and attention she needed. She decided to hire Brenda, a financial professional experienced with divorce issues.

In their first meeting, Brenda suggested that Claire consider enrolling in a program or series of seminars that would help give her a jump-start on financial issues. Brenda said that this way, Claire would learn some basics on her own time and be able to use her time with Brenda more effectively. Brenda presented Claire with some information about upcoming courses, and Claire was attracted to a finance "boot camp" program for women at the local community college. Claire thought that in the all-woman environment she would feel more comfortable asking questions. Brenda wholly endorsed her choice and laughingly asked her to keep good notes so Brenda could pick up some pointers.

Claire's first assignment at the "boot camp" course was to create a written inventory of her current financial status. Guided by her instructor, she arranged to have the house appraised by a real estate agent, requested a recent valuation of various investments, and researched how much the family cars, artwork, and jewelry were worth. She also added in the value of the Aspen time-share and annual golf club memberships.

By working with Brenda, Claire began to understand what steps she would need to take to create a financial life for herself independent of

Donald. Her instinct was to invest very conservatively, and Brenda helped point out the risks—yes, risks—of this approach. Together, they began to define her risk tolerance and create a growth strategy for an individual portfolio. Brenda helped coordinate Claire's work with her accountant, tax, and legal advisors.

Fortunately for Claire, she and Donald had agreed to keep a number of separate accounts during their marriage. In Donald's first marriage, everything was held jointly, and it made for messy transactions. During those divorce proceedings, Claire observed how joint accounts are truly joined. There were daily battles over purchases, responsibility for payments, accusations about missing money, and a lot of drama. So at least Claire felt she had cleared that hurdle and wouldn't be at Donald's mercy. The problem was, he had always filled her account with household money. Now, he had stopped.

Claire consulted her attorney because she was concerned about the impact on her credit rating if she couldn't pay her own bills. Just the day-to-day expense of maintaining the house and gardens surrounding it was staggering. Claire needed some sort of interim agreement from Donald until they could finalize the terms of the divorce. Although in general the separation had been amicable, Claire realized how vulnerable she was. Plus, there was the pre-nup, which she hadn't reviewed in years.

At Claire's next class, the instructor handed out a checklist of contracts or documents where both spouses might be jointly named. She suggested reviewing and revising all legal documents that listed the spouse as the primary beneficiary. Typically, this might include life insurance coverage and IRA accounts. She also recommended checking for any power of attorney papers. Claire followed these instructions and arranged for appropriate changes.

Claire was deeply concerned about health insurance. She had been covered under Donald's policy all their married life. She knew from experience that it is almost always cheapest to obtain insurance through an employer. Her tiny organization did offer health insurance, but it was a limited plan and Claire was concerned about the payments. But she had no idea if she was forced to find a better-paying job whether insurance would be part of the benefits package. Brenda counseled her to approach her short-term needs first. Claire explored whether she was entitled to receive health benefits under Donald's policy. She made a note to ask her attorney to make sure to ask that monthly premiums be included as part of her settlement.

A year after her separation began, Claire found herself having traveled far. Donald had been fairer than she might have guessed in dividing up their assets, and she was given enough resources to continue working at her nonprofit position. She and Brenda had put together a plan based on their many discussions about Claire's financial goals and priorities for the future. This plan included a budget and short-term strategies for covering cash flow while she adjusted to life on her own, and longer-term strategies for preparing for her own retirement. Claire felt as if she had been handed a new lease on life and was now ready to face the world on her own. The teacher of her "boot camp" course asked whether she would be willing to give a talk to the next semester's class on the topic of "Your Financial Life During and After Divorce." Claire agreed enthusiastically and wondered whether perhaps she might make a second career out of lecturing other women about "How to Handle a Divorce over 50."

Commonsense Considerations

Here are some of the major points of Claire's presentation. They might help you, too, when planning your financial future after a divorce.

- Educate yourself as thoroughly as possible about the financial implications of your divorce. The more you learn, the more in control of your financial future you'll become. You should explore all sources: books and magazines, Web sites, support groups, classes, and advisory services. Your lawyer will keep you informed of the legal aspects, but it's up to you to keep your lawyer informed of your financial situation.
- Assets are typically divided on a percentage basis. The more specifically you identify them, the more assets you are likely to be awarded. Make a list and gather as much documentation as you can to support it, including receipts, insurance appraisals, invoices, or credit card statements.
- Review beneficiary designations. Be systematic about considering the need to remove the name of your ex-spouse (or about-to-be-ex-spouse) from documents that in the event of your death might have financial

implications, such as retirement plans, insurance policies, and power of attorney or living will forms. While you're at it, sit down and review your will and estate plan for possible revision.

- Make sure you will have continued health insurance coverage after the divorce. If your health insurance was covered by your spouse's policy, try to negotiate continuing coverage or the expense of obtaining new health insurance, possibly as part of any child support and/or spousal payments. Begin to look into what you will do to afford the difference if a limit is set for this coverage.

- Negotiate child support. Each state has its own guidelines for determining child support. It also may be useful to consider prefunding of such agreed-upon expenses as college and graduate school tuitions, down payments for a first house, and weddings.

- Remember, your financial needs and preferences come first now. Just because as a couple you invested in a certain way does not mean that this strategy is right for you as a single person. And, conversely, if a particular investment yielded good results, don't reject it just because it was part of your former life.

An Unhappy Divorce

Neil was a physician's assistant at a university hospital in New England, near where he had grown up. His wife, Francie, was a general surgeon there who worked a part-time schedule. She had been raised on the West Coast and attended college and medical school there before she came east to do her residency. Neil supported his wife's desire to acquaint their two young daughters with her family and friends across the country. Over the winter holidays the family traveled west, and for two months in the summer, Francie took the girls on an extended visit.

Neil was never comfortable in Francie's native surroundings and signed up for double shifts while she was gone. It all seemed quite idyllic to Neil—which made it all the more painful when, one April day, Francie told him that she really didn't enjoy living on the East Coast any more and that she wished to move back to California with the girls at the end of the school year. She said she didn't care whether Neil accompanied them or not. If he didn't want to relocate, she said, it might make sense for them to divorce so she could get on with her life. She then asked him to immediately move to the guest room over the garage of their house.

Neil asked his wife whether she would agree to see a marriage counselor, but it was clear Francie had already made up her mind. He felt like he was on a roller-coaster speeding out of control. Moving seemed out of the question for him; he was not comfortable with the notion of uprooting and couldn't imagine adjusting to life beyond his familiar surroundings. At the same time, he suspected that if he filed for divorce, he would lose custody of his girls, though still be financially responsible for them. It was almost too much to think about. He ignored the situation as long as he could, hoping his wife would change her mind. He finally contacted a lawyer when he realized that Francie had withdrawn funds from their joint checking account to pay for three one-way airline tickets.

Neil's attorney prepared the case thoroughly, but because Neil did not want to contest his wife's request for custody, she could not be prevented from moving out of town with the children. The attorney also advised Neil that even though his wife made more money than Neil did, Neil would still have to provide child support.

Neil told his attorney that he wasn't interested in fighting with his wife over details, so he was willing to meet her demands on virtually every point. This meant turning over his 401(k) plan assets, their joint savings account, and all proceeds from the sale of their house, plus providing child support at a level that Neil believed exceeded what they were presently spending. Secretly, Neil thought that if he were conciliatory and generous, maybe his wife would change her mind and agree to reconcile with him. He gave her everything except a small savings account that both of them acknowledged he had established before they were married. He suspected this account would be all but emptied out by his lawyer's bill, however.

Neil's best friend's wife suggested he join a support group to help him through the first few months, but Neil preferred to tough it out on his own. He turned to the Internet to research his options and double-check that his lawyer was covering all the bases. It appeared that the attorney was. After a marathon 18-hour negotiating session in a conference room at his lawyer's office, it was all over. What Neil had spent years building up was gone. Francie then packed up the china, the CDs, the pet hamster, and the girls and left for California.

Neil realized he would need several months, if not years, to get over this whole experience. He had no desire or energy to lead the life of a swinging bachelor, and he certainly didn't have the wherewithal to support such a lifestyle. He sold the house at a considerable loss and moved into a studio apartment near the hospital. He signed up for extra shifts, hoping to start to rebuild what he had just given away. He decided that even though the girls weren't around, he would try to start a college fund for them. Perhaps they might consider returning to live near him for their higher education.

Commonsense Considerations

Neil found out the hard way that divorce is at once a financial, legal, and emotional process. When embroiled in a divorce, it's important to be realistic and, as much as possible, to keep the lines of communications open with your about-to-be-ex. Here is some additional wisdom.

- Always put your children's best interests first. No matter what the damage is to your bank account, it is a lot easier to rebuild your finances than your children's respect for you.
- Don't let "lay lawyers," even experienced family and friends, advise you. That's your attorney's job. Get a good one, and stick by his or her advice.
- Don't use money as a weapon.
- Remember to figure in the tax implications of financial decisions, or you may end up with the one-two punch of a higher tax bill once the assets are split.
- Divide up and conquer. Determine what's worth a fight and let the rest go. Try to keep your financial and emotional lives separate.
- Watch those lawyer fees. You don't want to end up paying higher attorney bills simply because it took you 20 hours to negotiate ownership of the cappuccino maker.

CHAPTER 22

Blending Finances in a Blended Family

If the odds are tough that a first marriage will survive, they are even tougher for the second. While many couples may enthusiastically remarry feeling older and wiser the second, third, or even fourth time around, there are emotional and financial complications that neither partner may anticipate.

For instance, lots of baggage is brought to second marriages, not the least of which includes children, ex-spouses, and bad debts. Finances take on a geometric complexity when there are assets and dependents from a first marriage on one or both sides. For this reason, it is especially important to find common ground on financial matters. Financial settlements from a previous marriage may have split up your financial resources, lowering your net worth. You may have to rely on your new spouse's former spouse to balance the

Half of all Americans will live in a stepfamily at some point in their lives, according to U.S. Census statistics. In the United States, an average of 1,300 new stepfamilies form every day. Some 22 million stepfamilies presently exist, and more than 20 percent of children under age 18—about 10 million— live in blended families.

family budget. Or there may be alimony or child support payments representing new liabilities. And divorce can leave deep emotional scars that you don't want to exacerbate with added financial stress.

Starting Over

Nancy was looking for a fresh start. Her modeling career hadn't really worked out, and neither had her first marriage. Then she met Joe, fell head over heels in love, and eloped a mere 6 months later. They shared each other's hopes and dreams about the future, but, in their excitement and rush to tie the knot, forgot to discuss finances.

One day, while they were still newlyweds, Joe inadvertently discovered that Nancy had received a large inheritance from her grandmother. When he asked her about it, Nancy immediately became defensive. Although she and Joe had often discussed their goal of buying their first home, Nancy insisted that the money from her grandmother was off-limits.

Nancy's grandmother had lost everything she owned during the Depression and through hard work and frugality had managed to become a wealthy woman before she died. Because of this history, Nancy felt that spending her grandmother's money was something she could only do in the case of an emergency. Nancy had never explained her rationale for not touching her grandmother's inheritance, so Joe wound up assuming that Nancy not only didn't trust him, but also lacked commitment to their future together. Before too long, Nancy's new marriage was fraying at the edges.

Nancy didn't want another marriage to end, so she proposed to Joe that they seek professional help. After discussions, he agreed. They sought a financial advisor to counsel them about different ways to keep their money separate but equal.

The financial advisor they hired immediately suggested that Nancy and Joe backtrack and face some of the financial issues they should have discussed before they tied the knot. He insisted it was never too late to have these talks, gently proposing that they would do best to first try to eliminate the "easy questions" where there was agreement before delving into the more complex. Nancy was surprised to learn that Joe had promised to support his aging father, and while he was still single had even thought about asking his dad to move in with him. Joe was unaware that Nancy had strict rules about how much debt she would carry. Happily, they found much common ground on many of the topics their advisor raised, particularly about planning for the future and the importance of budgets and savings.

After several months of hard work, Nancy and Joe truly understood each other's point of view. Nancy agreed to free up some of her money from her inheritance to put toward the purchase of a house. The financial advisor helped the couple draft a post-nuptial agreement so that in the remote event of a divorce, or if one of them were to die, it would be clear who owned what property. Joe and Nancy also realized that they should continue to maintain separate accounts for their money. This compromise allowed Nancy to retain her sense of independence, just as her contribution to the down payment restored Joe's confidence that she trusted him.

The bottom line for Nancy and Joe was that they were willing to meet each other halfway to make the marriage work. Their determination to live happily ever after was key to making this not just a dream but a reality.

Commonsense Considerations

Communication is key in any marriage—but especially in blended families. The best approach is to talk about your finances up front, preferably before the remarriage occurs. Even if you skip the discussion before you head down the aisle, it's never too late to have it, as Nancy and Joe discovered. Here are a few topics to get you started.

- What are your financial obligations? Answer questions such as: What is your total credit card debt? Have you filed bankruptcy? Are you paying alimony? If so, how much for how many more years?
- At what age are you planning on retiring?
- Do you have major medical expenses that you still owe or any that will be ongoing?
- Are you planning an entrepreneurial venture? If so, what kind of investment will be required?

- Do you have major maintenance costs associated with your house (new roof) or car (on its last legs)?
- How should you assign roles for your financial life together? For example, who should be the bread winner? One person, both parties? Who will take the lead in bill paying, storing financial records, and overall money management?
- Regarding banking, will joint or separate checking and savings accounts be established?
- What is your comfort level with carrying debt obligations? Do you have no debt tolerance or a high level?
- Should you file your income taxes jointly or separately?
- Should your assets be held jointly or separately?

If children are involved, further questions are necessary.

- What is the amount of child support that is owed to you or that you owe? When does the obligation end?
- What are the typical monthly expenditures for your children? Do you pay costs such as private tuition, an allowance, or their car insurance?
- What are your children's financial expectations? Do they expect you to cover all their living expenses until their marriage? Do they want to live at home rent-free during college? Do they expect a new car upon high school graduation?
- What is the plan for unexpected expenses for the children, such as a study abroad trip to Spain or math tutoring?
- What about college expenses? Do you expect your children to help pay for college through work-study or by receiving grants and loans?
- Are there any other financial promises or long-term commitments that should be disclosed?

Figuring It All Out

Kayla was a young mother of toddler twins. Her first husband, Tim, had not been a good provider or partner, emotionally or financially. After 4 years, Kayla realized she needed to get out of the marriage.

A few years after divorcing Tim, Kayla met Dylan and, over time, fell in love again. Dylan also had two children, older than Kayla's, who lived with his first wife. After Kayla and Dylan wed, they kept their finances separated. They agreed that Kayla would pay for all of her children's expenses and Dylan for his out of their respective accounts. They would then divvy up shared expenses, though Dylan would shoulder more because he earned more. They also decided it would make sense to review their financial arrangements every 4 months as a regular matter, whether or not a problem arose. They might even find a better way to manage their money.

This worked fine for a while, but then a problem arose. Kayla's ex, Tim, began to skip his child support payments. Because she wanted to maintain a good relationship with her children's father, Kayla didn't confront Tim or report the nonpayment to the authorities. However, when she ran out of money for the children and asked her new husband for help, Dylan was resentful. It wasn't that he didn't like his new stepchildren; it was just that he felt that Kayla should confront Tim about the missed payments.

Meanwhile, one of Dylan's daughters decided to enroll in a community college near where Kayla and Dylan lived, and she asked whether she could move into their spare bedroom for a year. This required further discussion between the couple, centering on whether Dylan's daughter ought to pay rent. Dylan thought it was a ridiculous idea, since whatever money she would be paying for rent would have come from him, via child support payments. Kayla felt it was important to teach Dylan's daughter the important lesson that nothing in life is free. They went round and round with this argument.

After continual prodding from Dylan, Kayla reluctantly broached the subject of the missing payments with Tim. It turned out that Tim's mother was ill, and he had been helping her pay her rent while she was out of work. He had no money left for the child support payments that had originally been ordered. Kayla agreed to go back to court to amend the support agreement, with the stipulation that Tim would repay the overdue amount when his mom got back on her feet. Dylan agreed to step in to help make up the difference in the interim. He appreciated that

Tim felt responsible enough to help his mother out, even though it had economic consequences for Kayla and her kids.

Dylan and Kayla, having failed to see eye to eye on the rent issue for Dylan's daughter, challenged each other to try to come up with an alternative solution. They decided it was fair to ask if the teen would be willing to watch Kayla's children twice a week, after school. This meant Kayla could withdraw them from an expensive after-school care program. When they presented the plan to Dylan's daughter, she was more than happy to swap baby-sitting for rent, and she volunteered to add a weekend night to the schedule, in case Dylan and Kayla might like to go out on the town.

The week after Dylan's daughter moved in, Dylan and Kayla had their first Saturday night out in years. As they clinked their wine glasses in the restaurant where they'd had their first date, they resolved to never give up trying to find solutions to their financial disputes, no matter how difficult the challenges. They certainly felt their marriage was on stronger ground for having faced and resolved these two recent situations.

Commonsense Considerations

Dylan and Kayla's marriage was off to a good start because they recognized the importance of open, honest communication. Couples in blended families need to make the effort to regularly discuss their attitudes toward money and plan their finances, even if everything appears rosy. Here are some guidelines.

- Openly discuss your track record in dealing with money—both the high points and the low. When you reveal your typical spending and saving habits, your "style" of managing money will become more apparent.
- Keep children out of discussions about child support, but do talk with them, at developmentally appropriate levels, about your family's financial situation.
- Develop a spending plan and regularly assess whether you are staying within its limits. Determine financial goals and make financial decisions together as a team.
- Test various approaches to managing your money in an effort to discover the most workable arrangement. There is no set prescription for

one method that works. Whether you decide on separate accounts, joint accounts, or some combination of the two, it is a personal decision.

- Share at least some of your assets. If you keep everything in your name, your new spouse may not feel trusted or a full partner in the relationship.
- Grab the opportunity of a new marriage to break bad financial habits. Watch that you don't abuse your credit. Although it might be tempting to buy furnishings or electronics for your new home (to add your imprint), especially if it belonged to your spouse and his or her ex, impulse purchases can really add up and harm you down the road.
- Stay in regular communication with your children's other parent to discuss how to pay for expected and unexpected expenses.
- Don't harm your children's welfare by contributing less than the required amount to their child support. Conversely, don't contribute more that what is required, in an effort to assuage remorse or worry over not spending more time with your kids.
- Child support is for expenses related to the children's care and welfare and not to pay debts or expenditures incurred for the parent's personal wants.
- Resist the temptation to exert power through money. For example, visitation rights must still be honored even if a child support payment is not received. And try to respect the wishes of the other parent who might not want their child to have a certain item that the child is insisting upon.
- Review, discuss, and revise your estate plan. If you don't have a will, the state will order the distribution of your property. This may result in your stepchildren inheriting nothing. Additionally, if you die without a will and have children who are minors, their surviving biological parent may automatically assume custody, which could force the breakup of their current living arrangement.
- You should also consider whether your life insurance coverage is adequate to protect all your dependents.

See also Chapter 10, "Sharing a Financial Life" for additional ideas.

23

Losing a Spouse

Losing a spouse is devastating at any time and under any circumstances, bringing intense emotional issues related to loss, grief, and life without your partner. This new paradigm can be overwhelming. The paperwork, logistics, and financial decisions that must be dealt with after a death can initially seem unmanageable.

Experience has shown that the grieving process is best taken one day at a time. It helps, when sorting through financial matters after the death of a spouse, to divide priorities into short-term, immediate, and long-term needs. Take time. It can be difficult, if not impossible, to make sound financial decisions when you are emotionally stressed. You don't need to make every decision all at once. Sometimes it's best to postpone decisions until you've had a chance to carefully think through your goals and priorities.

Focusing on the Present

It was a huge blow to Melinda, who hadn't turned 30 yet, when her husband Charles died suddenly in a boating accident. Charles left behind not only Melinda but a daughter who had just turned 2 years old and a son who was 5. Charles was a year older than Melinda and had worked as an engineer for an architectural consulting firm. He made a comfortable salary that had enabled Melinda to work part-time and devote more time to raising their children than would have been possible if she worked 40 hours a week. He loved to sail, and everyone was at a loss to explain or understand what happened. But one day he was there—and the next, he was gone.

Charles had handled all the family's financial decisions, including their mortgage and car payments, as well as savings. He had just begun to discuss with Melinda college funds, and retirement plans were still on the horizon. He made sure there was money in their joint checking account for day-to-day expenses, like groceries and pocket money. Melinda had several credit cards that she used freely. Charles never complained about the bills.

Melinda knew Charles had a life insurance policy through work, but did not know where it was or its value. It was one of the first things she thought about once she collected herself after the accident. The stack of bills in the wooden box on Charles's desk, where she still placed his mail out of habit, was growing every day. Melinda realized she had to take some action sooner rather than later.

Melinda thought she knew where Charles had kept some of his files, so she started there. She looked for several hours, but then gave up and called the human resources coordinator at his office, apologizing for disturbing her. She learned that the policy was modest, but would probably see them through the first year at least. Charles had apparently not gotten around to updating it when their second child arrived. He did have a will, as well, that directed that the bulk of his estate go to Melinda.

Melinda did not know if Charles was entitled to any pension, so she took the opportunity to ask the human resources contact about this. Apparently, Charles had not worked long enough at the firm to qualify. Going through his mail, however, she found a statement for a 401(k) plan from a previous employer. Melinda hadn't known about that retirement account. She contacted the company, but discovered that since the plan had been established in Charles's bachelor days, he had named his mother as the beneficiary and never changed it.

Melinda needed immediate cash flow to replace her husband's paycheck. To get access to her husband's life insurance policy, she went through the process for claiming benefits. This involved providing a certified copy of Charles's death certificate and other identifying information in order to prove that she was the bona fide beneficiary of the life insurance policy.

Melinda received the insurance check within 2 weeks. Having the money was comforting, and she was able to use it to pay some of the bills that had been piling up. Once she had done that, however, there remained a substantial amount, and she wasn't quite sure what to do with it. Invest it? Put it in savings? Buy herself something nice to cheer her up? She tried to deposit it into Charles's investment account, but found it was frozen. His financial advisor indicated he was more than happy to open an account in her name, though.

Meanwhile, she was trying to track down other sources of income. Melinda was entitled to Charles's Social Security benefits because her dependent children were under age 18. When she herself reached retirement age, she would receive her own benefits. She called Charles's company again to inquire about any other benefits or assets and was told, gently, there weren't any.

Three weeks after Charles's death, Melinda started to feel disoriented and anxious. The funeral was over; the condolence cards that had arrived by the dozens at first were now only a trickle. She had scores of thank-you notes to write to people who had come by to offer their support and to others who had made donations to Charles's favorite charities. Her sister, who had immediately flown in from across the country to be at her side, had returned to her own family.

The numbness and shock of Charles's sudden death, which initially allowed her to function on automatic pilot, was wearing off. Melinda felt completely alone. She knew she had to stay strong for the children, but the more she tried, the weaker she felt. And there seemed to be so many details to take care of. Her youngest child continued to ask where dada was, and although she had tried to explain it didn't seem to be sinking in. Finally, she reached for the phone to call a referral service for a child psychologist and suddenly realized she hadn't made any insurance payments over the previous months. Was the family even covered under Charles's health insurance anymore?

It wasn't as if she needed advice, either. Between Charles's accountant, his best friend, the estate attorney, and his brother, she felt like she was getting advice from all directions. Everyone was trying his or her best, to be sure, but she couldn't sort through it all clearly, and it seemed like sometimes the information she got was contradictory.

One afternoon, a neighbor stopped by with a casserole for Melinda and the children. The youngest was napping and Melinda was sitting at Charles's desk staring at the piles of bills when Brooke walked in. Brooke was an older woman who herself had been widowed just 2 years earlier. Immediately recognizing Melinda's pain, she sat in the roomy leather armchair across from the desk and spoke with Melinda in a low, soothing voice. She told her there was absolutely no reason to feel pressured about making a definitive plan for the future. She gently asked if Melinda had enough cash to cover the monthly essentials: mortgage, groceries, the car, and insurance.

Melinda nodded. The life insurance would pay for these basics over the next few months to come, even if costs rose. Brooke then asked if Melinda had uncovered all sources of income, like Social Security and pensions. Melinda said she had found out that Charles had no pension, and she had applied for his Social Security benefits, though she hadn't received a payment yet. "Well, then," Brooke told her, "you are all set for now." So long as the family's basic financial needs were taken care of— bills paid, income hunted down, the children's cares secured, Social Security being processed, and Charles's will moving through the legal system—Melinda really shouldn't worry about much for the next 6 months. That should give her plenty of time to meet with her advisors individually and maybe even arrange a group meeting or two to go through her options.

Melinda immediately felt like a huge weight had been lifted. She got up to walk Brooke to the door, stopping along the way to put the casserole in the kitchen. She thanked her neighbor for the thoughtful gifts— dinner for the family and the valuable advice.

Commonsense Considerations

Melinda would have appreciated having a list of financial tasks to follow in the first days and weeks after her husband's death. Here's a checklist you can use if you're faced with the death of a spouse.

- Notify the life insurance company of the death. File a claim according to their instructions.
- Make a three-column list of your immediate expenses (like mortgage, car payments, household, credit card payments), your intermediate financial obligations (insurance payments, tuition), and your long-term responsibilities (college funds, retirement). As you determine your financial position, use this list to prioritize your needs and decision-making.
- Locate and centralize important papers: bank and investment accounts, lists of property, income tax returns, insurance policies (life, health, home, and auto), marriage and birth certificates, birth certificates of any minor children, Social Security numbers of all immediate family members, and W-2 forms.
- Review insurance coverage and make sure there are no gaps—check life, auto, or medical—now that you are on your own. Find out if you will need to pay premiums on health insurance coverage offered through your spouse's employer to ensure continuity of coverage.
- Request at least a half-dozen death certificates from the funeral director. You will need these to apply for benefits.
- Contact Social Security and the Veterans Administration (if appropriate). They won't contact you.
- Call your spouse's employer to discuss pensions or other benefits due and status of health insurance.
- Inform all creditors of the death. Follow up in writing and keep copies.
- Cancel credit cards in your spouse's name.

Bud's Big Plans

Bud and Miriam met and married in their late 40s. It was a second marriage for both. Each had grown children living on their own. Right after they were married, Miriam inherited a small manufacturing business from her father, took the helm, and ran it successfully for more than 20 years. When she died following a brief illness, her will named Bud, who had by then retired from his teaching job, as the sole beneficiary of her entire estate. Bud became the owner, free and clear, of the house where

Miriam had raised her children during her first marriage and of her father's business. Although he knew that the business was his wife's largest asset, they had never discussed any details of its day-to-day operations. Suddenly, he had a business to run or sell and lots of pressure from many sides to make numerous decisions on complex financial matters.

Miriam's investors pressed Bud to make an immediate decision about selling the business. They were concerned that without Miriam's stewardship, the company might fail. Her children, on the other hand, were terribly upset at the thought of a sale, but neither of them was in a position to help run the company. Bud found out from Miriam's attorney that he had a full year from his wife's death to sort out what was best. By waiting, he might be able to find some advisors who would undertake an independent valuation of the company, rather than simply accept the offer that certain investors had initially proposed. And there was the question of what to do about the house.

The first thing Bud did, then, was to assure Miriam's children, his own children, and the five employees of the business that he wasn't going to make any major changes for at least 6 months. The general manager of the company told him that even without Miriam's leadership, the company would stay open and profitable for that period of time.

Because Miriam had known that her illness might be terminal, she had been able to make some advance preparations. She had explained to Bud her filing systems, so after her death he was able to access copies of their insurance policies, financial accounts, deeds, vehicle registrations, and income tax returns for both the business and their household. Reviewing these documents, Bud confirmed that the bulk of his wife's assets were tied up in the business.

Bud's day-to-day living expenses were not a great concern, as he had his own pension and his and Miriam's Social Security checks, and the house was mortgage-free. He was more focused on the long-term question of whether he would have enough to last through his lifetime. Although he was in his 70s, he was in good health. His own mother had lived to age 100. He also thought he would like to contribute to his future grandchildren's college expenses. And he and Miriam had volunteered for local charities for several years. Now he might be in a position to make a difference through donations.

While there were many professionals available to Bud to help analyze his long-term needs and resources, Bud decided to try to work
independently on a plan. He took a few books out of the library, and,
following their checklists, made an inventory of all his assets, including the house and the business, which he valued based on a number
provided by the company's bookkeeper. Then he made a list of all his
expenses, real and anticipated. He realized that after he sold the business, he was going to have a substantial lump sum (this is sometimes
called a "liquidity event") that he should not just deposit in his bank
account. He might be facing some tax issues as well as choices about
how to invest this money so that it would provide income for his lifetime. He was also thinking he might sell the house and find smaller,
more manageable living quarters, perhaps even in another town, which
would further add to his cash pot.

All the while, Bud's own children and his wife's were in constant
touch with him, offering their support and opinions. Their interest in his
future plans ranged from benevolent curiosity to nagging that annoyed
him. Bud decided he needed to find a way to communicate quickly and
fairly, so he signed up for a course at the library to learn to use e-mail
and indulged himself in his first major purchase since his wife's death:
Internet DSL service. By establishing a group list, he was able to let all
the children know at the same time what he was doing. He also for-
warded cartoons and jokes that he found amusing, so that his correspon-
dences weren't all business. The children enjoyed the "Bud-o-grams"
they received from him nearly every day and openly aired their opinions
and concerns through this forum.

Through the local Chamber of Commerce, Bud was able to find the
name of a professional who would undertake an appraisal of his wife's
company. He signed a contract to start this process. Then, he asked a
family friend who was a licensed real estate broker for her assessment
about the value of the house. She promised to work something up for
him in a few days.

Through his research, Bud decided that the best way to set up a college fund for his theoretical grandchildren would be through a trust that
he could administer through his lifetime. He was also starting to feel
anxious about tax issues. He knew he was obligated to file a return for

the state within 9 months of Miriam's passing, but he wasn't sure whether that would be his only responsibility. It seemed to be the right time to start to consult some professionals.

Six months after Miriam's death, Bud had the completed appraisal of his wife's business. The general manager of the company approached Bud and told him that the employees were interested in buying it themselves, but needed some time to come up with a financial plan. Bud told him this would be fine. He was even willing to cut them a deal, since he knew his wife would have been happy to have the business continue on in familiar hands. He planned to start the educational trust with about half the proceeds and to invest the other half in a conservative portfolio that would provide him with money for his living expenses. His attorney and financial planner stepped in to help him realize this plan.

As for the house, Bud informed his children and stepchildren that he had decided to put it on the market in the spring and move to an apartment once it was sold. He hoped that before this happened everyone would make at least one visit to discuss what furniture they might like from the house. He also told them that he had decided to divide the money he received from the house sale five ways, so that each of them could get a share. It was his hope (but not his requirement) that they use the money to support or supplement their own housing needs, either to buy their own houses or to renovate their existing homes.

"Miriam loved this house and it was a special place for her," he wrote to them all in an e-mail. "I'd like to think that she is helping each of you create your own special places too." With his share, he planned to start a Charitable Remainder Unitrust. This is a trust that will allow Bud to receive income for the rest of his life from a contribution of cash or assets (such as stock or real estate) to a charity, with certain tax benefits as well. After his death, the money would be the charity's to keep.

Bud was satisfied with the outcome of his plan for Miriam's money, and he felt she would have been too. He missed Miriam terribly, but felt her values would live on through the college fund and the charitable contributions. This way he was able to honor her in death as much as he had loved her in life.

Commonsense Considerations

As Bud discovered, even with some instructions, long-term planning can be challenging after the death of a spouse. Once your short-term needs are satisfied, you need to make a long-term plan that will accommodate your priorities. Where you want to live, whether you wish (or need) to work or not, and how you can protect the assets you have are all part of this plan. You must also think through your financial obligations to your children and your own estate plan. Here is a checklist that will help you organize these tasks.

- **Review your financial plan relative to where your life is today.** Review it periodically to make sure it stays relevant to your changing life.
- **Find trusted financial professionals.** Listen to what they say, and ask questions. If you get conflicting advice, get a second opinion. Get a third opinion if you need to.
- **Prepare for your own potential long-term-care needs.** If you expect to be responsible for others, such as your children or your own parents, consider how you would pay for theirs. Long-term-care insurance may offer a good alternative to raiding retirement savings or having to rely on your children. Speak with a knowledgeable professional about long-term-care and life insurance policies. It's important to select the right policies and coverage amounts for you and to review those policies regularly.
- **Get your own affairs in order.** After having been through this process, you will have a greater understanding of how certain planning techniques could have eased the transition for you, and you will now be able to make those plans for your heirs. Make sure your estate plan and other key documents, such as your will, living will, and healthcare proxy, are current. Make sure any 401(k) plan, IRA, and insurance beneficiary designations are also up-to-date.
- **Protect your estate by developing an estate plan.** This will help to minimize taxes and make sure your assets are distributed according to your wishes. The marital deduction allows one to pass an unlimited amount of property to a spouse, free of estate tax. However, upon

death of the surviving spouse, taxes will become due on the value of the estate.

- **Gift away what you don't need.** Find out how much you are entitled to transfer annually to an individual without incurring any federal gift tax.
- **Speak regularly to your financial professionals.** This will help you keep on top of things and continue to educate you about financial matters.

CHAPTER **24**

Managing Inherited Money

Inherited money is inherently different. Deep, complex emotions are often attached to it, reflecting childhood memories, traditions, values, and relationships. To many, an inheritance is more than just money, jewelry, or an equity portfolio. It is often impossible to separate an inheritance from the memories connected with it. This is what makes inherited money so unique. It is a link to the past and, sometimes, a hope for the future.

The dynamics of inheritances have changed in recent years, thanks to demographic and economic factors. People are living longer lives. Today, a 65-year-old can have a reasonable expectation of living another 20 years, which means another 20 years of living expenses and possibly high-end healthcare and supervised-living costs as well. Not only is money being passed on to older heirs, they are also receiving less. In addition, the intricacies of inheritance taxes have affected inheritance patterns. More people are gifting their money during their lifetimes.

While occasionally benefactors create trusts that give specific instructions or rules for dispensing money, most inheritances come with no strings attached. An inheritance is usually a gift, to be spent as the heir sees fit. What you do with it depends on several factors, including how much has been left to you and in what form (cash or non-cash assets or valuables, including businesses and real estate), how old you are, your present financial position, and those deep-rooted values that are passed on with the legacy.

Matt's Legacy

Matt was in his mid-40s when his Great-aunt Ethel passed away. It came as a complete surprise when he received notice he would be receiving $400,000 from her estate. He had no idea she had that kind of money and even less of an idea why she would leave it to him.

After speaking with the attorney for his aunt's estate, Matt learned it might take a year or even more before he would see the check for the money. Although the lawyer advised him not to count his chickens, Matt did not heed his advice. He spent the next year whipping out his credit cards and taking out loans to make purchases that he would never before have considered.

He bought a sports car right off the showroom floor (even though he had a perfectly serviceable sedan), a huge high-tech flat screen television that required expensive additional cable service, and a time-share at a ski resort in the Rocky Mountains. He had an architect draw up plans for an addition to his house and a swimming pool, and he signed up for a two-week Mediterranean cruise. He began to anxiously look forward to the day his Aunt Ethel's check would arrive. Within just a few months, he was having a hard time juggling the payments for these new acquisitions and slipped behind several months in paying his mortgage. When finally the check arrived, Matt deposited it into his bank account and took the rest of the day off from work to decide what to do next.

Matt organized his bills into piles. With a sigh of relief, he wrote checks to pay off the credit card debt that he had run up over the last few months refurbishing his wardrobe and paying for expensive dinners for friends. He then caught up on his mortgage payments for the current month and for the 3 months for which he was delinquent. His car loan was next to go. The cruise required payment in full, and there were other, miscellaneous bills he had amassed in anticipation of receiving his money. His legacy was dwindling fast.

With all good intentions of doing something sensible with the balance of his inheritance, Matt made an appointment to meet with his aunt's longtime financial advisor. But when he arrived at Joel's office he was disappointed at how shabby it was and found Joel himself to be somewhat of an antique. When he mentioned some of the investments he thought he might like to make, Joel shook his head slowly in disapproval. He recommended a far more conservative portfolio that had the potential to result in enough income in 20 years for Matt to retire comfortably. But it would also require foregoing the new additions to his house and a return to a more modest lifestyle than Matt had been leading, which Matt was unwilling to do. He thanked Joel for his time and headed to the door, never intending to return to this office.

On his way out, he met Joel's associate, an energetic woman named Grace, who was just leaving for a lunchtime jog. She apologized for being in exercise clothes and said there was a health club in the basement of the building, where she would shower after running. Joel felt more of a connection with Grace than he had with Joel, and he mentally made a note to call her up soon to discuss moving his inheritance from his bank savings account to an investment portfolio. But for the moment, he had a contractor to meet, so that conversation would have to wait.

Construction began on Matt's house and he moved to a luxury hotel for a month to escape the noise and dirt. It took longer and cost more than he had ever imagined. It was completed the day before he left on vacation. He had a great time and tried not to think about the remark one of his neighbors made before he left, questioning why Matt had to go to the Mediterranean to swim when he now had a Mediterranean-like pool right in his backyard. After he returned from his vacation, he paid the bills for the contractor and realized he had about half of his original inheritance left to his name.

Out of the blue, he received a call from Grace, the financial advisor he'd met briefly in Joel's office. She said Joel had asked her to call to see how he was doing. Since Matt had never acted on his intention to invest the balance of his money, he told Grace he would come in and meet with her.

If Joel was surprised to see Matt again, he didn't show it. He told Matt that he was in good hands with Grace and retreated to his office. After exchanging pleasantries about their mutual jogging habit, Grace asked Matt how he felt his investments were doing. Sheepishly, he confessed he really hadn't done much with the money except spend it. Of the original $400,000 he inherited, he only had $200,000 left.

After that stunning revelation, Grace calmly worked out a plan to recoup his inheritance. She showed him simple calculations that demonstrated his remaining $200,000, invested for 19 years earning an average annual 10 percent rate of return, could grow to be slightly more than $400,000. Matt was stunned that it would take 19 years to recoup the sum he had received just 19 months earlier. He wondered if it even made any sense to bother investing it.

Grace recognized that Matt might not have the patience or the discipline to wait for the long-term results of his investment, so she offered suggestions that might help him. For example, he could accelerate the growth of his money by arranging for a small but consistent automatic deposit from his bank account to his investment account every month, right after he was paid. She also suggested that once every year, Matt arrange for a distribution out of his invested funds of a fixed amount that he was free to spend as he wished. Although this payout would slow the growth of his assets, she felt it would provide a critical incentive for Matt to keep saving without feeling totally deprived of enjoying his money.

Matt hesitantly agreed to give it a try. The first year was rough—the stock market was flat and there wasn't much to show for what Matt felt were deprivations. He was tempted to pull the money out of the investment account to pay off his credit card bills, which were looming large yet again. But Matt felt he owed it to himself—and his late aunt—to give it another year. At the end of the second year, the results were more satisfying, and Matt was able to use his distribution to subsidize his holiday shopping list. Using it this way helped him avoid running up his credit.

He also started to show some interest in the investments in the portfolio that Grace had set up. Every few months, when his statements arrived, he called her to discuss them. He set up an online tracking system and told Grace that he was reading, from cover to cover, the prospectus materials as well as the annual reports of the companies in which he owned shares. He even voted on the proxy ballots, which were sent out once a year before the annual meetings of the companies in which he owned shares. The proxy forms are mailed to shareholders, usually along with the Annual Report, and list the names of directors hoping to take a seat on the company Board of Directors. They also outline issues that shareholders may have a say in, such as compensation packages for executives.

The third year, when Grace called to tell Matt it was time to issue his distribution, he asked her to wait a minute. Her heart sank. She wouldn't have been the least bit surprised if he had directed her to liquidate the account. Instead, Matt told Grace he'd rather leave the distribution money in the account this year. He felt his debts were under control and he had enough disposable income to pass up the distribution. It would do him more good, he told her, to keep it in the portfolio. And, by the way, he added, he had a few ideas he'd like her to look into for investments in the coming year.

When Grace told Joel about this conversation, he thought to himself, but did not say aloud, "Matt's aunt would have been proud of him."

Commonsense Considerations

If you are fortunate enough to receive a substantial inheritance—one in excess of your annual earnings, for example—you should consider seeking the help of professionals to explain your options. If the money is invested, you will want to touch base with the financial advisor, though you are not under any obligation to use this individual for advice. However, the financial advisor could be very instrumental in helping you transfer or liquidate the portfolio.

If your windfall is a somewhat smaller sum, you might want to consider using it in one of these ways.

- **Pay off some credit card balances.** This way, your benefactor has helped you lower your debt burden and improve your credit profile.
- **Jump-start a special savings fund.** Even if the inheritance isn't enough to buy the car of your dreams, it could be the beginning of your saving to do so.
- **Form a family investment fund.** If you inherit securities out of a large portfolio that's been divided up, you might see if other inheritors would like to pool their shares. You will have to contact an attorney to

draw up the partnership papers and find a financial advisor to help manage the fund.

- **Consider making a charitable donation in the name of the deceased.** You may wish to do this with all or part of the money.

Learning on the Job

Like many women of her generation, Hannah had never taken a very active role in managing money. Her husband had handled all the family finances. When he left her a widow in her late 60s, she felt awkward and ignorant about managing their large investment portfolio. She was further intimidated because friends and family often talked about what a brilliant stock-picker her husband had been and how he had grown a modest sum into a family fortune. She felt she could never live up to his talents and was likely to lose the entire amount if she took over managing it.

Lots of Hannah's friends had suggestions about ways she should handle these new funds. Hannah confided to Stephen, her husband's best friend and financial advisor, that she was confused and scared. She realized she had been left this money to provide her with financial security. Meanwhile, she was feeling very insecure. Having to deal with so much at once was overwhelming.

Stephen invited Hannah to come to his office, where he described his firm's financial planning process. He suggested that Hannah might want to start from the beginning, rather than just jump in and try to manage the money without a solid base of understanding about how it all worked. He also thought she might do better to start fresh with a financial planner and new financial advisor, though he was happy to help her out any time she needed him.

The process, Stephen explained, would entail a series of meetings and discussions that would lead to a written financial plan with detailed recommendations. The objective would be to teach Hannah to make informed decisions based on her own specific financial objectives, risk tolerance, time frame, and investable assets. Once a financial plan is determined, picking the specific investments naturally falls into place.

Stephen related to Hannah that this process was a good way to counteract the common tendency to quickly invest the funds.

At Hannah's second meeting Stephen introduced her to Sarah, a colleague who was a financial planner. Sarah encouraged Hannah to openly explore her feelings about her new financial position and what the inheritance truly meant to her and the people and organizations in her life. This was the first time that anyone had ever asked Hannah questions about what role money and investments played in her life. What was important to her? If money were no object, what would she want to see happen? Would she like to live in a larger or more expensive home? Would she like to be able to provide homes for her daughters and education funds for her grandchildren? What about providing for charitable organizations she cared about?

Sarah probed further, asking about Hannah's past experience with investments. Were there specific types of investments that she considered off-limits based on past experience or what she had heard from others? Were there companies she preferred to invest in—or to not invest in, due to personal feelings about their products?

Living expenses were also covered in this meeting. Sarah and Hannah put pencil to paper to figure out how much it currently cost her to live, how much she spent for housing, travel, food, home upkeep, and clothing, and how much more she would like to spend in various areas if she could afford it. The balance of the time they had together allowed Sarah to talk about safe ways to temporarily invest the funds so that they would earn a competitive investment return while giving Hannah time to evaluate her choices.

A third meeting was arranged. When Hannah arrived, she realized she was already feeling more comfortable about being able to take charge of the family finances. Sarah presented a first draft of a financial model that estimated annual income, annual expenses, and net worth year-by-year. This was based on a set of initial assumptions. They then discussed how adjusting these assumptions would affect the conclusions. What if Hannah increased her current spending level? What if she wanted to purchase a second home, a place where she could invite her daughters and their families on vacations for many years in the future? What if the stock market experienced a period of underperformance relative to the historical experience? Or what if she chose to invest in a relatively conservative manner?

Sarah outlined in detail the various types of risk associated with investments, such as principal risk, or the risk of losing the original amount invested. Separate from earnings, liquidity risk stems from the lack of marketability of an investment that cannot be bought or sold quickly enough to prevent or reduce a loss. There were also interest rate risk and inflation risk, both of which Hannah was able to grasp quickly. This led to a discussion about diversified portfolios.

While she and Sarah discussed risk management as part of a comprehensive financial plan, Hannah raised a question about adjusting her present life insurance and liability policies. Sarah was able to offer advice, but also suggested Hannah consult with the family's insurance broker for further ideas. Finally, they came around to talking about Hannah's estate planning. Hannah noted that her family had worked too hard to simply let the government decide how their wealth would ultimately be distributed. She was also firmly convinced that once the portfolio was established, she wanted to bring her daughters in to meet Sarah, so that when they faced their own inheritances, they would already be knowledgeable about the process.

Commonsense Considerations

Receiving an inheritance should be an impetus for you to review your own estate plan, whether or not you think there will be money left from your legacy to pass on to your own family. An estate plan is much more than just a will, though this document is an important part of it. Hannah already knew she needed to reconsider her insurance requirements. Here's what else she—and you—should do:

- **Reexamine and, if necessary, rewrite your will.** Are you still confident about your choices for executor, guardian of any minor children, and trustees of any funds you have put in trusts? Are there new charitable contributions you might like to make, or different instructions you would like to leave for distribution of your assets?
- **Review trusts you have established**, both under your will and external to it.

- **Put in order other estate paperwork.** This should include your healthcare directive, power of attorney, or living will.
- **Check your beneficiary forms.** This money will be passed directly to your designees and is not handled through your estate.
- **Make a plan to cover your funeral expenses.** And be specific about your wishes for a service and type of burial.
- **Collect, copy, and store all documents related to your estate.** They should be kept in a safe but accessible place. Don't lock them in a safe deposit box, since your survivors may not have access to that until several weeks after your death.

PART 3 SUMMARY

The third and final part of *The Citi Commonsense Money Guide* considers several real life situations that could throw even the best intentioned and designed financial plans off track. You may have diligently worked your way out of debt (or successfully avoided going overboard in the first place) and made yourself a reasonable financial plan. You may have set up a workable budget to help you reach your goals and built yourself a firm financial foundation. You may have adequate insurance to protect you and your family, a manageable mortgage on your home, a college fund for the kids, and a retirement plan for yourself. And then . . . out of nowhere comes an event that threatens to undo years of hard work. The question is, how do you prepare for the unforeseeable?

The unforeseeable might not necessarily be negative, but it will affect your finances. Here are a few suggestions. You should try to stay flexible. Maybe your budget can be adjusted to accommodate the new expense. Maybe it will be 3 years, not 2, before you get that new car.

Saving for That Rainy Day

Another trick to weathering financial storms, even those that seem to come out of nowhere, is to consider maintaining an adequate emergency savings fund. This may be easier said than done. Most experts recommend a minimum of 3 months' living expenses be kept for emergencies, and this can be a substantial amount to accumulate. And while it may not be enough to cover your costs in a true catastrophe, it is a start.

Louise had a hard time saving for her emergency fund, but was dedicated to the notion of having a cushion. Although the way she figured out how to do this, by making sure she would receive a once-a-year tax refund, meant she had to forfeit interest she might have potentially earned on setting aside the money herself, she preferred to use the government as her piggy bank, and this worked well for her. While it wasn't a stretch for Ray and Meg to set aside savings, they were concerned that this money shouldn't lie dormant, so they explored investment options that would put their money to work while keeping it close at hand should they need it.

Happy Holidays on a Budget

Holidays can create special stress on budgets. Some families are able to absorb the impact of several hundred (or perhaps even thousands) of dollars of extra spending over the holidays, and others find themselves in a debt hole that may take them months to climb out of. Anticipating these expenses is the smartest approach; however, even then you can get caught short. Stephanie's family had experienced hard times that depleted their holiday funds, so she and her husband had to scramble late in the year to make sure they would be able to purchase presents for their children. To make up the difference, Stephanie found non-monetary ways to celebrate.

Special events, such as anniversaries, big-number birthdays, and graduations are typically foreseeable, as are weddings. However, they also can fall into the category of budget busters since they have strong emotional connections that might push the limits of financial sensibility. Carlos and Belkis had started to plan financially for the two events they had known were coming up in the year ahead when a third, their daughter's wedding, dropped on them out of nowhere. Through their measured response to the three-way tug-of-war on their financial resources, they were able to consider all the options and make the best decision possible for all involved.

Out of Work—But Not Down and Out

Losing your job can be an emotionally traumatic event—and one that is financially devastating as well. Jessica's experience, though, demonstrates a rational reaction to the inevitable. It involved cutting back and preparing for her period of unemployment as thoughtfully as she might prepare for a special event like a wedding or large purchase. Planning, budgeting, and saving were all called into action. Her former colleagues gave her additional insight into possible benefits she might ask for, and as she discovered, if you don't ask, you won't get. It wasn't even a matter of landing on her feet—Jessica stayed on her feet throughout her period of unemployment and when she became reemployed was able to pick up where she left off.

Sharon wasn't so fortunate. Her debts continued to burden her even once she started working again. She had to face up to them and figure out a way to get them paid off. Only by confronting her debts in black and white on paper, through making a list, was she able to start on a path of rehabilitation.

Watching Your Wallet

Pickpockets have been around for centuries. Modern-day pickpockets can take more than just your wallet—they may assume your identity. Credit fraud and identity theft are crimes where you, and your financial stability, are the victim. These are crimes on the rise, and there are several ways to reduce your vulnerability. By the time this book is published, it is inevitable that new forms of credit fraud or identity theft may emerge, so it is important to continue to be on the lookout so as not to become a target.

It was devastating to Sheila to realize that her trusted companion was stealing from her, using her credit cards and forging checks. Her story illustrates yet again why it is so important to stay on top of your finances on a monthly basis. In Gary's story, he was victimized by a career criminal. But this didn't make the experience any easier. He still had to devote time and energy to figuring out what accounts had been infiltrated and make sure that his credit report would not be marred. And Cynthia learned to be a better watchdog over her personal information—and reputation.

Surviving Splitsville

Divorce can, and often does, wreak havoc on the best of financial plans. Claire's divorce left her marooned emotionally and financially, but she was able to catch up on a lifetime of financial ignorance through hard work and good counseling from a financial advisor. It's critical to separate your finances as quickly and thoroughly as possible in a divorce, and be systematic about removing your spouse's name from important documents that might have financial consequences, such as retirement plans, insurance policies, and power of attorney forms.

Neil's experience was further compounded by his wishful thinking that there might be a reconciliation if he ceded to his wife's demands. Instead, he was left with virtually nothing and would be spending the next several years of his life rebuilding what took just a few months to dissolve.

Life in a Blender

When one or both partners in a marriage or cohabitation arrangement have previously been married, and may even have children from that prior union, financial mayhem can take hold. Second marriages, it appears, are even more fragile than first ones. Nancy and Joe needed to work through a number of financial issues (as well as emotional ones) that they might have been better off confronting before they tied the knot, but were able to make up for lost time thanks to their determination to make their marriage work.

While it may seem decidedly unromantic, previously married individuals may want to sit down and run through a financial checklist before remarrying, just to make sure that everything is out in the open about individual financial responsibilities. If children are involved, even more questions should be discussed. Kayla and Dylan were able to weather their financial difficulties because they were candid about their differing points of view and willing to compromise. In their case, things worked out even better than either of them might have foreseen.

Losing a Loved One

Losing a spouse to death is yet another life event with deeply entangled emotional and financial implications. Melinda, a young widow, was advised to deal first with her immediate financial needs before facing the family's long-term plans. Perhaps these would need considerable adjustment—perhaps not. But she would be on presumably more stable footing 6 months or even a year down the road to make long-term decisions and would do best to separate the financial issues accordingly.

For Bud, circumstances were somewhat different. He had his long-term planning to contend with rather quickly, since his wife's business needed to be addressed. Bud was able to educate himself thoroughly in order to make the best decisions possible that both benefited him and also honored his late wife's memory.

Coming Into Money

Lastly, inheriting money, stocks, or property might seem to be an event outside the scope of this section dealing with financial curveballs. But this too can throw off your financial planning and must be accommodated. Matt's extravagant spending turned out to extend far beyond the cash his aunt left him. Through the experience, he learned how to invest responsibly. As for Hannah, her husband's estate required her to think through how she wanted to live the rest of her own life.

It would be impossible to capture every circumstance that threatens to destabilize your financial life, but these few have some common themes that should help you meet any situation confidently. Preparation and facing the situation are important. Above all else, educating yourself through whatever means are most efficient and comfortable can help you make the right choices and get back on track.

GLOSSARY

30-day-late payment
> A payment that is made 30 days after the due date.

401(k) plan
> A tax-deferred savings plan set up by an employer to allow employees to save for retirement; may also include contributions from employers. Income taxes are paid upon withdrawal, usually after age 59. Early withdrawal can trigger a penalty tax. 401(k) is the IRS section that describes the program.

529 Savings Plan
> Every state offers one or more 529 Savings Plan choices that allow parents, grandparents, or others to make tax-free contributions for college tuition. Some 529 plans enable families to lock-in future tuition at in-state public colleges at current prices. Others allow savings of up to $250,000 per child for tuition at any college, in or out of state. 529 is the section of the IRS code that provides the special tax incentives to fund education.

Accountant
> A professional who is trained to document, record, and analyze financial information in order to provide accurate payroll, tax, income, and other reports.

Account number

The unique number that identifies a bank, brokerage, charge, credit, or other financial account.

ACH transaction

A payment that uses Automatic Clearing House (ACH), the national electronic network that banks and other financial institutions use to record credits and debits relating to funds transferred between financial accounts.

Activate credit card or credit line

Call, complete an online registration, or otherwise fulfill a creditor's requirements for making a credit account active and able to be used.

Adjustable life insurance (See Universal life insurance)

Adjusted gross income (AGI)

The income used to calculate federal income tax liability, after approved deductions and before standardized or itemized deductions and exemptions. Approved deductions include 401(k), individual retirement account, Simplified Employee Pension (SEP), Keogh or other qualified retirement or education contributions, alimony, capital losses up to $3,000, unreimbursed business expenses, and interest penalties from premature withdrawals from a certificate of deposit or tax-deferred savings. Once the AGI is determined, medical expenses (including health insurance), as well as state, local, and real estate taxes and other itemized deductions are subtracted from it to determine federal income tax liability.

Advance (Also called Cash advance, See also Claim advance)

A loan or payment made against a credit line or payout from an insurance claim, payroll, bonus, or other funds that will be due in the future.

AGI (See Adjusted gross income)

Amortization

To pay off a loan or other debt, such as a mortgage, by making regular payments each month or on some other agreed upon schedule. Each payment includes funds to pay a percentage of the debt plus the interest on that debt. Usually the payments at the beginning of the payoff period include more interest than principal.

Annual Fee

The cost or charge for having credit available to use for a year. Some credit cards charge an annual fee while others do not. The annual fee is in addition to the cost of using credit, interest.

Annual percentage rate (APR)

The cost of credit on a yearly basis, expressed as a percentage rather than a dollar amount.

Asset

Something of value. Personal assets are divided into two main categories: liquid assets (cash-on-hand and savings) and capital assets (investments including 401(k) retirement funds, a house, or other valuable property).

Asset allocation

A key concept in financial planning and money management, asset allocation is a method of using various types of investments to improve the chance of profit, protect against loss, and preserve the current value of assets. Asset allocation begins with a thorough review of a person's financial goals, risk aversion, and investment timeline. Next, it is important to make a through analysis of current assets, including income and savings, stocks, bonds, real estate, art, or other valuables. Finally, an asset allocation plan is created to use current assets or replace some of them, as necessary, with other investments to meet financial goals. Asset allocation does not guarantee a profit or protect against a loss.

ATM (automatic teller machine)

A computer that allows consumers to learn balances, get cash, make deposits, and do other banking chores. ATMs are located in banks, stores, malls, drive-in centers, colleges, hospitals, airports, service stations, and many other locations for 24-hour convenience. If you use an ATM that is not sponsored by your bank, there may be a fee for using it.

Automobile insurance

Insurance to cover the expenses or losses related to an automobile accident or malfunction, including health, life, and damages to driver's car or other passengers and vehicles involved in an accident or malfunction.

Average annual return

The rate of return on investments averaged over a specific period of time (example: the previous 20 years). It is determined by adding together the rates of return for each year and dividing by the number of years in the calculation.

Balance sheet

A financial snapshot of assets and liabilities to show net worth at a specific point in time. A personal balance sheet would include all checking and savings account balances and investments, as well as loans and other debts on a certain date, such as the end of a quarter or year.

Bankruptcy

When a borrower cannot pay debts and cannot work out a payment plan with credit card companies or other creditors, he/she can file with the court to be released from debts. This is a serious situation that may have profound effects on the consumer. It may require the sale of the debtor's property and/or a court-approved plan for repayment of debts. It can also reduce or eliminate, for many years, the consumer's ability to get a job, buy a car or home, or get additional credit.

Banks

Corporations chartered by state or federal government to offer numerous financial services, such as checking and savings accounts, loans, and safe deposit boxes. The Federal Deposit Insurance Corporation (FDIC) insures accounts in federally chartered banks.

Bank statement

A monthly record of all activity within an account, provided by the bank.

Beneficiary

An individual or group named to receive the income, funds, or payment from an investment, trust, retirement, or insurance fund. Example: A husband may name his wife as the beneficiary of his life insurance policy.

Bill (See also Treasury bill)

A statement that explains the payment terms and conditions, including current or past due amounts, total debt, due date, annual percentage rate, and other details.

Billing dispute resolution

The procedures involved in reporting, checking, verifying, and solving billing questions or problems. It is important to follow these procedures to clear up billing disputes quickly and efficiently. Problem-solving procedures are available on the back of each billing statement, on the creditor's Web site, through the toll-free consumer service information telephone line, and on the application forms signed to open the account.

Billing statement (See Bill)

Bond

One of several investment instruments sold to consumers and business investors. A bond is a long-term financial instrument that is designed to raise capital for a business, a charitable or educational institution, or local, state, and federal government agencies. Investors buy bonds (lend money) for one year or longer, in exchange for the promise by the issuer to pay interest (coupon rate) and return the principal (loaned amount) at maturity (when the bond expires). Some bonds pay interest on a regular basis, usually every 6 months; others do not pay interest but are purchased at a "discount price," and the mature bond pays the "face value" price at maturity. Government bonds may be exempt from federal, state, and local taxes. Bonds are rated for investment quality based on tax status, issuer's credit, maturity, and many other factors. A bondholder does not have ownership rights, like a stockholder does, but bondholders do have preferred status in a claim against a bond issuer's assets, in the event of default. Bonds can be an important part of a consumer's financial portfolio because they can offer regular income with limited risk.

Budget

A financial plan that summarizes future income and expenditures over a period of time.

Cancelled check

A check that has been stamped to show that the payee has received the designated amount from the bank and that amount has been deducted from the account holder's checking account.

Capital gain

A positive difference between an asset's price when bought and its price when or if sold; the opposite of capital loss.

Capital loss

A negative difference between an asset's price when bought and its price when or if sold; the opposite of capital gain.

Cash advance (See Advance)

Cashier's check

A check that is paid for by a customer—with either cash or funds transferred from a savings or checking account—then issued by a bank, drawn on the bank's own funds and signed by the cashier. A cashier's check is often required for large financial transactions where the title to property is transferred. Example: A cashier's check is required by the seller to finalize the closing of a home sale.

Cash value

The savings or accumulated investment value of an asset, such as an insurance policy.

Certificate of deposit (CD)

A timed deposit that may be protected by the FDIC, incurs penalty charges if money is withdrawn before the maturity date, and usually has a higher rate of return than other interest-bearing savings options.

Certified public accountant (CPA)

An accountant who is a graduate of an accredited college accounting program, has several years' professional accounting experience, and has passed an exam to certify skills, integrity, and objectivity in reporting financial information. A CPA also needs to take continuing education programs to have current knowledge of tax laws and other developments that affect financial reporting.

CESA (See Coverdell Educational Savings Account)

Chapter 7 bankruptcy

One type of bankruptcy in which a consumer asks the court to forgive all unsecured debts, such as credit card or revolving credit lines. Usually a Chapter 7 bankruptcy requires the sale of personal assets to pay as much of the outstanding debt as possible but stops foreclosure, repossession, and other debt collection efforts. Each state has specific regulations about what items (home, retirement or pension funds, car, household furnishings) are exempt from liquidation in a Chapter 7 bankruptcy. Chapter 7 does not eliminate debts due to taxes, child support, alimony, student loans, court fines, or payments related to judgments for fraud, personal injury, property damage, or other claims and penalties. A Chapter 7 filing remains on a credit report for 10 years and makes it very difficult to get credit during that time. Federal law protects a person who files Chapter 7 from discrimination in hiring, public housing, or qualifying for a driver's license.

Check

A paper form used to pay bills against funds held in a bank or credit union account.

Checking account

An account from which the account holder can write checks.

Check register (Also called Ledger)

A record of all activity that happens within a checking account; maintained by the checking account holder.

Claim advance

A demand made by the insured, or the insured's beneficiary, for payment of a portion of the benefits prior to final claim settlement, as provided by the policy. Example: A person who has a homeowners' insurance policy that provides $100,000 for repairs may request a claim advance as a deposit against repairs due to a fire. The final costs of repair will be used to calculate the final claim settlement, but the claim advance will help the policyholder proceed with the repair.

COBRA (See Consolidated Omnibus Budget Reconciliation Act)

Collision auto insurance coverage (Also called Property auto insurance coverage)

Pays for damage to your car resulting from a collision with another car or any other object, or as a result of flipping over. Even if you are at fault for the accident, your collision coverage will reimburse you for the costs of repairing your car, minus the deductible. Collision coverage is usually sold with a deductible ranging from $250 to $1,000.

Commission

A fee to a third party for assisting a business transaction, such as buying or selling an asset. Example: A real estate agent who sells a home receives a commission—a percentage of the cost of the home—for the work done to make the sale. A commission on a $200,000 home could be 5 percent, or $10,000.

Compensation (See also Income)

The total wage or salary and benefits that an employee receives.

Compound interest

Interest credited daily, monthly, quarterly, semi-annually, or annually on both principal and previously credited interest.

Comprehensive auto insurance coverage

Reimburses you for theft or for damage caused by something other than a collision with another car or object (for example, fire, earthquake, windstorm, hail, vandalism, or contact with animals). It will also reimburse you if your windshield is cracked or shattered. Comprehensive coverage is generally sold with a $100 to $300 deductible.

Consolidated Omnibus Budget Reconciliation Act (COBRA)

A federal law that requires an employer with 20 or more employees to offer, for up to 18 months, continued healthcare coverage for employees who leave their jobs. The employee pays for the healthcare insurance at the same rate that the employer had paid.

Constant dollar plan (See Dollar cost averaging)

Consumer

A person who buys and/or uses a product.

Coverdell Educational Savings Account (CESA or ESA)

Formerly known as the Educational IRA. This account is designed to save for a child's education, including elementary school, high school, and college. Contributions are made from after-tax money (no income tax deduction is allowed), but the earnings (capital gains, interest, and dividends) are not taxable if used for qualified educational expenses. The account is transferable among family members, but the entire account has to be disbursed before the beneficiary's 30th birthday. Withdrawals after that date, or for non-qualified educational expenses, are subject to income taxes and a penalty. Eligibility to make contributions to a CESA are based on one's income level.

Note: The Economic Growth and Tax Relief Reconciliation Act of 2001 is scheduled to "sunset," or expire, effective December 31, 2010. The sunset will not affect the taxation of distributions from a CESA for higher education expenses. However, beginning in 2011, the tax treatment of distributions for grades K-12 expenses is uncertain. Other provisions may also be affected by the sunset.

CPA (See Certified public accountant)

Credit

Trust given to another person for future payment of a loan, credit card balance, etc.

Credit card

A small plastic card that is encoded with a credit account number and other information to allow a person to charge expenses against a credit line.

Credit counseling

Professional guidance from trained credit counselors, who will work with an individual to help him or her get out of debt and establish a sound financial management plan.

Credit laws

Bankruptcy Reform Law—Credit Counseling

The recently enacted Bankruptcy Reform Law includes a provision that consumers be fully informed about the bankruptcy process, alternatives to bankruptcy, and the potential consequences of filing for bankruptcy. The new law also requires debtors, prior to receiving a bankruptcy discharge, to complete a financial management instructional course. Providing consumers in bankruptcy with education and training, as well as the necessary skills and tools, will enable them to better prepare for their financial future and to avoid future financial problems.

Equal Credit Opportunity Act

Federal law that ensures that consumers are given an equal chance to receive credit. Prohibits discrimination on the basis of gender, race, marital status, religion, national origin, age, or receipt of public assistance. Lenders cannot ask about your plans for having children or refuse to consider consistently received alimony or child support payments as income. If you are denied credit, you have a legal right to know why.

Fair and Accurate Credit Transactions (FACT) Act

This federal legislation was enacted in 2003 to establish and strengthen national standards for collecting, reporting, and safeguarding credit information. FACT gives consumers, companies, consumer reporting agencies, and regulators more and better resources to expand access to credit and other financial services, improve accuracy of consumers' financial information, and help fight identity theft. FACT provides strong consumer protection, gives consumers free annual credit reports, and specific rights and procedures for correcting inaccurate credit report information.

Fair Credit and Charge Card Disclosure Act (1989)
A part of the Truth in Lending Act that mandates a box on credit card applications that describes key features and costs (i.e., annual percentage rate, grace period for purchases, minimum finance charge, balance calculation method, annual fees, transaction fees for cash advances, and penalty fees such as over-the-limit fees and late payment fees).

Fair Credit Billing Act (1975)
Federal law that covers credit card billing problems. It applies to all open-end credit accounts (for example: credit cards and overdraft checking). States that consumers should send a written billing error notice to the creditor within 60 days (after receipt of first bill containing an error); creditor must acknowledge in 30 days; creditor must investigate; and creditor may not damage a consumer's credit rating while a dispute is pending.

Fair Credit Reporting Act (as amended 1997)
Federal law that covers the reporting of debt repayment information. It establishes when a credit reporting agency may provide a report to someone; states that obsolete information must be taken off (after 7 or 10 years); gives consumers the right to know what is in their credit report; requires that both a credit bureau and information provider (example: department store) have an obligation to correct incorrect information; gives consumers the right to dispute inaccurate information and add a 100-word statement to their report to explain accurate negative information; and gives consumers the right to know what credit bureau provided a report when they are turned down for credit.

Fair Debt Collection Practices Act (1978)

Federal law that prohibits debt collectors from engaging in unfair, deceptive, or abusive practices when collecting debts. Collectors must send a written notice telling the amount owed and name of the creditor; collector may not contact consumer if he or she disputes in writing within 30 days (unless collector furnishes proof of the debt); collectors must identify themselves on the phone and can call only between 8 am and 9 pm unless a consumer agrees to another time; and collectors cannot call consumers at work if they are told not to.

Truth in Lending Act (1968)

Federal law that mandates disclosure of information about the cost of credit. Both the finance charge (i.e., all charges to borrow money, including interest) and the annual percentage rate, or APR (i.e., the percentage cost of credit on a yearly basis), must be displayed prominently on forms and statements used by creditors. The law provides criminal penalties for willful violators, as well as civil remedies. It also protects you against unauthorized use of your credit card. If a card is lost or stolen, the maximum amount you have to pay is $50.

Credit line (Also called Line of credit)

Amount or limit of credit available in a specific account.

Creditor

A company that offers credit and is owed payment when that credit is used.

Credit protection

Insurance, security codes, emergency payment systems, or other programs that preserve credit and make sure that it is only used by the authorized persons.

Credit rating (Also called Credit score)

A number that indicates a person's creditworthiness based on the use of credit, credit payments, employment, and other information.

Credit report

Financial information collected by businesses and used by lenders to determine creditworthiness of individuals. This information contains an individual's personal and employment history, as well as payment history of all debts.

Credit score (See Credit rating)
Credit union
> Not-for-profit cooperative of members with some type of common bond (example: an employer), which provides a wide array of financial services, often at a lower cost than banks.

Custodial account
> A bank, brokerage, insurance, or other financial account that is managed by a trustee or competent adult on behalf of another, such as a minor child or a disabled adult. The term also applies to retirement accounts managed for eligible employees or mutual funds managed by a custodian or fiduciary committee.

Customer service
> Programs and policies established to help inform and assist a company's customers about products, use, guarantees, and repair. Customer service contact information is on credit cards and billing statements, applications, and typically online at the company's Web site.

Debit card
> A card that uses the same payment system as a credit card but does not provide credit. Instead, the payment for goods and services purchased with the card is subtracted directly from a person's bank account.

Debt percentage
> A measure of debt calculated by dividing total outstanding debt, excluding a first mortgage, by total assets. The higher the percentage, the more debt, which may indicate a higher level of credit risk.

Debt-to-income ratio
> A measure used by creditors or lenders to determine a person's creditworthiness or ability to pay current and future credit obligations. To calculate the debt-to-income ratio, the total amount of monthly payments for credit debts (including auto or student loans, credit card balances, and other loans) is divided by the pretax income. The closer the amount is to 1, the more pretax income is needed for current credit expenses and the less likely the person is able to manage additional credit expenses.

Deductible
> An agreed upon amount that an insurance policy owner has to pay before reimbursement begins. As a rule, the larger the deductible, the

lower the premiums. Example: An auto insurance policy with a $1,000 deductible would be less expensive than one with a $500 deductible.

Deed in lieu

A legal transaction in which, to avoid the foreclosure process, a debtor delivers a property deed to a tender holding a mortgage.

Deficiency balance

The amount a creditor owes to a lender after a car, home, or other asset is returned to the lender and sold due to the creditor's inability to afford the obligation.

Deflation

A broad overall drop in the price of goods and services; the opposite of inflation.

Direct deposit

A person signs an agreement to have payments such as salary, Social Security, investment income, or other funds sent directly into a bank account. This is a safe, convenient way to have immediate access to money.

Disposable income

Income remaining after income taxes and payroll taxes are deducted from gross pay; income available to spend or save.

Diversification

An investment strategy designed to reduce risk and generate consistent performance by investing in a variety of stocks, bonds, real estate, and other assets. Diversification does not guarantee a profit or protect against a loss.

Dividend

A payment to shareholders that a company's board of directors approves from earnings.

Dollar cost averaging (Also called Constant dollar plan)

Investing regular sums of money (example: $50) at regular time intervals (example: quarterly) regardless of whether security prices are moving up or down. Dollar cost averaging is designed to reduce the average cost of investing over time, because if security prices rise, fewer units are bought, and as prices fall, more units are bought. A periodic investment plan such as dollar cost averaging does not assure a profit or protect against a loss.

Due date

The date a bill must be paid to keep an account current and avoid penalty fees.

Earned income

Payment received for work, such as wages, salaries, commissions, and tips.

Educational IRA

Now known as the Coverdell Education Savings Account (CESA or ESA). See Coverdell Education Savings Account.

Emergency fund

Cash on hand, including savings or liquid assets, to handle a personal or family emergency. Financial management specialists recommend having enough savings to cover at least 3, but ideally 6, months of living expenses including rent or mortgage, insurance, credit card bills, and other regular expenses, in case of disability or unemployment.

Endorsement

Signature on the back of the check, entitling the payee to either receive or transfer payment.

Employee benefit

Something of value that an employee receives in addition to a wage or salary. Examples include health insurance, life insurance, discounted childcare, and subsidized meals at the company cafeteria.

Employer-sponsored retirement savings program

Tax-deferred savings plan offered by an employer, providing a federal tax deduction, tax deferral of contributions and earnings, and, in some cases, employer matching. Such programs include 401(k) plans for corporate employees, 403(b) plans for employees of schools and nonprofit organizations, and Section 457 plans for state and local government employees.

Employer-sponsored savings plan

A government-approved program through which an employer can assist workers in building their personal retirement funds.

Entrepreneur

A person who starts a business.

Equifax (See also Experian, TransUnion)

One of the three major consumer credit reporting companies. Stores, credit card companies, and others who offer credit or other consumer services provide and access information on their customers' use and payment of credit. An individual consumer may have several credit or other accounts reported on by one or more of the credit reporting companies.

Equity mutual funds

A mutual fund that contains several different equities, or stocks. An equity mutual fund may be set up to mirror a market index, such as the S&P500 or NASDAQ; an industry, such as telecommunications or healthcare; or to meet specific investment goals, such as growth or income.

ESA (See Coverdell Educational Savings Account)

Expense

The cost of a good or service.

Experian (See also Equifax, TransUnion)

One of the three major consumer credit reporting companies. Stores, credit card companies, and others who offer credit or other consumer services provide and access information on their customers' use and payment of credit. An individual consumer may have several credit or other accounts reported on by one or more of the credit reporting companies.

Fair Isaac Corporation (FICO) score

A FICO score is a measure of a consumer's creditworthiness that is calculated from information provided by the three major credit reporting companies, Equifax, Experian, and TransUnion. A FICO score includes both positive and negative information about payment history, amounts owed, length of credit use, and new credit applications, as well as the types of credit used. The higher the FICO score, the more credit-worthy or credit-reliable a consumer is judged to be and the more likely to receive better credit values. The FICO score was developed by the Fair Isaac Corporation, a research company, and adopted for use by major creditors and financial institutions because of its reliability in predicting creditworthiness.

Federal Deposit Insurance Corporation (FDIC)

A federal agency, established in 1933, that protects bank depositors against certain losses of up to $100,000.

Federal Insurance Contributions Act (FICA)

The legislation that funds Social Security. FICA deductions are made from each individual's paycheck, then sent by employers to the government.

Federal Trade Commission (FTC)

The federal agency responsible for promoting free enterprise and preventing monopolies or the restraint of trade, as well as protecting the consumer.

Fee-for-service health insurance

Patients choose their own doctors and, after satisfying a deductible, pay a portion of each bill (typically 20 percent or more). Claims are filed by either the medical provider or the patient, and generally accidents or illnesses—not preventive care—are covered.

FICA (See Federal Insurance Contributions Act)

FICO score (See Fair Isaac Corporation score)

Fiduciary

A term used to describe an obligation or trust related to financial management for another. Example: A trustee has a fiduciary responsibility to manage funds prudently for the best interest of heirs, retirees, or others beneficiaries.

Finance charge

All charges to borrow money, including interest.

Financial advisor (Also called Financial planner)

A person who gives financial advice. Check the credentials to be sure a financial advisor or planner is a qualified and/or certified professional, such as a certified financial planner (CFP) designation.

Forbearance

Postponement of payments or reduction in monthly payments for a limited, specified period of time during which a borrower is unable to make payments. The plan can include making higher than normal payments once the borrower resumes payments, in order to cure the delinquency.

Foreclosure

The legal process of seizing and selling a home or other real estate property when the buyer is in default for not paying the mortgage or loan according to the agreed upon terms of contract. Usually the lender sells the property at a public auction, and the proceeds are used to pay off the outstanding debt on the property.

Fraud

A seller's intentional deception of a buyer, which is illegal.

FTC (See Federal Trade Commission)

Garnishment

A court order requesting that an employer deduct a percentage of an employee's paycheck and send it to a creditor before the paycheck is given to the employee.

Government transfer payments

Payments by governments, such as Social Security, veterans' benefits, and welfare, to people who do not supply current goods, services, or labor in exchange for these payments.

Grace period

A time period during which a borrower can pay the full balance of credit due and not incur any finance charges.

Gross pay

The total amount of your pay before deductions for FICA, health insurance, taxes, and other expenses.

Growth mutual funds

Growth funds have stocks in companies with excellent prospects for future growth in revenues.

Health Insurance Portability and Accountability Act (HIPAA) release

A release that everyone is required to sign at their doctor's office to authorize the release of health records only to those named on the form.

Health Maintenance Organization (HMO)

A prepaid healthcare enrollment program that establishes contracts with hospitals, clinics, physicians, pharmacists, rehabilitation specialists, and other wellness or healthcare resources to provide comprehensive preventive and medical care for individual and group members.

High cap (Also called Large cap)

The term used to describe a company or stock that has a value of $5 billion or more. The total value of a company or stock is found by multiplying the number of shares outstanding by the current price per share.

HIPAA release (See Health Insurance Portability and Accountability Act release)

HMO (See Health Maintenance Organization)

Home equity loan (Also called Home equity line of credit)

A loan or line of credit issued on the current value of your home minus the outstanding mortgage. Example: If your home cost $150,000 and now has a market value of $200,000, you may qualify for a home equity loan or line of credit for $50,000 or more, depending on how much of a down payment you made and how much of your mortgage principal is outstanding.

Homeowner's/renter's insurance

Insurance that protects a person from liability or catastrophic losses due to injury or damages to a person or property caused by accident, fire, or other specific events. Generally insurance coverage for floods, earthquakes, hurricanes, windstorms, mold, and sewer damage must be purchased separately. Experts recommend that a homeowner's/renter's insurance policy have a deductible of $1,000 or more; this reduces the premium cost.

IDA (See Individual development account)

Identity theft

Crime committed when someone gains access to and uses another person's credit card numbers, Social Security number, birth date, checking and savings account numbers, driver's license, automobile records, or other important personal information to buy items or get loans.

Income (See also Compensation)

Earnings from work or investment.

Individual development account (IDA)

Special savings accounts that help low-income consumers build financial assets. IDA savings deposits are increased with matching funds from sponsoring community-based organizations and financial institutions, and can be used to buy homes, pay for post-secondary education, start a small business, or save for retirement.

Individual retirement account (IRA)

An IRA is a tax-deferred personal savings account designed to help people save for their retirement. Many people are eligible to set up an IRA, including those who are not enrolled in an employer's pension program or who meet IRA requirements for taxable income or tax status. An annual deposit of up to $2,000 is tax deductible, and the earned interest accumulates without being taxable until it is withdrawn, at age 59½ or later. Withdrawals must begin at age 70. There are penalties for earlier withdrawal, so it is important to know and follow all the IRA guidelines. The IRA specialist at a bank, credit union, brokerage, or mutual fund company can provide detailed facts about IRA advantages, costs, and other policy features.

Inflation

A broad, overall rise in the price of goods and services; the opposite of the less common deflation.

Insurance

Protection against the loss of life, health, home, car, or other valuables.

Insurance agent or broker

An individual who is authorized to sell insurance. In most states a person must complete requirements to be a licensed insurance agent or broker.

Insurance rider

A supplement or addition to an insurance policy, which becomes part of the policy when it is agreed to by both parties, the insurer and the insured. A rider can be used to expand, limit, or waive a policy's coverage.

Insurance underwriter

A person trained to evaluate insurance risks and decide what coverages will be available for them, at what cost or premium, and with what deductibles or other qualifications.

Interest

Money paid to savers and investors by financial institutions, government, or corporations for the use of their money (example: 5 percent interest on a certificate of deposit or 6 percent interest on a bond).

Interest-only loan

A loan that is structured so that the payments are only interest; no part of the principal is paid. Example: The monthly cost of an interest-only loan for a home mortgage would be just the monthly interest rate; at the end of the loan term, the original purchase price of the home is still due.

International equity

A stock or bond issued by a company incorporated or established outside the United States.

Investing

The process of setting aside money to increase wealth over time and accumulate funds for long-term financial goals, such as retirement.

Investors

People who buy securities, such as stock and bonds, to achieve long-term financial goals.

IRA (See Individual retirement account)

Large cap (See High cap)

Ledger (See Check register)

Liability insurance coverage

Insurance that pays for injuries, damage, or other losses caused by the insured person.

Lien

A court order that allows a creditor to place a claim on property, investments, funds, or other types of security owned by the debtor who is in default. A lien lets a creditor recover the losses from unpaid debt.

Line of credit (See Credit line)

Liquidity

The quality of an asset that permits it to be converted quickly into cash without loss of value.

Loan assumption

To take on or accept the responsibilities of a loan contract. Example: A parent or guardian may assume the payment and other responsibilities for a car loan, tuition, or other debt; a buyer may purchase a house by assuming the responsibilities of the current mortgage.

Loan modification

A change in the terms or conditions of a loan agreed upon by both the person or the company that grants the loan and the person who receives it.

Loan repayment plan

The stated and legal agreement or contract to pay a loan in full, including credit, service, and other costs as outlined and explained.

Loan-to-value (LTV) ratio

LTV is a measure of the market value of an asset compared to the value of the loan used to purchase it. The LTV allows the lender to calculate how much will be lost or can be reclaimed if the borrower defaults. An LTV is found by dividing the market value by the amount of the loan. As a rule, the higher the LTV, the lower the interest rate or more favorable the loan terms will be.

Long-term-care insurance

Insurance that helps pay for personal or custodial care, nursing home care, or other non-medical services required by a person who has been certified to be disabled. Long-term-care policies vary by coverage, types of services covered for reimbursement, qualifications for disability, per diem payment, and length of time coverage and payments are provided.

Loss

The reduction or decrease in value of an investment.

Low cap (Also called Small cap)

The term used to describe a company or stock that has a value of $1 billion or less. The total value of a company or stock is found by multiplying the number of shares outstanding by the current price per share.

LTV ratio (See Loan-to-value ratio)

Managed care health insurance

These policies can include: health maintenance organizations (HMOs), preferred provider organizations (PPOs), and point-of-service (POS) plans. Patients pay a co-payment when using doctors in the plan, and preventive care is usually covered.

Market cycles

The collective movement of the stock market as the value of investments rises or falls. A bull market occurs when investment prices rise faster than their historical average as a result of an economic recovery or growth. The opposite of a bull market is a bear market, a prolonged period when investment prices fall, accompanied by widespread pessimism. Bear markets often happen when inflation is rising or the economy is in recession and unemployment is high.

Medicaid

The federal health insurance program for disabled and low-income consumers.

Medical auto insurance coverage

Pays for the cost of treating injuries, the cost of rehabilitation, lost wages, or funeral costs.

Medicare

A federal government program of transfer payments for certain healthcare expenses for citizens 65 or older. The Social Security Administration manages the program.

Money market account

A type of savings account that may be protected by the FDIC, with minimum balance requirements and usually higher interest rates than other types of savings accounts.

Money order

A certificate that can be bought at the post office or another institution and used to pay bills, instead of cash; legal receipt for bill payment.

Money wire (Also called Transfer)

The process of sending money from one individual or bank to another, sometimes internationally.

Mortgage

A loan to pay for a property, usually a house. For most people, a mortgage is the largest financial obligation they apply and qualify for in their lifetime.

Mortgage protection insurance (See Private mortgage insurance)

Mutual fund

An investment company that pools money from shareholders to invest in a variety of securities, including stocks, bonds, and short-term money market assets.

NASDAQ index

A computerized index that tracks current bid and asking prices for equities and securities, mainly technology stocks.

National Credit Union Administration (NCUA)

A federal agency that charters and oversees federal credit unions. The

NCUA insures against certain losses any deposits at federal credit unions and at some state credit unions.

Needs

Those economic goods and services that are considered basic, such as food, clothing, and shelter.

Net pay (Also called Take-home pay)

The amount of money in your paycheck; total wage or salary (plus bonuses) minus payroll deductions.

No-fault insurance coverage

A type of auto insurance, in place in 12 states, in which each driver's auto insurance coverage pays for injuries and damage, no matter who caused the accident. No-fault insurance also reduces insurance costs by limiting lawsuits and damage claims.

Online banking

Computer systems that allow consumers to check balances, pay bills, transfer funds, and complete other banking activities on the Internet.

Opportunity cost

The opportunity cost of a choice is the value of the best alternative given up. Example: If a person sells an investment worth $40,000 and earning 8 percent per year—$3,200—to buy a new car, the opportunity cost is $3,200 because that is how much the person gives up by using the investment. Most likely in this situation, the cost of financing the car would be higher than 8 percent, so the buyer might be willing to pay this opportunity cost, compared with paying higher car-loan finance fees.

Ordinary life insurance (See Whole life insurance)

Overdraft

Lack of sufficient funds in a checking account to cover the full amount of a check. A bank or credit union will charge a service charge called an overdraft fee to cover expenses involved in returning a check and handling other procedures caused by an overdraft.

Overdraft protection

Procedure agreed upon in advance by an account holder and a bank to transfer funds from a savings or credit account to a checking account to cover insufficient funds.

Paycheck

The paper form or check that is the amount of money a person has earned during a specific period after taxes and other deductions.

Payroll deduction (Also called Salary deduction)

An amount subtracted from a paycheck as the government requires or the employee requests. Mandatory deductions include various taxes. Voluntary deductions include loan payments or deposits into savings accounts.

Permanent life insurance (See also Whole life insurance)

Any of the several types of life insurance that remain in effect for the insured person's lifetime, if premiums are paid as the policy requires. Examples: universal life insurance, variable life insurance, adjustable life insurance, and whole life insurance.

Personal identification number (PIN)

A secret code that a consumer creates to access online or ATM bank or investment accounts. Experts suggest that PINs should be changed often to protect consumers from fraud or theft.

Phishing

An illegal search for credit information on the Internet by sending false e-mails to consumers and asking for or capturing financial information or codes. A growing problem that can result in identity theft, financial loss, and damage to a victim's credit history.

PIN (See Personal identification number)

Point-of-service (POS) plan

A healthcare insurance plan that requires a patient to choose a primary-care doctor who coordinates care and refers the patient to specialists within the POS plan as needed. POS plans offer complete health services to members, including education, preventive care, and continuing medical care.

PPO (See Preferred provider organization)

Preferred provider organization (PPO)

A healthcare insurance plan that allows members to visit any doctor within the PPO network. Patients generally do not need to have a primary-care physician to make referrals. Patients are required to pay a co-pay for each doctor visit. A member who goes to a doctor outside the PPO generally pays the difference between what the medical provider charges and what the plan will pay.

Premium

A payment on an insurance policy, as per the terms of the contract.

Principal

The amount of money borrowed or invested, not including fees, interest, or dividends. Example: A new car may cost $23,000, but if you make a down payment of $5,000 and get $3,000 credit for your old car, the principal of your car loan will be $15,000, the actual amount borrowed.

Private mortgage insurance (PMI)

Also called mortgage protection insurance, this protects a lender if the borrower defaults on a mortgage. Sometimes a potential homeowner can negotiate a larger down payment, purchase life insurance with a mortgage payment benefit, or provide savings and other assets to guarantee the mortgage in place of a PMI policy.

Profit

The positive difference between total revenue from a business or investment minus total expense.

Pro rate (Also called Pro rata)

Fee or payment based on a defined time period or measure. Example: A pro rata insurance fee would be payable on a monthly, quarterly, or annual basis, and coverage would extend only for the paid period. Or, interest on a revolving credit line may be charged on a pro rata basis, that is, daily, monthly, or quarterly and paid only for the time and amount of credit used.

Property auto insurance coverage (See Collision auto insurance coverage)

Proportional allocation or distribution

Divided according to percentage ownership. Example: Stockholders receive dividends based on the number of shares of stock owned—that is, dividends are proportionally allocated or distributed.

Prospectus

An official document that contains information required by the Securities & Exchange Commission to describe a mutual fund.

Protecting on the downside

An investment that is designed to limit or manage the potential loss in the event of a price or market decline.

Purchasing power

A measurement of the relative value of money in terms of the quality and quantity of goods and services it can buy. Inflation decreases purchasing power; deflation increases it.

Qualified tuition account (See 529 Savings Plan, Educational IRA)

Tax-free savings or investment account that allows parents, grandparents, or others to make contributions for college tuition.

Rate of return (Also called Yield)

The amount earned as a return on an investment, expressed as a percentage of its cost. Example: If you earn $3 annual return on a $24 investment, $3 divided by $24 equals 0.125, or a 12.5 percent rate of return.

Remittance

A payment or transfer of money, by mail, e-mail, or wire payment.

Repossession

When a creditor takes back an item that has not been paid for according to the credit agreement.

Reverse mortgage

A mortgage that allows a homeowner who is at least 62 years of age to receive payments based on the current market value of a property. Example: The Johnsons' home has a current market value of $200,000 and no mortgage. A reverse mortgage would allow them to receive regular monthly payments against a portion of the market value. When the home is sold, the bank will be paid back the amount that the Johnsons received, plus bank charges as agreed upon in the reverse mortgage contract.

Revolving credit

A credit agreement that makes credit available again after the payment for its use. Example: A $500 overdraft credit account will have $500 available after all the interest and outstanding principal are paid.

Risk

Exposure to loss of investment capital due to a variety of causes, such as business failure, stock market volatility, and interest rate changes. In business, the likelihood of loss or reduced profit.

Risk management

Procedures to minimize the adverse effect of a possible financial loss by: (1) identifying potential sources of loss; (2) measuring the financial consequences of a loss occurring; and (3) using controls to minimize actual losses or their financial consequences.

Rollover

Moving funds from one investment to another. When used in relation to 401(k), IRA, or other tax-deferred funds, a rollover means that the funds move from trustee to trustee, from one institutional account to another, without going directly to the consumer.

Roth IRA

A type of individual retirement account that lets people within certain income limits save for retirement while their savings grow tax-free. Contributions are taxable, but withdrawals, subject to certain rules, are not taxed at all.

Rule of 72

A quick way to calculate how long it will take to double a sum of money. Divide 72 by the expected interest rate to determine the number of years (example: 72 ÷ 8 percent = 9 years).

Salary (See also Wage)

Payment for work, usually calculated in periods of a week or longer. Salary is usually tied to the completion of specific duties over a minimum but not maximum number of hours.

Salary deduction (Also called Payroll deduction)

An amount subtracted from a paycheck as the government requires or the employee requests. Mandatory deductions include various taxes. Voluntary deductions include loan payments or deposits into savings accounts.

Savings account

An account at a financial institution that allows regular deposits and withdrawals. The minimum required deposit, fees charged, and interest rate paid varies among providers.

Savings and loan association (S&L)

A financial institution that provides loans and interest-bearing accounts. Accounts in federally chartered S&Ls are federally insured.

Savings bond

A bond is a certificate representing a debt. A U.S. Savings Bond is a loan to the government. The government agrees to repay the amount borrowed, with interest, to the bondholder. Two types of savings bonds are Series EE and inflation-adjusted I bonds. Savings bonds are often purchased through payroll deduction or at financial institutions in denominations of $50 to $10,000.

Secured creditor

A lender who holds an interest such as a lien or mortgage against property owned by the borrower. Example: A customer's ownership of his vehicle may be used as collateral to qualify for a loan.

Short sale

An investing technique based on the assumption that a security or commodity will fall in price. The investor borrows a security or commodity futures contract with the agreement to return it on a specific date. The borrower sells the investment on the market. If the price falls by the time it must be returned to the financial advisor, the borrower has made a profit. If the price has increased, he will have lost money. Example: An investor sells short 200 shares of a company because he thinks it is overpriced. If he is correct and the price falls before the stocks need to be replaced, he'll make a profit. If it rises, he can lose money.

Simple interest

Interest credited daily, monthly, quarterly, semiannually, or annually on principal only, not previously credited interest.

Small cap (See Low cap)

Social Security

A federal government program of transfer payments for retirement, disability, or the loss of income from a parent or guardian. Funds come from a tax on income, a payroll deduction labeled "FICA."

Standard & Poor's (S&P) index

An index created by weighting the market value and performance of 500 stocks identified as widely held. The S&P 500 index represents the stock market as a whole to provide a broad snapshot of the overall U.S. equity market. Over 70 percent of all U.S. equity is tracked by the S&P 500, and it is generally considered the most accurate measure of the total equity market's performance.

Straight life insurance (See Whole life insurance)

Stocks

A type of investment where investors hold shares of a corporation, which may rise or fall in value.

Subprime loan

The extension of credit to a person considered to be a high-risk borrower due to lack of or damaged credit history. A subprime loan has a higher-than-average interest rate. Subprime lenders reduce their risks in making loans by charging borrowers a higher interest rate and, in some cases, additional fees.

SWIFT (Society for Worldwide Interbank Financial Telecommunications) Transaction

A movement of funds over the SWIFT worldwide dedicated computer network that includes 7,800 financial institutions in more than 200 countries. The SWIFT infrastructure allows the secure, standardized, and fast communication and transfer of payments, securities, and trade. Examples: A U.S company relies on a SWIFT transaction to purchase inventory from an overseas company, or the government of one country can buy bonds or other investments from another government.

Take-home pay (See also Net pay)

The pay actually received by an employee after adding bonuses and deducting taxes, healthcare premiums, and retirement savings plans.

Tax

A government fee on business and individual income, activities, or products.

Taxable income

Income subject to tax; total income adjusted for deductions, exemptions, and credits.

Tax credit (See also Tax deduction, Tax exemption)

An amount that a taxpayer who meets certain criteria can subtract from tax owed. Examples include a credit for earned income below a certain limit and for qualified post-secondary school expenses.

Tax deduction (See also Tax credit, Tax exemption)

An expense that a taxpayer can subtract from taxable income. Examples include deductions for home mortgage interest and for charitable gifts.

Tax-deferred

A savings or investment plan allowing tax payment to be postponed until a later date. Examples include IRA, 401(k), Keogh Plan, annuity, savings bond, and employee stock ownership plan.

Tax-exempt (Also called Tax-free)

Investments (example: municipal bonds) whose earnings are free from tax liability.

Tax exemption (See also Tax Credit, Tax Deduction)

An amount that a taxpayer who meets certain criteria can subtract from taxable income. Examples include exemptions for each dependent or for life insurance proceeds.

Tax-free (See Tax-exempt)

T-bill (See Treasury bill)

Term

The period of time during which a loan must be paid or during which an investment accrues interest. Examples: The term of an auto loan can be 4 or 5 years; the term of a Treasury bill can be 1 year.

Term life insurance

A life insurance policy that provides coverage for a defined time, such as 1 year, 5 years, 20 years, or more. At the end of the term, the insurer must requalify for a new policy.

Time value of money

Comparison of a lump sum of money, or a series of equal payments, between two different time periods (example: present and future), assuming a specified interest rate and time period.

Transfer (See Money wire)

Transfer payments (See Government transfer payments)

TransUnion (See also Experian, Equifax)

One of the three major consumer credit reporting companies. Stores, credit card companies, and others who offer credit or other consumer services provide and access information on their customers' use and payment of credit. An individual consumer may have several credit or other accounts reported on by one or more of the credit reporting companies.

Travelers' checks

Documents that function as cash but can be replaced if lost or stolen. Travelers' checks are often used when traveling to other countries.

Treasury bill (Also called Bill, T-bill, or U.S. Treasury bill)

Short-term U.S. government debt investments that are sold at a discount and paid at face value; the difference is interest. For example, a person could pay $970 for a T-bill and receive $1,000 at maturity. Treasury bills mature in various time periods, from several days up to 26 weeks. Treasury Bills are exempt from state and local taxes. Consumers can buy T-Bills directly at www.treasurydirect.gov or through their financial advisor, bank, credit union, or other investment resource.

Trust

A legal agreement that gives an organization or individual, the trustee, responsibility for the financial management and administration of funds or property for the benefit of others, such as heirs, retirees, an institution, or other beneficiaries.

Trustee

An organization or individual appointed by a company or individual to manage and administer funds or property for beneficiaries.

UGMA account (See Uniform Gifts to Minors Act account)

Unbanked

A person without any kind of deposit relationship at a formal financial institution.

Unearned income

Money received for which no exchange was made, such as a gift.

Uniform Gifts to Minors Act (UGMA) account

The federal law, which most states have adopted, that permits an adult to give a child irrevocable gifts of money or investments by transferring them to a custodial account. This allows financial assets to be passed to a child without establishing a trust or legal guardian. Withdrawals are taxed based on the minor's tax status. The custodian of a UGMA account assumes responsibility for the prudent management of it until the child reaches 21 and becomes the legal owner with full right to use and manage the assets.

Uniform Transfers to Minors Act (UTMA) account

Similar to the Uniform Gift to Minors Act, the UTMA extends the types of assets (real estate, fine art, patents, royalties, other valuables) that can be transferred to minors in custodial accounts. In some states the UTMA replaces the UGMA; in others, it works in combination with it.

Uninsured

People who do not have insurance to cover healthcare, disability, auto or personal liability, or other expenses or losses.

Universal life insurance (See also Permanent life insurance)

This is a flexible life insurance policy that allows the policy owner to change the face value, premiums, and cash value of the policy. Example: If the saving (cash value) portion of the policy is earning a low return, it can be shifted to pay for the premium, or the face value can be increased or reduced, depending on the insurance needs of the owner, so a larger percentage of the premium can be applied to savings.

Unsecured creditor

A lender who provides credit without requiring security such as a cash deposit, deed, or other collateral.

U.S. Treasury bill (See Treasury bill)

UTMA account (See Uniform Transfers to Minors Act account)

VantageScore℠

A consumer credit scoring model developed jointly by the three major consumer credit bureaus (Equifax, Experian, and TransUnion). VantageScore ratings range from 501 to 990 with a corresponding letter grade assigned, similar to those you would receive in a school (A to F).

Variable life insurance (See also Whole life insurance)

A life insurance policy that pays benefits and provides for the growth of cash value by allowing a choice of investment opportunities and premium payment options.

Wage (See also Salary)

Payment for work, usually as calculated in periods of an hour rather than longer.

Waiver of premium benefit

A provision included in most life insurance and some health insurance policies that keeps an insurance policy in effect even though the insured person is exempt from paying premiums because of disability. In life insurance policies, the waiver of premium benefit usually takes effect 6 months after the insured is certified disabled by a doctor and the insurance company; in healthcare policies, it is usually effective 90 days after the insured is certified disabled.

Wants

Desires for economic goods or services, not necessarily accompanied by the power to satisfy them.

Wealth

Accumulated assets such as money and/or possessions, often as a result of saving and investing.

Whole life insurance

Life insurance that combines insurance protection with cash savings and that remains in effect for the insured person's lifetime, if premiums are paid as the policy requires. Usually the premiums, benefits, and cash value remain the same over the life of the policy. Also known as ordinary life insurance, straight life insurance.

Withdrawal

Take money from a bank or credit union account.

Yield (Also called Rate of return)

The amount earned as a return on an investment, expressed as a percentage of its cost. Example: If you earn $3 annual return on a $24 investment, $3 divided by $24 equals 0.125, or a 12.5 percent rate of return.

APPENDIX

Setting Financial Goals Worksheet

SHORT-TERM FINANCIAL GOALS

GOAL	AMOUNT NEEDED	TIME FRAME

LONG-TERM FINANCIAL GOALS

GOAL	AMOUNT NEEDED	TIME FRAME

(continued)

Setting Financial Goals Worksheet (cont.)

FINANCIAL STRATEGIES

For Short-term Goals:

1. _____

2. _____

3. _____

For Long-term Goals:

1. _____

2. _____

3. _____

Debt Total Worksheet

CREDITOR'S NAME	TOTAL BAL	MIN DUE	DUE DATE	APR
	$	$		
	$	$		
	$	$		
	$	$		
	$	$		
	$	$		
	$	$		
	$	$		
	$	$		
	$	$		
	$	$		
	$	$		
	$	$		
TOTAL	$	$		

Monthly Debt Percentage Worksheet

DEBTS	AVERAGE MONTHLY PAYMENTS
	$
	$
	$
	$
	$
	$
	$
	$
	$
	$
	$
	$
	$
	$
	$
	$
	$
	$

1. Total your monthly debt payments $_____
2. Enter your monthly gross income (income before taxes and other deductions, such as medical and retirement plan contributions)
   $_____
3. Divide #1 by #2 to calculate your debt percentage   _____%

Budget Worksheet

FOR MONTH:_____

CATEGORY	AMOUNT BUDGETED	AMOUNT SPENT	SURPLUS (+)/ SHORTAGE (-)
Fixed Expenses			
HOUSING			
Rent or Mortgage	$	$	$
2nd Mortgage/Equity Loan	$	$	$
Other (explain)	$	$	$
TRANSPORTATION			
Vehicle Loan Payment	$	$	$
Other (explain)	$	$	$
INSURANCE			
Health	$	$	$
Life	$	$	$
Disability/Long-Term care	$	$	$
Other (explain)	$	$	$
CHILD CARE			
Child Care/Babysitters	$	$	$
Child Support/Alimony	$	$	$
Other (explain)	$	$	$
Fixed Expenses Subtotal	$	$	$
Periodic Fixed Expenses			
HOUSING			
Property Tax/Real Estate Taxes	$	$	$
Insurance (Homeowner/Rental)	$	$	$
Other (explain)	$	$	$

(continued)

Budget Worksheet *(cont.)*

CATEGORY	AMOUNT BUDGETED	AMOUNT SPENT	SURPLUS (+)/ SHORTAGE (-)
Periodic Fixed Expenses (cont.)			
TRANSPORTATION			
Primary Vehicle	$	$	$
License Plate	$	$	$
Registration	$	$	$
Insurance	$	$	$
Secondary Vehicle	$	$	$
License Plate	$	$	$
Registration	$	$	$
Insurance	$	$	$
Driver's License	$	$	$
Gas/Public Transportation/Parking	$	$	$
Other (explain)	$	$	$
Periodic Fixed Expenses Total	$	$	$
Variable Expenses			
HOUSING			
Utilities			
Heat	$	$	$
Electricity	$	$	$
Water	$	$	$
Sewer	$	$	$
Trash	$	$	$
Recycling	$	$	$

CATEGORY	AMOUNT BUDGETED	AMOUNT SPENT	SURPLUS (+)/ SHORTAGE (-)
Telephone			
Basic Service	$	$	$
Long Distance Charges	$	$	$
Cell Phone(s)	$	$	$
Other (explain)	$	$	$
FOOD			
General Food & Groceries	$	$	$
Food Outside the Home	$	$	$
Work Lunches	$	$	$
School Lunches	$	$	$
Meals at Restaurants	$	$	$
Other (explain)	$	$	$
MEDICAL			
Doctor	$	$	$
Dentist	$	$	$
Prescriptions	$	$	$
Glasses	$	$	$
Medical Bills Above and Beyond	$	$	$
Other (explain)	$	$	$
CLOTHING			
New Purchases	$	$	$
Cleaning (laundry + dry cleaning)	$	$	$
Repairs/Alterations	$	$	$
Other (explain)	$	$	$

(continued)

Budget Worksheet *(cont.)*

CATEGORY	AMOUNT BUDGETED	AMOUNT SPENT	SURPLUS (+)/ SHORTAGE (-)
Variable Expenses (cont.)			
EDUCATION			
Tuition, Registration Fees, Training Classes	$	$	$
Supporting Books, Magazines, Newspapers, Supplies	$	$	$
DONATIONS			
Religious	$	$	$
Charities	$	$	$
Other (explain)	$	$	$
PERSONAL			
Hairdresser	$	$	$
Children's Allowance	$	$	$
Gifts/Flowers (birthdays, anniversaries)	$	$	$
Tobacco	$	$	$
Alcohol	$	$	$
Other (explain)	$	$	$
ENTERTAINMENT			
Movies, Concerts, Sporting Events	$	$	$
Cable/Satellite Service	$	$	$
Internet Service	$	$	$
Gambling/Lottery	$	$	$
Health Clubs/Gyms	$	$	$
Vacations/Trips	$	$	$
Other (explain)	$	$	$

CATEGORY	AMOUNT BUDGETED	AMOUNT SPENT	SURPLUS (+)/ SHORTAGE (-)
RECREATION/SPORTS/HOBBIES	$	$	$
MISCELLANEOUS			
Pet Care/Supplies	$	$	$
Landscaping	$	$	$
Mailing/Postage	$	$	$
Fees for Checking Accounts, Checks, Money Orders, etc.	$	$	$
Other (explain)	$	$	$
Variable Expenses Subtotal	$	$	$
Debts			
Education Loans	$	$	$
Personal Loans	$	$	$
Credit Card #1	$	$	$
Credit Card #2	$	$	$
Credit Card #3	$	$	$
Other (explain)	$	$	$
Debts Subtotal	$	$	$
Savings & Investments			
Savings	$	$	$
Investments	$	$	$
Savings & Investments Subtotal	$	$	$

Budget Summary

CATEGORY	AMOUNT BUDGETED	AMOUNT SPENT	SURPLUS (+)/ SHORTAGE (-)
Fixed Expenses	$	$	$
Periodic Fixed Expenses	$	$	$
Variable Expenses	$	$	$
Debts	$	$	$
Savings & Investments	$	$	$
TOTAL MONTHLY ACCOUNTING	$	$	$

Event Budgeting Form

Name of Event: _____

Date of Event: _____

Venue: _____

Total Budget Goal:_____

CATEGORY	ESTIMATED	ACTUAL	SURPLUS (+)/ SHORTAGE (-)
Venue Rental	$	$	$
Invitations & Postage	$	$	$
Decorations	$	$	$
Food	$	$	$
Drinks	$	$	$
Entertainment	$	$	$
Service & Tips	$	$	$
Goody Bags/Gifts	$	$	$
Other	$	$	$
Other	$	$	$
TOTAL	$	$	$

Net Worth Worksheet

Assets	
INVESTABLE ASSETS	
Cash: Checking/Savings/Money Market Accounts/CDs/T-Bills	$
Bonds: Taxable; Tax-Exempt	$
Stocks	$
Mutual Funds	$
Life Insurance (Face Amount)	$
Annuities	$
Limited Partnerships	$
Real Estate	$
Collectibles/Personal Assets	$
Retirement Assets	
IRAs	$
Qualified Retirement Plans	$
Pensions	$
Other	$
TOTAL ASSETS	$

Liabilities	
Credit Card Debt	$
Margin Debt	$
Personal Loans	$
Mortgages	$
Auto Loans	$
Other	$
TOTAL LIABILITIES	$

Total Assets $_____ – Total Liabilities $_____ = Net Worth $ _____

INDEX

C